MySQL for Python

Integrate the flexibility of Python and the power of
MySQL to boost the productivity of your applications

Albert Lukaszewski, PhD

[PACKT] open source *
PUBLISHING   community experience distilled

BIRMINGHAM - MUMBAI

MySQL for Python

First published: September 2010

Production Reference: 1160910

Published by Packt Publishing Ltd.
32 Lincoln Road
Olton
Birmingham, B27 6PA, UK.

ISBN 978-1-849510-18-9

www.packtpub.com

Cover Image by Vinayak Chittar (vinayak.chittar@gmail.com)

Credits

Author
Albert Lukaszewski

Reviewers
Swaroop C H
Andy Dustman
Geert JM Vanderkelen

Acquisition Editor
Steven Wilding

Development Editor
Wilson D'souza

Technical Editors
Prashant Macha
Charumati Shankaran

Indexer
Hemangini Bari

Editorial Team Leader
Aanchal Kumar

Project Team Leader
Priya Mukherji

Project Coordinator
Prasad Rai

Proofreader
Aaron Nash

Production Coordinator
Shantanu Zagade

Cover Work
Shantanu Zagade

About the Author

Albert Lukaszewski is principal consultant for Lukaszewski Consulting Services in southeast Scotland. He has programmed computers for 30 years. Much of his experience has related to text processing, database systems, and **Natural Language processing (NLP)**. Currently he consults on database applications for companies in the financial and publishing industries.

In addition to MySQL for Python, Albert Lukaszewski has also written "About Python", a column for the New York Times subsidiary, About.com.

Many people had a hand in this work beyond my typing at the keyboard. Some contributed by their effort and others by their sacrifice. Thanks to the team at Packt for their consistent understanding and support. I am particularly thankful to Steven Wilding for help and support above and beyond the call of duty.

Thanks also to Andy Dustman, Geert Vanderkelen, and Swaroop for their helpful review of this book and for making so many significant and helpful recommendations. This book would be much the poorer were it not for their suggestions.

To Richard Goodrich, who first introduced me to Python, thank you for liberating me from bondage to that other P-language. Funny what a little problem can lead to.

My heartfelt thanks and appreciation go to my wife, Michelle, and my sons, Cyrus and Jacob. The latter was born during the writing of this book and consistently brightens even the darkest Scottish weather with his smile. I appreciate your sacrifice. I could not have written this book without your support.

Finally, my thanks to my brother, Larry, who first introduced me to the world of computing. I would probably not know anything about computer programming if you had not left me your TRS-80. So this is all your fault, and I am glad you did it.

About the Reviewers

Swaroop C H has previously worked at Yahoo! and Adobe, has co-founded a startup, has written two technical books (one of which is used as a text book in more than ten universities worldwide), writes a popular blog that has been consistently rated one of the top ten blogs in India, and is a marathoner. More details at `http://www.swaroopch.com/about/`.

He has written two technical books — A Byte of Python and A Byte of Vim — beginner books to Python and Vim respectively. They are freely available under the Creative Commons license on his website `www.swaroopch.com`.

Andy Dustman (`http://profiles.google.com/farcepest`) is the primary author of MySQLdb, the MySQL interface for Python.

The MySQL-Python project is supported and funded purely by volunteers and donations by the user community at (`http://sourceforge.net/projects/mysql-python/`).

Andy has been using Python since 1997, and currently works on Django applications (using MySQL, of course) when not doing system and network administration. In his spare time, he rides motorcycles.

> I would like to thank Kyle VanderBeek, who has recently become a co-developer on MySQLdb, and has helped to push me a bit to get some things done. 12 years is a long time to be working on a project, and motivation is sometimes hard to come by.
>
> Ed Landa, for taking a chance on a grad school dropout, and for giving me the opportunity to release MySQLdb under an open source license.
>
> Laura Michaletz, who encourages me and somehow manages to make me feel like a superstar.
>
> And my wife, Wendy, for being there for me for three decades.

Geert JM Vanderkelen is a member of the MySQL Support Team at Sun, a wholly-owned subsidiary of Oracle. He is based in Germany and has worked for MySQL AB since April, 2005. Before joining MySQL he worked as developer, DBA and SysAdmin for various companies in Belgium and Germany. Today Geert specializes in MySQL Cluster and works together with colleagues around the world to ensure continued support for both customers and community. Geert is also the maintainer of MySQL Connector/Python.

Table of Contents

Preface

Python is a dynamic programming language, which is completely enterprise ready, owing largely to the variety of support modules that are available to extend its capabilities. In order to build productive and feature-rich Python applications, we need to use MySQL for Python, a module that provides database support to our applications.

This book demonstrates how to boost the productivity of your Python applications by integrating them with the MySQL database server, the world's most powerful open source database. It will teach you to access the data on your MySQL database server easily with Python's library for MySQL using a practical, hands-on approach. Leaving theory to the classroom, this book uses real-world code to solve real-world problems with real-world solutions.

The book starts by exploring the various means of installing MySQL for Python on different platforms and how to use simple database querying techniques to improve your programs. It then takes you through data insertion, data retrieval, and error-handling techniques to create robust programs. The book also covers automation of both database and user creation, and administration of access controls. As the book progresses, you will learn to use many more advanced features of Python for MySQL that facilitate effective administration of your database through Python. Every chapter is illustrated with a project that you can deploy in your own situation.

By the end of this book, you will know several techniques for interfacing your Python applications with MySQL effectively so that powerful database management through Python becomes easy to achieve and easy to maintain.

What this book covers

Chapter 1, Getting Up and Running with MySQL for Python, helps you to install MySQL for Python specific software, how to import modules into your programs, connecting to a database, accessing online help, and creating a MySQL cursor proxy within your Python program. It also covers how to close the database connection from Python and how to access multiple databases within one program.

Chapter 2, Simple Querying, helps you to form and pass a query to MySQL, to look at user-defined variables, how to determine characteristics of a database and its tables, and program a command-line search utility. It also looks at how to change queries dynamically, without user input.

Chapter 3, Simple Insertion, shows forming and passing an insertion to MySQL, to look at the user-defined variables in a MySQL insertion, passing metadata between databases, and changing insertion statements dynamically without user input.

Chapter 4, Exception Handling, discusses ways to handle errors and warnings that are passed from MySQL for Python and the differences between them. It also covers several types of errors supported by MySQL for Python, and how to handle them effectively.

Chapter 5, Results Record-by-Record, shows situations in which record-by-record retrieval is desirable, to use iteration to retrieve sets of records in smaller blocks and how to create iterators and generators in Python. It also helps you in using `fetchone()` and `fetchmany()`.

Chapter 6, Inserting Multiple Entries, discusses how iteration can help us execute several individual `INSERT` statements rapidly, when to use or avoid `executemany()`, and throttling how much data is inserted at a time.

Chapter 7, Creating and Dropping, shows to create and delete both databases and tables in MySQL, to manage database instances with MySQL for Python, and to automate database and table creation.

Chapter 8, Creating Users and Granting Access, focuses on creating and removing users in MySQL, managing database privileges with MySQL for Python, automating user creation and removal, to `GRANT` and `REVOKE` privileges, and the conditions under which that can be done.

Chapter 9, Date and Time Values, discusses what data types MySQL supports for date and time, when to use which data type and in what format and range, and frequently used functions for handling matters of date and time.

Chapter 10, Aggregate Functions and Clauses, shows how MySQL saves us time and effort by pre-processing data, how to perform several calculations using MySQL's optimized algorithms, and to group and order returned data by column.

Chapter 11, SELECT Alternatives, discusses how to use HAVING clauses, how to create temporary subtables, subqueries and joins in Python, and the various ways to join tables.

Chapter 12, String Functions, shows how MySQL allows us to combine strings and return the single, resulting value, how to extract part of a string or the location of a part, thus saving on processing, and how to convert cases of results.

Chapter 13, Showing MySQL Metadata, discusses the several pieces of metadata about a given table that we can access, which system variables we can retrieve, and how to retrieve user privileges and the grants used to give them.

Chapter 14, Disaster Recovery, focuses on when to implement one of several kinds of database backup plans, what methods of backup and disaster recovery MySQL supports, and how to use Python to back up databases

What you need for this book

The content of this book is written against MySQL 5.5, Python 2.5.2, and MySQL for Python 1.2.2. Development of the examples was done with MySQL 5.0, but everything was confirmed against the 5.5 documentation. As for operating systems, any of the main three will do: Microsoft Windows, Linux, or Mac. Any additional requirements of modules are discussed in the book as they come up.

Who this book is for

This book is meant for intermediate users of Python who want hassle-free access to their MySQL database through Python. If you are a Python programmer who wants database-support in your Python applications, then this book is for you. This book is a must-read for every focused user of the MySQL for Python library who wants real-world applications using this powerful combination of Python and MySQL.

Conventions

In this book, you will find a number of styles of text that distinguish between different kinds of information. Here are some examples of these styles, and an explanation of their meaning.

Code words in text are shown as follows: "We can include other contexts through the use of the include directive."

A block of code is set as follows:

```
import MySQLdb
mydb = MySQLdb.connect(host = 'localhost',
                       user = 'skipper',
                       passwd = 'mysecret',
                       db = 'fish')
```

Any command-line input or output is written as follows:

```
>>> print results
((1L, 'tuna', Decimal('7.50')), (2L, 'bass', Decimal('6.75')), (3L,
'salmon', Decimal('9.50')), (4L, 'catfish', Decimal('5.00')),
```

New terms and **important words** are shown in bold. Words that you see on the screen, in menus or dialog boxes for example, appear in the text like this: "clicking the **Next** button moves you to the next screen".

Reference to a particular section or chapter are shown in italics.

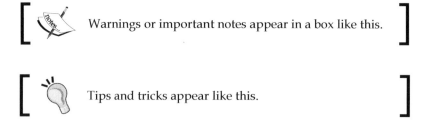

Warnings or important notes appear in a box like this.

Tips and tricks appear like this.

Reader feedback

Feedback from our readers is always welcome. Let us know what you think about this book—what you liked or may have disliked. Reader feedback is important for us to develop titles that you really get the most out of.

To send us general feedback, simply send an e-mail to feedback@packtpub.com, and mention the book title via the subject of your message.

If there is a book that you need and would like to see us publish, please send us a note in the **SUGGEST A TITLE** form on www.packtpub.com or e-mail suggest@packtpub.com.

If there is a topic that you have expertise in and you are interested in either writing or contributing to a book on, see our author guide on www.packtpub.com/authors.

Customer support

Now that you are the proud owner of a Packt book, we have a number of things to help you to get the most from your purchase.

> **Downloading the example code for this book**
>
> You can download the example code files for all Packt books you have purchased from your account at http://www.PacktPub.com. If you purchased this book elsewhere, you can visit http://www.PacktPub.com/support and register to have the files e-mailed directly to you.

Errata

Although we have taken every care to ensure the accuracy of our content, mistakes do happen. If you find a mistake in one of our books—maybe a mistake in the text or the code—we would be grateful if you would report this to us. By doing so, you can save other readers from frustration and help us improve subsequent versions of this book. If you find any errata, please report them by visiting http://www.packtpub.com/support, selecting your book, clicking on the **errata submission form** link, and entering the details of your errata. Once your errata are verified, your submission will be accepted and the errata will be uploaded on our website, or added to any list of existing errata. Any existing errata can be viewed by selecting your title from http://www.packtpub.com/support.

Piracy

Piracy of copyright material on the Internet is an ongoing problem across all media. At Packt, we take the protection of our copyright and licenses very seriously. If you come across any illegal copies of our works, in any form, on the Internet, please provide us with the location address or website name immediately so that we can pursue a remedy.

Please contact us at copyright@packtpub.com with a link to the suspected pirated material.

We appreciate your help in protecting our authors, and our ability to bring you valuable content.

Questions

You can contact us at questions@packtpub.com if you are having a problem with any aspect of the book, and we will do our best to address it.

1
Getting Up and Running with MySQL for Python

It may seem rather unnecessary to start a book on MySQL for Python with a chapter on setting it up. There are, in fact, several ways to get MySQL for Python in a place such that your local Python installation can use it. Which one you use will depend as much on your familiarity with your operating system and with Python itself, as it will on which operating system and version of Python you are running.

In this chapter we will cover the following:

- Where you can get MySQL for Python
- Installing MySQL for Python
- Importing the module into your programs
- Accessing online help about the MySQL for Python API and its accompanying modules
- How to connect to a database
- How to create a MySQL cursor proxy within your Python program
- How to close the database connection from Python
- How to access multiple databases within one program

Getting MySQL for Python

How you get MySQL for Python depends on your operating system and the level of authorization you have on it. In the following subsections, we walk through the common operating systems and see how to get MySQL for Python on each.

Using a package manager (only on Linux)

Package managers are used regularly on Linux, but none come by default with Macintosh and Windows installations. So users of those systems can skip this section.

A package manager takes care of downloading, unpacking, installing, and configuring new software for you. In order to use one to install software on your Linux installation, you will need administrative privileges.

Administrative privileges on a Linux system can be obtained legitimately in one of the following three ways:

- Log into the system as the root user (not recommended)
- Switch user to the root user using `su`
- Use `sudo` to execute a single command as the root user

The first two require knowledge of the root user's password. Logging into a system directly as the root user is not recommended due to the fact that there is no indication in the system logs as to who used the root account. Logging in as a normal user and then switching to root using `su` is better because it keeps an account of who did what on the machine and when. Either way, if you access the root account, you must be very careful because small mistakes can have major consequences. Unlike other operating systems, Linux assumes that you know what you are doing if you access the root account and will not stop you from going so far as deleting every file on the hard drive.

Unless you are familiar with Linux system administration, it is far better, safer, and more secure to prefix the `sudo` command to the `package manager` call. This will give you the benefit of restricting use of administrator-level authority to a single command. The chances of catastrophic mistakes are therefore mitigated to a great degree.

 More information on any of these commands is available by prefacing either `man` or `info` before any of the preceding commands (`su`, `sudo`).

Which package manager you use depends on which of the two mainstream package management systems your distribution uses. Users of RedHat or Fedora, SUSE, or Mandriva will use the **RPM Package Manager (RPM)** system. Users of Debian, Ubuntu, and other Debian-derivatives will use the `apt` suite of tools available for Debian installations. Each package is discussed in the following:

Using RPMs and yum

If you use SUSE, RedHat, or Fedora, the operating system comes with the yum package manager. You can see if MySQLdb is known to the system by running a search (here using sudo):

```
sudo yum search mysqldb
```

If yum returns a hit, you can then install MySQL for Python with the following command:

```
sudo yum install mysqldb
```

Using RPMs and urpm

If you use Mandriva, you will need to use the urpm package manager in a similar fashion. To search use urpmq:

```
sudo urpmq mysqldb
```

And to install use urpmi:

```
sudo urpmi mysqldb
```

Using apt tools on Debian-like systems

Whether you run a version of Ubuntu, Xandros, or Debian, you will have access to **aptitude**, the default Debian package manager. Using sudo we can search for MySQLdb in the apt sources using the following command:

```
sudo aptitude search mysqldb
```

On most Debian-based distributions, MySQL for Python is listed as python-mysqldb.

Once you have found how apt references MySQL for Python, you can install it using the following code:

```
sudo aptitude install python-mysqldb
```

Using a package manager automates the entire process so you can move to the section *Importing MySQL for Python*.

Using an installer for Windows

Windows users will need to use the older 1.2.2 version of MySQL for Python. Using a web browser, go to the following link:

```
http://sourceforge.net/projects/mysql-python/files/
```

This page offers a listing of all available files for all platforms. At the end of the file listing, find **mysql-python** and click on it. The listing will unfold to show folders containing versions of MySQL for Python back to **0.9.1**. The version we want is **1.2.2**.

 Windows binaries do not currently exist for the 1.2.3 version of MySQL for Python. To get them, you would need to install a C compiler on your Windows installation and compile the binary from source.

This is outside the purpose of the present book, but tips for how to do this are contained in the README file that accompanies the 1.2.3 version.

Click on **1.2.2** and unfold the file listing. As you will see, the Windows binaries are differentiated by Python version—both 2.4 and 2.5 are supported. Choose the one that matches your Python installation and download it. Note that all available binaries are for 32-bit Windows installations, not 64-bit.

After downloading the binary, installation is a simple matter of double-clicking the installation EXE file and following the dialogue. Once the installation is complete, the module is ready for use. So go to the section *Importing MySQL for Python*.

Using an egg file

One of the easiest ways to obtain MySQL for Python is as an egg file, and it is best to use one of those files if you can. Several advantages can be gained from working with egg files such as:

- They can include metadata about the package, including its dependencies
- They allow for the use of egg-aware software, a helpful level of abstraction
- Eggs can, technically, be placed on the Python executable path and used without unpacking
- They save the user from installing packages for which they do not have the appropriate version of software
- They are so portable that they can be used to extend the functionality of third-party applications

Installing egg handling software

One of the best known egg utilities — **Easy Install**, is available from the PEAK Developers' Center at http://peak.telecommunity.com/DevCenter/EasyInstall. How you install it depends on your operating system and whether you have package management software available. In the following section, we look at several ways to install Easy Install on the most common systems.

Using a package manager (Linux)

On Ubuntu you can try the following to install the easy_install tool (if not available already):

```
shell> sudo aptitude install python-setuptools
```

On **RedHat** or **CentOS** you can try using the yum package manager:

```
shell> sudo yum install python-setuptools
```

On Mandriva use urpmi:

```
shell> sudo urpmi python-setuptools
```

You must have administrator privileges to do the installations just mentioned.

Without a package manager (Mac, Linux)

If you do not have access to a Linux package manager, but nonetheless have a Unix variant as your operating system (for example, Mac OS X), you can install Python's setuptools manually. Go to:

```
http://pypi.python.org/pypi/setuptools#files
```

Download the relevant egg file for your Python version.

When the file is downloaded, open a terminal and change to the download directory. From there you can run the egg file as a shell script. For Python 2.5, the command would look like this:

```
sh setuptools-0.6c11-py2.5.egg
```

This will install several files, but the most important one for our purposes is easy_install, usually located in /usr/bin.

On Microsoft Windows

On Windows, one can download the setuptools suite from the following URL:

```
http://pypi.python.org/pypi/setuptools#files
```

From the list located there, select the most appropriate Windows executable file.

Once the download is completed, double-click the installation file and proceed through the dialogue. The installation process will set up several programs, but the one important for our purposes is `easy_install.exe`. Where this is located will differ by installation and may require using the search function from the **Start Menu**.

On 64-bit Windows, for example, it may be in the `Program Files (x86)` directory. If in doubt, do a search. On Windows XP with Python 2.5, it is located here:

```
C:\Python25\Scripts\easy_install.exe
```

Note that you may need administrator privileges to perform this installation. Otherwise, you will need to install the software for your own use. Depending on the setup of your system, this may not always work.

Installing software on Windows for your own use requires the following steps:

1. Copy the **setuptools** installation file to your Desktop.
2. Right-click on it and choose the **runas** option.
3. Enter the name of the user who has enough rights to install it (presumably yourself).

After the software has been installed, ensure that you know the location of the `easy_install.exe` file. You will need it to install MySQL for Python.

Installing MySQL for Python from an egg file

After installing `EasyInstall`, you still need to install the MySQL for Python `egg`. The `egg` files for MySQL for Python can be downloaded from the following URL:

```
http://sourceforge.net/projects/mysql-python/files/
```

There you will see a list of all available files relevant to MySQL for Python.

Which one you use depends on your operating system and your installed Python version. Currently, the only `egg` files available for MySQL for Python version 1.2.3c1 are for Linux running either Python 2.5 or 2.6. Mac users should use a `tarball` (`tar.gz`) file as discussed in the next section.

To get an `egg` file for Windows, click on the **MySQL-python** directory and select the **1.2.2** version. This is the same directory used for the Windows binaries discussed earlier in this chapter. This time, however, you need to select an `egg` for Windows that fits either Python 2.4 or 2.5. There is no 2.6 version.

Once you have the `egg` file for MySQL for Python, you simply need to invoke `EasyInstall` over the newly-downloaded `egg` file. How you do that will depend on the permissions you have for your operating system.

With administrator permissions, you can simply call the `EasyInstall` binary. For Linux, it will look like this:

```
shell> easy_install <name of egg file>
```

For Windows, you will use a command similar to this one:

```
C:\Python25\Scripts\easy_install.exe <name of egg file>
```

Note that you must have administrator privileges to do this. Otherwise, Windows users will have to install the software locally. Linux users can use `sudo`.

`EasyInstall` will then unpack the archive, install it in your default Python installation folders, and configure it for immediate use.

For Windows users, if you had to install `setuptools` locally, you may also require a local installation of Python itself in order to install MySQL for Python. See the section *On Microsoft Windows* under *Installing egg-handling software*, for help with this. If you need to go through this process, all of your configurations will be local, so you are best to use full path command-line calls.

If your system has MySQL, Python, and `setuptools`, but you still don't have administrative access, it is advisable to unpack the `egg` file manually and call it as a local module. To do this, use an archiving program to unzip the file.

The content listing for the Windows egg will look like this:

- `Egg-info`
- `MySQLdb`
- `_mysql_exceptions.py`
- `_mysql_exceptions.pyc`
- `_mysql.py`
- `_mysql.pyc`
- `_mysql.pyd`

And the Linux egg unpacks to the following files:

- `Egg-info`
- `MySQLdb`
- `_mysql_exceptions.py`
- `_mysql_exceptions.pyc`
- `_mysql.py`
- `_mysql.pyc`
- `_mysql.so`

With the exception of the `egg-info` directory, the contents are the basic ingredients of a Python module and can be imported locally if one's program resides in the same directory as the files are located.

Using a tarball (tar.gz file)

Due to the need for certain programming libraries, this method of installation applies only to users of Unix-derived operating systems. This method involves installing from the source files and so requires the necessary C libraries to compile a binary version. Windows users should therefore use one of the other methods discussed previously.

If you cannot use `egg` files or if you use an earlier version of Python, you should use the `tar.gz` file, a `tar` and `gzip` archive. The `tar.gz` archive follows the Linux `egg` files in the file listing. The current version of MySQL for Python is 1.2.3c1, so the file we want is as following:

```
MySQL-python-1.2.3c1.tar.gz
```

This method is by far more complicated than the others. If at all possible, use your operating system's installation method or an `egg` file.

This version of MySQL for Python is compatible up to Python 2.6. It is worth noting that MySQL for Python has not yet been released for Python 3.0 or later versions. In your deployment of the library, therefore, ensure that you are running Python 2.6 or earlier. As noted, Python 2.5 and 2.6 have version-specific releases. Prior to Python 2.4, you will need to use either a `tar.gz` version of the latest release or use an older version of MySQL for Python. The latter option is not recommended.

Most Unix-derived operating systems (Linux, Mac) come with the `tar` and `gzip` utilities pre-installed. For users of these systems, unpacking the archive is as simple as the following command:

```
shell> tar xvzf MySQL-python-1.2.3c1.tar.gz
```

The archive will then unpack into a directory called `MySQL-python-1.2.3c1`.

Windows users can use any of the following archive programs to unpack the `tarball`:

- PowerArchiver 6.1
- 7-Zip
- WinZip

Once the file is unpacked, you need to ensure that you have the program `mysql_config` in your path. For Mac users, this usually comes with the MySQL installation itself. For Linux, if you are using **bash** or another shell with command-line completion, you can check this by typing the following in a terminal:

```
shell> mysql_conf
```

Then press the **tab** key. If the command is completed to `mysql_config`, there are no issues, otherwise your operating system does not know of any such command, and you need to either find it or install it.

An alternative way of checking is to use the `whereis` command. Type the following from the command-line:

```
shell> whereis mysql_config
```

If it is installed, the system will return its location. Then echo your current PATH value by typing:

```
shell> echo $PATH
```

and compare the results. If the location of `mysql_config` is one of the values in your path, there are no issues otherwise, we need to either find it or install it.

The `mysql_config` program comes with the MySQL client development libraries. If you have these installed, check the directory that holds the MySQL client binary (use `whereis mysql` if necessary). If you are unsure, you can check with a package manager using the following commands:

```
shell> aptitude search mysql | grep client | grep dev
```

This will work for Debian-based systems. Users of RPM-based systems should substitute either yum search or urpmq for aptitude search. This query will return results for the development files and for the MySQL client, and you can then see if the appropriate package is installed. If it is not, you can install it with the install argument (for either aptitude or yum) or by using urpmi.

If the mysql_config program is installed, but is outside your path, you need to indicate its location to the MySQL for Python setup configuration. Navigate to the MySQL-python-1.2.3c1 directory and open the file site.cfg in your favorite text editor. The file is not large, and the following section is easily seen as the second part of the file:

```
#The path to mysql_config
#Only use this if mysql_config is not on your PATH,
    or you have some weird setup that requires it
#mysql_config = /usr/local/bin/mysql_config
```

If mysql_config is outside of your path, uncomment the last line of the part cited here and enter the correct path. So, if mysql_config is installed to:

```
/usr/local/bin/mysql/bin/mysql_config
```

The last line should read:

```
mysql_config = /usr/local/bin/mysql/bin/mysql_config
```

Then save the file and close it.

Next, we should build the package using the instructions that came with it in setup.py. Use the following command to attempt a build without installing it:

```
shell> python setup.py build
```

If the process goes through without error, which it usually does, the build is successful. If there is an error, it usually involves the lack of a module or software package. In which case, confirm that you have all the prerequisites needed for the task by checking the list in the readme file that comes with the archive.

 Be sure to read the readme file that comes with the source code. It contains a lot of help on the installation process.

Once the build is successful, installation can be done with the following command:

```
shell> python setup.py install
```

Note that you will need **super user** access for this. If you do not have administrative access to your system, you need to use one of the other methods.

Importing MySQL for Python

The name of the project MySQL for Python is the current version of a project that began under the rubric MySQLdb. Consequently, unlike most Python modules, the MySQL for Python module is not called by its name, but by its historic handle. To import the module, insert the following into a Python program or simply type it in a following Python shell:

```
import MySQLdb
```

To make working with the module easier, you can also import it with an alias:

```
import MySQLdb as mysql
```

This allows us to use mysql instead of MySQLdb when we access parts of the module.

When you do this, several things will occur. You need not be concerned about most of them, but you should be aware that MySQLdb depends upon a module called _mysql. The _mysql module is largely a Python adaptation of the **MySQL C API**.

 This is important to note because it is this API that you will access through MySQL for Python.

MySQL for Python is a wrapper for accessing the _mysql API. A wrapper is essentially a system of macros, or trusted code, that allows you to do common tasks quickly. It allows you to program without having to repeat commonly used or accessed variables and functions. The _mysql module is a powerful and proven way of accessing a MySQL database. However, controlling it within a Python program can pose a challenge for some, like driving a Formula 1 car for the first time. So consider MySQL for Python as a system that allows you to harness the power of a Formula 1 racing car even if you're merely driving a Hyundai.

Unlike some systems of macros, MySQL for Python still allows you to access the classes and functions of _mysql. This is due to the nature of Python's import functionality.

Accessing online help when you need it

As with other modules, Python is able to provide online help about MySQL for Python. In the following sections, we look at the MySQLdb and _mysql modules in greater depth using Python's built-in help() function.

MySQLdb

After importing MySQLdb, you can read over the documentation that accompanies the module. In a Python shell, type:

```
help(MySQLdb)
```

You will then see a manual page detailing all of the functions and classes of MySQL for Python. It is well worth giving this a cursory read to familiarize yourself with the module. In the course of this book, we will cover most of these items from various angles.

As the help page indicates, MySQLdb includes the following modules:

- **connections**: Initiating, maintaining, and closing a connection to MySQL
- **cursors**: Managing the execution of queries
- **converters**: For converting between MySQL data types as well as between data types in MySQL and Python
- **times**: Converting date and time values between MySQL and Python

Each of these is abstracted to the point of its own module in the source tree. Without a doubt, the most important part of the module is connections.py, without which we could not interface with MySQL. Where the others are static, the conversion module, convertors.py, allows you to define your own convertor on-the-fly.

The MySQLdb module itself has only one operating class that does not pertain to errors—**DBAPISet**. This is MySQLdb's internal object class for processing data. To interface with MySQL, however, we use functions. Of the several listed at the end of the MySQLdb help page, one uses connect() in every MySQLdb program.

At first glance, it may here be confusing to see that MySQLdb seems to have three ways of connecting with a database. In the list of functions, these are as follows:

- connect()
- Connection
- Connect

Knowing the ins and outs of these functions is not necessary. It is, however, important to know that they exist and to recognize that the latter two are simply different ways of transferring data to the first. `Connect()` then passes the arguments to the `connections.Connection()` class, MySQLdb's MySQL database connection class, in the `connections.py` module.

_mysql

In looking over the module, you may also note that reference is made to the `_mysql` module, but it is not explicitly detailed. This is because it is a dependency and not part of the module itself. However, you can access the documentation for `_mysql` without importing it directly by using the MySQLdb namespace:

```
help(MySQLdb._mysql)
```

In the previous discussion about `connections.Connection()`, we stopped following the trail of the connection and any ensuing data transmission where MySQLdb stopped. In reality, however, the data does not stop there. When a connection or operational request is received by `connections.Connection()`, it is processed and passed to `_mysql` and subsequently to the MySQL API in C to perform it.

To handle this interface, `_mysql` uses two classes:

- `connection`
- `result`

The first is used to establish communication with MySQL and thus returns a `connection` object. The second, as the name implies, returns a set containing the results from a MySQL command that a program sends. These results can be either the query results or an error. `_mysql` naturally passes the error to the calling process. In the case of MySQLdb, we then have a comprehensive toolbox to handle the errors that may arise.

Connecting with a database

In making a phone call, one picks up the handset, dials a number, talks and listens, and then hangs up. Making a database connection through MySQL for Python is nearly as simple. The four stages of database communication in Python are as follows:

- Creating a `connection` object
- Creating a `cursor` object
- Interacting with the database
- Closing the connection

Creating a connection object

As mentioned previously, we use `connect()` to create an object for the program's connection to the database. This process automates logging into the database and selecting a database to be used.

The syntax for calling the `connect()` function and assigning the results to a variable is as follows:

```
[variable] = MySQLdb.connect([hostname], [username], [password],
                              [database name])
```

Naming these variables as you assign the values is not required, but it is good practice until you get used to the format of the function call. So for the first few chapters of this book, we will use the following format to call the `connect()` function:

```
[variable] = MySQLdb.connect(host="[hostname]",
                             user="[username]",
                             passwd="[password]",
                             db="[database name]")
```

Let's say we have a database-driven application that creates the menu for a seafood restaurant. We need to query all of the fish from the menu database in order to input them into a new menu. The database is named **menu**.

If you do not have a database called menu, you will obviously not be able to connect to it with these examples. To create the database that we are using in this example, put the following code into a text file with the name menu.sql:

```
CREATE DATABASE `menu`;
USE menu;

DROP TABLE IF EXISTS `fish`;
SET @saved_cs_client     = @@character_set_client;
SET character_set_client = utf8;
CREATE TABLE `fish` (
  `ID` int(11) NOT NULL auto_increment,
  `NAME` varchar(30) NOT NULL default '',
  `PRICE` decimal(5,2) NOT NULL default '0.00',
  PRIMARY KEY  (`ID`)
) ENGINE=MyISAM AUTO_INCREMENT=27 DEFAULT
CHARSET=latin1;
SET character_set_client = @saved_cs_client;

LOCK TABLES `fish` WRITE;
INSERT INTO `fish` VALUES (1,'catfish','8.50'),(2,'catf
ish','8.50'),(3,'tuna','8.00'),(4,'catfish','5.00'),(5
,'bass','6.75'),(6,'haddock','6.50'),(7,'salmon','9.50
'),(8,'trout','6.00'),(9,'tuna','7.50'),(10,'yellowfin
tuna','12.00'),(11,'yellowfin tuna','13.00'),(12,'tuna'
,'7.50');
UNLOCK TABLES;
```

Then log into your MySQL session from the directory in which the file menu.sql is located and type the following:

```
source menu.sql
```

This will cause MySQL to create and populate our example database.

For this example, the database and program reside on the same host, so we can use **localhost**. The user for the database is **skipper** with password **mysecret**. After importing the MySQL for Python module, we would call the connect() function as follows:

```
mydb = MySQLdb.connect(host="localhost",
                       user="skipper",
                       passwd="mysecret",
                       db="menu")
```

The `connect()` function acts as a foil for the `connection` class in `connections.py` and returns an object to the calling process. So in this example, assigning the value of `MySQLdb.connect()` to `mydb` renders `mydb` as a `connection` object. To illustrate this, you can create the necessary database in MySQL, connect to it as shown previously, then type `help(mydb)` at the Python shell prompt. You will then be presented with large amounts of information pertinent to `MySQLdb.connections` objects.

Creating a cursor object

After the `connection` object is created, you cannot interact with the database until you create a cursor object. The name *cursor* belies the purpose of this object. Cursors exist in any productivity application and have been a part of computing since the beginning. The point of a cursor is to mark your place and to allow you to issue commands to the computer. A cursor in MySQL for Python serves as a Python-based proxy for the cursor in a MySQL shell session, where MySQL would create the real cursor for us if we logged into a MySQL database. We must here create the proxy ourselves.

To create the cursor, we use the `cursor()` method of the `MySQLdb.connections` object we created for the connection. The syntax is as follows:

```
[cursor name] = [connection object name].cursor()
```

Using our example of the menu database above, we can use a generic name `cursor` for the `database` cursor and create it in this way:

```
cursor = mydb.cursor()
```

Now, we are ready to issue commands.

Interacting with the database

Many SQL commands can be issued using a single function as:

```
cursor.execute()
```

There are other ways to issue commands to MySQL depending on the results one wants back, but this is one of the most common. Its use will be addressed in greater detail in future chapters.

Closing the connection

In MySQL, you are expected to close the databases and end the session by issuing either quit or exit.

To do this in Python, we use the close() method of the database object. Whether you close a database outright depends on what actions you have performed and whether MySQL's **auto-commit** feature is turned on. By default, MySQL has **autocommit** switched on. Your database administrator will be able to confirm whether **auto-commit** is switched on. If it is not, you will need to commit any changes you have made. We do this by calling the commit method of the database object. For mydb, it would look like this:

```
mydb.commit()
```

After all changes have been committed, we can then close the database:

```
mydb.close()
```

Multiple database connections

In MySQL for Python, all database objects are discrete. All you need do is to connect with each under a different name. Consider the following:

```
mydb1 = MySQLdb.connect(host="localhost",
                        user="skipper",
                        passwd="mysecret",
                        db="fish")
mydb2 = MySQLdb.connect(host="localhost",
                        user="skipper",
                        passwd="mysecret",
                        db="fruit")
cursor1 = mydb1.cursor()
cursor2 = mydb2.cursor()
```

The objects then function like any other variable or object. By calling their methods and attributes separately, you can interact with either or even copy from one to the other.

Summary

In this chapter we have looked at where to find MySQL for Python, as it is not part of Python by default. We have also seen how to install it on both Windows and non-Windows systems—UNIX-like and Linux distributions. The authors of MySQL for Python have taken the pain out of this by providing a very easy way to install through an **egg** utility like EasyInstall.

Like most modules, MySQL for Python must be imported before you can use it in Python. So we then looked at how to import it. Unlike most modules, we saw that MySQL for Python needs to be imported by its earlier moniker, MySQLdb.

After that, we took a peek at what is waiting for us under the MySQL for Python covers using help(). We saw that MySQL for Python is not an interface to MySQL itself but to a MySQL Database API that is built into Python. It has a large number of classes for handling errors, but only one for processing data (There are different kinds of cursors). Further, it does not even use classes to access MySQL, but uses functions to process and pass information to _mysql, which then passes it to the C MySQL database interface.

Following this trail, we also saw that _mysql does not have a robust facility for handling errors, but only passes them to the calling process. That is why MySQL for Python has such a robust error handling facility.

Next, we saw how to connect to a MySQL database. As with most parts of Python, this is easy for beginners. But the function used is also sufficiently robust to handle the more complex needs of advanced solutions.

After connecting, we created a MySQLdb cursor and prepared to interact with the database. This showed that, while there are many things that MySQLdb will take care of for us (like connection closure), there are some things we need to do manually. In this instance, it is creating the cursor object that represents the MySQL cursor.

Finally, we saw that one can connect to multiple databases by simply using different object names for each connection. This has the consequence of necessitating different namespaces as we refer to the methods and attributes of each object. But it also allows one to bridge between databases across multiple hosts seamlessly and to present a unified interface for a user.

In the next chapter, we will see how to form a MySQL query and pass it from Python using variables from the system, MySQL, and the user.

2
Simple Querying

Record retrieval is without doubt the most common activity employed with regard to MySQL and other relational databases. Like most computer programs, MySQL functions on the basis of being invoked with parameters and returning results in accordance with them. As we seen, Python acts as an intermediary to that process. We can use it to access MySQL, login, and connect to a database of our choice.

In this chapter, we will look at the following:

- Forming a MySQL query directly
- Passing a query to MySQL
- User-defined variables in a MySQL query
- Determining characteristics of a database and its tables
- Changing queries dynamically, without user input

Working through each of these points will help you at the end of the chapter, when we get to the project: a command-line search tool.

A brief introduction to CRUD

The four basic functions of any persistent storage system like MySQL spell **CRUD**:

- Create
- Read
- Update
- Delete

These are key concepts, which each of the basic MySQL commands reflect.

There is nothing technical about the words themselves, but the concepts are very important. They represent the four activities that you can expect to be able to do in every relational database system you use. There are several alternatives to this acronym and keyword series (for example, SCUD for "select, create, update, and delete" or SIDU for "select, insert, delete, and update"). The point of each of these is that database functionality boils down to two sets of opposing activities:

- Creating and deleting database objects (for example, databases, tables, records)
- Inserting and reading data (that is writing and reading)

Each of these will be addressed in the coming chapters. In this one, we start with reading data using SELECT.

Forming a query in MySQL

In order to best understand how to submit a query through MySQL for Python, it is important to ensure you understand how to submit a query in MySQL itself. The similarities between the two outnumber the differences, but the first may seem confusing if you don't properly understand the second.

MySQL statements have a basic structure. In following a set structure, they are formed like natural language statements. Being a computer program, it understandably responds very poorly to informational statements and only moderately well to questions. Almost all MySQL statements have an imperatival tone, expressing your command. This is reflective of the client-server relationship. The computer is the servant who exists to do the bidding of yourself as the client or, if you prefer, master.

The syntactic structure of a simple MySQL statement is not that different from the language you use every day. Where English would have:

- Give me everything from the staff table!

MySQL would need to hear:

- SELECT * FROM staff;

Let's look at the MySQL statement, comparing it to the English in detail.

SELECT

MySQL does not support natural language searching like *Give me*. Rather, like other programming languages including Python, MySQL has a set of reserved key words. These are largely single synonyms for common, core actions. For data retrieval, the key word is SELECT. It could have been GIMME or any of a score of similar ways of saying the same thing, but MySQL is consonant with the Zen of Python:

> *There should be one — and preferably only one — obvious way to do it*

Therefore, the MySQL developers settled on a single keyword — one that just happens to be compliant with the SQL standard.

* (asterisk)

Being read up on your regular expressions, I am sure you recognize this universal quantifier. While it is one of the most commonly used, MySQL supports several metacharacters that you can use to nuance your searches.

MySQL supports different kinds of metacharacters in different contexts. The following is a full list of metacharacters. (Note that not all of them may be supported in a given situation.)

- .: To match any single character
- ?: To match zero or one character
- *: To match zero or more characters
- +: To match one or more characters
- {n}: To match an expression n times
- {m,n}: To match an expression a minimum of m and a maximum of n times
- {n, }: To match an expression n or more times
- ^: Indicates the bit-level indicator at the beginning of a line
- $: Indicates the bit-level indicator at the end of a line
- [[:<:]]: To match the beginning of words
- [[:>:]]: To match the ending of words
- [:class:]: To match a character class
- [:alpha:]: For letters
- [:space:]: For whitespace
- [:punct:]: For punctuation
- [:upper:]: For upper case letters
- [abc]: To match one of the enclosed characters
- [^xyz]: To match any character other than those enclosed
- |: Separates alternatives within an expression

In the case of the SELECT command, the asterisk is the only metacharacter supported. In addition to the asterisk, however, SELECT also supports several arguments used to quantify results:

- **ALL**: All matching rows (synonymous to using an asterisk (*)
- **DISTINCT**: Sort the results set into unique values
- **DISTINCTROW**: Where the entire record is unique

Each of these can be prefaced before the field to be quantified as illustrated here using the database structure from the last chapter:

```
SELECT DISTINCT id FROM menu;
```

This would return the values of the id column from the menu table and remove any duplicates from the results.

FROM

As with the English equivalent, MySQL needs some context in order to retrieve anything. In English, if one simply said Give me! without non-verbal cues for the intended context, the listener would rightly be confused. So here we tell MySQL from which table in the current database we want it to extract information.

Note that this is technically optional. Leaving it off, however, typically means that you are using MySQL's built-in datasets. For example, here is a statement using the built-in functions for the current date, user, and version (the \G is the same command as \g, but it tells MySQL to display the results vertically):

```
mysql> SELECT NOW(), USER(), VERSION()\G
*************************** 1. row ***************************
    NOW(): 2009-08-29 12:29:23
   USER(): skipper@localhost
VERSION(): 5.1.31-1ubuntu2
1 row in set (0.00 sec)
```

staff

This is merely the name of the table to be searched. In English, there are many locations from which one may desire something. That is why we would need to clarify that we want the items from the far table. MySQL, on the other hand, only understands things in terms of databases and tables and so understands as the name of a table whatever immediately follows the FROM keyword.

; (semicolon)

The semicolon is the default statement delimiter in MySQL. When creating a MySQL script or interacting with MySQL dynamically through its shell, leaving off a semicolon at the end of a statement will result in either a second prompt or, if you press the matter, an error being thrown. As we will see shortly, the syntax of MySQL for Python and Python itself mandates a different way of showing the end of the line. Therefore when passing MySQL queries in Python, we do not need to end any statements with the semicolon.

You may wonder why certain portions of the MySQL query are capitalized. It is a standard presentation format for MySQL statements to present the static or standard elements of a MySQL statement in capitals. Variable parts of the statement, however, are case sensitive and must be called with the same case in which they were created (otherwise, MySQL will throw an error). This matter of capitalization is not significant if you interact with MySQL directly, from a MySQL prompt. There, MySQL will understand your statements whether they be in all caps or lowercase. However, in your code, proper capitalization is critical to making your SQL statements readable to the next developer—both in Python and in MySQL scripts.

Where the semicolon is the statement delimiter in the MySQL shell, the backslash (\) is used to delimit lines within a statement. So, if you want to break up a statement but not have it executed when you press return, simply use a backslash at the end of each line of the statement. For example:

```
mysql> SELECT \
    -> * \
    -> FROM \
    -> menu;
```

Other helpful quantifiers

The previous discussion offers an overview of the SELECT command and its most common arguments. There are many other ways to nuance the data. In addition to FROM, you can also employ SELECT with the following optional arguments.

WHERE

WHERE is used to declare a condition under which MySQL is to narrow the results of the search. The basic syntax of the clause is:

```
[WHERE where_condition]
```

For example:

```
mysql> SELECT * FROM menu WHERE id='5';
+----+-------+-------+
| id | name  | price |
+----+-------+-------+
|  5 | trout |  6.00 |
+----+-------+-------+
1 row in set (0.00 sec)
```

GROUP BY

GROUP BY allows you to group results according to one of the following three parameters:

- col_name: Is the name of one of the table's columns
- expr: Is a regular expression
- position: Is a position in the table

Once grouped, you can then tell MySQL to list the results in either ASCending or DESCending order through ASC and DESC, respectively. The former is the default. Additionally, MySQL provides for a summative line at the end of the results through the use of WITH ROLLUP.

The syntax of a GROUP BY clause is:

```
GROUP BY {col_name | expr | position} [ASC | DESC], [WITH ROLLUP]
```

To appreciate the effect of GROUP BY, you can retrieve all of the values from a table.

```
mysql> SELECT * FROM menu;
```

```
+----+----------------+-------+
| ID | NAME           | PRICE |
+----+----------------+-------+
|  4 | catfish        |  5.00 |
|  2 | bass           |  6.75 |
|  6 | haddock        |  6.50 |
|  3 | salmon         |  9.50 |
|  5 | trout          |  6.00 |
|  1 | tuna           |  7.50 |
|  7 | yellowfin tuna | 12.00 |
+----+----------------+-------+
7 rows in set (0.00 sec)
```

Using GROUP BY on just one column can give us the same list in alphabetical order:

```
mysql> SELECT * FROM menu GROUP BY name;
```

```
+----+----------------+-------+
| id | name           | price |
+----+----------------+-------+
|  2 | bass           |  6.75 |
|  4 | catfish        |  5.00 |
|  6 | haddock        |  6.50 |
|  3 | salmon         |  9.50 |
|  5 | trout          |  6.00 |
|  1 | tuna           |  7.50 |
|  7 | yellowfin tuna | 12.00 |
+----+----------------+-------+
7 rows in set (0.00 sec)
```

If we had multiple entries for some of the fish (for example, tuna and yellowfin tuna), it could also be used to give a count by field value.

```
mysql> SELECT name, count(*) FROM menu GROUP BY name;
+----------------+----------+
| name           | count(*) |
+----------------+----------+
| bass           |        1 |
| catfish        |        1 |
| haddock        |        1 |
| salmon         |        1 |
| trout          |        1 |
| tuna           |        2 |
| yellowfin tuna |        2 |
+----------------+----------+
7 rows in set (0.00 sec)
```

More on how to use the modifiers of GROUP BY can be found in Section *11.12* of the MySQL manual.

HAVING

As the WHERE clause has already been discussed, one might wonder rightly — what is the point of the HAVING clause? The WHERE clause is used for simple facts and does not support aggregate evaluations. The HAVING clause is used for aggregate functions. It can be used to replace WHERE, but to do so is generally viewed as poor coding because it violates the SQL standard.

The HAVING clause is used to quantify results according to aggregate functions. For this reason, it is usually used in conjunction with the GROUP BY clause.

The basic syntax of the HAVING clause is:

```
HAVING where_condition
```

Carrying on with the previous `menu` example, a basic example of this is:

```
mysql> SELECT * FROM menu GROUP BY name HAVING id>'3';
+----+----------------+-------+
| id | name           | price |
+----+----------------+-------+
|  4 | catfish        |  5.00 |
|  6 | haddock        |  6.50 |
|  5 | trout          |  6.00 |
|  7 | yellowfin tuna | 12.00 |
+----+----------------+-------+
4 rows in set (0.00 sec)
```

For an example closer to real life a video rental store that wants to know which customers rent the most videos might use a query like this one:

```
mysql> SELECT customer_id,count(*) AS cnt FROM rental GROUP BY customer_
id HAVING cnt> 40;
+-------------+-----+
| customer_id | cnt |
+-------------+-----+
|          75 |  41 |
|         144 |  42 |
|         148 |  46 |
|         236 |  42 |
|         526 |  45 |
+-------------+-----+
5 rows in set (0.05 sec)
```

This shows the customer number followed by the number of total rentals in the record of rentals for each customer whose aggregate custom exceeds 40 videos.

ORDER BY

As the name implies, the ORDER BY clause is used to tell MySQL how to order the results of a query. The basic syntactical structure of this clause is as follows:

```
[ORDER BY {col_name | expr | position} [ASC | DESC], ...]
```

While the ORDER BY clause can be used in conjunction with the GROUP BY modifiers, this is typically not necessary. The following two examples illustrate why:

```
mysql> SELECT * FROM menu GROUP BY name ORDER BY id DESC;
+----+----------------+-------+
| id | name           | price |
+----+----------------+-------+
|  7 | yellowfin tuna | 12.00 |
|  6 | haddock        |  6.50 |
|  5 | trout          |  6.00 |
|  4 | catfish        |  5.00 |
|  3 | salmon         |  9.50 |
|  2 | bass           |  6.75 |
|  1 | tuna           |  7.50 |
+----+----------------+-------+
7 rows in set (0.00 sec)


mysql> SELECT * FROM menu ORDER BY id DESC;
+----+----------------+-------+
| id | name           | price |
+----+----------------+-------+
|  7 | yellowfin tuna | 12.00 |
|  6 | haddock        |  6.50 |
|  5 | trout          |  6.00 |
|  4 | catfish        |  5.00 |
|  3 | salmon         |  9.50 |
|  2 | bass           |  6.75 |
|  1 | tuna           |  7.50 |
+----+----------------+-------+
7 rows in set (0.00 sec)
```

Because the ORDER BY is applied after the GROUP BY, it largely abrogates the need for the grouping.

LIMIT

The LIMIT clause is used to restrict the number of rows that are returned in the result set. It takes two positive integers as arguments. The first number indicates the point at which to start counting and counts from zero for that process. The second number indicates how many times to increment the first number by one in order to determine the desired limit.

The syntax of the LIMIT clause is as follows:

```
LIMIT {[offset,] row_count | row_count OFFSET offset}
```

The following four examples show how LIMIT may be used to reduce the returned results neatly. Used in an iterative fashion, incrementing the parameters of a LIMIT clause allows you to step through results.

In this first example, LIMIT is applied to an alphabetic listing of fish names. The table in question is the same one we used previously for GROUP BY. Note that the id numbers are out of sequence.

```
mysql> SELECT * FROM menu GROUP BY name LIMIT 3,4;
+----+----------------+-------+
| id | name           | price |
+----+----------------+-------+
|  3 | salmon         |  9.50 |
|  5 | trout          |  6.00 |
|  1 | tuna           |  7.50 |
|  7 | yellowfin tuna | 12.00 |
+----+----------------+-------+
4 rows in set (0.00 sec)
```

In order to get the id numbers sequenced correctly, we employ an ORDER BY clause to prep the data before applying the terms of the LIMIT clause to it.

```
mysql> SELECT * FROM menu ORDER BY id LIMIT 3,4;
+----+----------------+-------+
| id | name           | price |
+----+----------------+-------+
|  4 | catfish        |  5.00 |
|  5 | trout          |  6.00 |
|  6 | haddock        |  6.50 |
|  7 | yellowfin tuna | 12.00 |
+----+----------------+-------+
4 rows in set (0.00 sec)
```

These final two examples illustrate how to apply LIMIT to searches that could easily return scores, if not hundreds or thousands, of hits.

```
mysql> SELECT * FROM menu ORDER BY id LIMIT 2,3;
+----+---------+-------+
| id | name    | price |
+----+---------+-------+
|  3 | salmon  |  9.50 |
|  4 | catfish |  5.00 |
|  5 | trout   |  6.00 |
+----+---------+-------+
3 rows in set (0.00 sec)


mysql> SELECT * FROM menu LIMIT 2,4;
+----+---------+-------+
| id | name    | price |
+----+---------+-------+
|  3 | salmon  |  9.50 |
|  4 | catfish |  5.00 |
|  5 | trout   |  6.00 |
|  6 | haddock |  6.50 |
+----+---------+-------+
4 rows in set (0.00 sec)
```

LIMIT and HAVING may seem very similar as they both work to narrow the aggregate. The difference between them lies in the timing of their application by MySQL. HAVING is applied as a parameter of the search *before* MySQL actions the query. The LIMIT clause, on the other hand, is applied *after* the search results have been returned.

If you are programming for a web application and your database and web server are located on a single machine, you need to conserve your server resources. Therefore, you almost certainly want to use HAVING instead of LIMIT. If you are trying to reduce your search time, again, use HAVING. However, if your desired hits will comprise a sizable portion of the results otherwise, or your database server, application server, and web server are each discrete systems from each other, then you might consider using LIMIT. In the main, however, LIMIT allows MySQL to use more resources than HAVING because the former is applied after the query is already processed.

INTO OUTFILE

INTO OUTFILE allows for the rapid output of tabular results to a text file on the local host. Its basic syntax is as follows:

```
INTO OUTFILE 'file_name'
```

For example, one could use:

```
mysql> SELECT * FROM menu ORDER BY id LIMIT 3,4 INTO OUTFILE '/tmp/
results.txt';
Query OK, 4 rows affected (0.00 sec)
```

This would output the results of the query to a file results.txt in the /tmp directory of the server.

More information can be found in the MySQL manual, Section 12.2.8 (URL: http://dev.mysql.com/doc/refman/5.1/en/select.html). It is understood that MySQL for Python allows a program to process the data and output the results using Python's own I/O calls.

Passing a query to MySQL

We have just seen how to form a query for a generic MySQL session. While that was not particularly difficult, using MySQL for Python is even easier. For this next section, we will be working against a database fish with a table menu that has the following contents:

```
+----+---------------+-------+
| id | name          | price |
+----+---------------+-------+
|  1 | tuna          |  7.50 |
|  2 | bass          |  6.75 |
|  3 | salmon        |  9.50 |
|  4 | catfish       |  5.00 |
|  5 | trout         |  6.00 |
|  6 | haddock       |  6.50 |
|  7 | yellowfin tuna | 12.00 |
+----+---------------+-------+
```

As discussed in *Chapter 1, Python's interface with MySQL* requires a cursor. It is through the `cursor` object that we pass commands to MySQL. So, we import MySQL for Python, log into our database `fish` and create the cursor as follows:

```
import MySQLdb
mydb = MySQLdb.connect(host = 'localhost',
                       user = 'skipper',
                       passwd = 'mysecret',
                       db = 'fish')
cur = mydb.cursor()
```

A simple SELECT statement

To pass a command to MySQL, we use the `execute()` method that we briefly covered in the last chapter. The `execute()` method, as the name implies, expects an argument of what is to be executed by Python. In other words, it takes the MySQL sentence or statement as its argument. Its basic syntax is as follows:

```
results_variable = cursor_handle.execute('MySQL statement')
```

In practice, it looks like this:

```
command = cur.execute('SELECT * FROM menu')
```

As you might surmise from the previous discussion on SELECT, this returns all rows of the `table` menu.

You will notice that we did not have to specify the database in the `execute()` call. This is because it was already specified in the `MySQLdb.connect()` call. Each connection represents one database being accessed in the name of one user on one host. If any of those dynamics need to change, a new `connection` object becomes necessary. It is possible to create a connection without declaring a database at the outset, but a database must be specified before a cursor can be created or a query made.

Unlike in the MySQL shell, the `execute()` call here does not immediately return the results. They are held in system memory (RAM) until you tell MySQL for Python what you want to do with them. This is another reason why it is important to mind your use of system resources in the use of HAVING and LIMIT, as mentioned previously.

For the purposes of illustration, we can pull down all of the results in one go. To do this, we use the `fetchall()` method of the cursor object.

```
results = command.fetchall()
```

At this point, the results have now passed from MySQL for Python into the calling program's resource matrix. The `fetchall()` method returns its results as a series of tuples. Printing the value of `results` shows the following:

```
>>> print results
((1L, 'tuna', Decimal('7.50')), (2L, 'bass', Decimal('6.75')), (3L,
'salmon', Decimal('9.50')), (4L, 'catfish', Decimal('5.00')), (5L,
'trout', Decimal('6.00')), (6L, 'haddock', Decimal('6.50')), (7L,
'yellowfin tuna', Decimal('12.00')))
```

This is obviously far from human-friendly. However, we can now use Python's own data-handling resources to parse it. In programming terms, we now have greater control over our data and can present it as we want. So let's create a loop to iterate through the results and print the results in a formatted way.

```
>>> for record in results:
...          print record[0] , "-->", record[1] , " @", record[2], "each"
...
1 --> tuna   @ 7.50 each
2 --> bass   @ 6.75 each
3 --> salmon  @ 9.50 each
4 --> catfish  @ 5.00 each
5 --> trout  @ 6.00 each
6 --> haddock  @ 6.50 each
7        --> yellowfin tuna  @ 12.00 each
```

Modifying the results

The last query could easily have returned more results than we could use. As mentioned previously, this is why the SELECT command comes with a comprehensive suite of modifiers to nuance one's query and, hopefully, use a minimal amount of system resources.

To use GROUP BY, ORDER BY, or any of the other clauses that one can add to a SELECT statement, one simply adds them to the MySQL statement that is passed to the `execute()` method.

If you wanted to retrieve information only on fish whose price is greater than $7, you would need to sort through the data again and find the record with the matching name. Better to let MySQL do the dirty work. Using the preceding simple query (see *Where* under *Other helpful quantifiers*), we can do the following:

```
command = cur.execute("""SELECT * FROM menu WHERE price > 7""")
results = command.fetchall()
for record in results:
    print record[0], ". ", record[1], "(%s)" %record[2]
```

The results would be:

```
1 .  tuna (7.50)

3 .  salmon (9.50)

7 .  yellowfin tuna (12.00)
```

Similar statements can be passed for each of the SELECT clauses discussed above.

Using user-defined variables

What if you want to specify a different price floor every time you run the search? What if you didn't want to use a floor but specify the price exactly? What if you wanted to reuse part of the statement and automate queries by fish name instead of retrieving all of them at once? Under such circumstances, you need to be able to handle variables in your SELECT statements.

MySQL for Python passes variables to MySQL in the same way that Python formats other kinds of output. If we wanted to specify just the floor of the search, we would assign the variable as any other and pass it to the execute() method as a string. Consider the following snippet from a Python terminal session:

```
>>> value = "7.50"
>>> command = cur.execute("""SELECT * FROM menu WHERE price = %s"""
%(value))
>>> results = cur.fetchall()
>>> for record in results:
...     print record[0], ". ", record[1], "(%s)" %record[2]
...
...
1 .  tuna (7.50)
```

If we wanted the user to have the option of specifying the price precisely or using comparative expressions, we can add in that option along with making the previous variable user-defined.

```
>>> operation = input("operation: ")
operation: '='
>>> value = input("value: ")
value: 7.50
>>> command = cur.execute("""SELECT * FROM menu WHERE price %s %s"""
%(operation, value))
>>> results = cur.fetchall()
>>> for record in results:
...     print record[0], ". ", record[1], "(%s)" %record[2]
...
1 .   tuna (7.50)
```

As you may have surmised by now, the `execute()` method is simply passing the MySQL statement as a string to `_mysql`, which in turn passes it to the C database API, which in turn passes it to MySQL. This being the case, we can define the statement separately and pass it to `execute()` as a variable. Consider the following replacement for the latter half of the preceding code.

```
>>> statement = """SELECT * FROM menu WHERE price %s %s""" %(operation,
value)
>>> command = cur.execute(statement)
>>> results = cur.fetchall()
>>> for record in results:
...     print record[0], ". ", record[1], "(%s)" %record[2]
...
1 .   tuna (7.50)
```

Determining characteristics of a database and its tables

For reasons of security, one simply must not rely on the user to know the database structure in order to make a query. Even if the user does, one should never write code that assumes this. You never know who the user is and what nefarious results will be sought by the user. Given that there are more people than you know who want to break your code and exploit your data, it is best practice to restrict the user's knowledge of the database and to verify the integrity of any data the end user inputs into the program.

Without doubt, the best way to restrict the user's knowledge of the database is to provide set options for the user in a way that the user cannot edit. In **graphical user interfaces (GUIs)**, this is done most often by drop-down menus and radio buttons. In terminal-based programs, one lists the options. The former keeps the programmer in control of the environment and so funnels the user to the point of either choosing the set options or not using the application. In the case of a terminal-based program or in the case of the text boxes of a GUI, one still has to evaluate the data input by the user. Otherwise, a mishandled error opens the system up for technological vandalism or even burglary.

To evaluate data input from the user, one typically identifies parameters for the variable installed and then validates the input through a series of conditionals. Such parameters can include criteria such as string length, variable type, alphabet characters only, alphanumeric characters, or others. If the data fails anywhere along the way, the program prints a customized error message to the user. The error message is not the message thrown by Python or other, ancillary process. Rather, it is the message given when that error message is detected. The user is then directed to do a given action—contacting their administrator, changing their input, and so on.

The scenario works well for most cases. There are, however, instances in database-driven applications where one must implement more advanced measures. For example, if you had several tables that could be searched, you would not necessarily want to have a different program for each one. Instead, it makes better sense to abstract the problem of search to where the same search function can be applied to any of the tables at the user's discretion. The problem breaks down as follows:

1. Determine what tables exist
2. Assign a number to each one for a terminal-based program
3. Offer the options to the user
4. Allow the user to detail a search query
5. Ensure that the data input for the table is one of the options
6. Run the query
7. Print the results

Determining what tables exist

In a MySQL session, the tables of a database are available through the following command:

```
SHOW TABLES in <database name>;
```

This allows you to specify a different database from that which you are using at the time.

If you specify the database to be used in the argument to `MySQLdb.connect()`, then you do not need to specify the database name.

In Python, we pass the `SHOW TABLES` statement to `execute()` and process the returned data.

```
>>> statement = """SHOW TABLES"""
>>> command = cur.execute(statement)
>>> results = cur.fetchall()
```

Previously, here we would iterate over the results and output the parts we want. Instead, we will initiate a list and append the table names to it.

```
>>> table_list = []
>>> for record in results:
...     table_list.append(record[0])
```

Assigning each table a number

While we detailed a necessary part of the pseudocode in the last section, it is not wholly necessary for us in this process. Using a list, we can access each item discretely without having to give it a number. However, in order to ensure that the process is plain to see, we could process the list into a dictionary, using the item's ordinal place plus one as the key value.

```
>>> item_dict = {}
>>> for item in xrange(1,len(table_list)):
...     item_dict[item-1] = table_list[item-1]
```

The effect is that the first item of the list, which normally is accessed with subscript 0, is assigned the key value 1. All other tables are handled similarly, and we are set to scale to any number of tables in the database.

Offering the options to the user

Offering the options to the user, we simply print out the key value as the indicator for the table name.

```
>>> for key in item_dict:
...     print "%s => %s" % (key, item_dict[key])
>>> choice = input("Please enter your choice of table to be queried. ")
```

To verify the input, we would then check that the value is an integer within the same range as those offered. As shown below, however, we can also code the program to be self-validating. Note, however, that this should be complementary to proper security checks. One never knows with what haste the next person who edits the code will approach the task.

Allowing the user to detail a search query

Now, the user can be allowed to input a value for which he or she would like to search. As shown previously, this can be any value in the database. However, realistically speaking, we need to give structure to the choice-making process. We can do this at the same time that we validate the user's choice of database by requesting of MySQL the names of the columns for the given table.

```
>>> try: table_choice = item_dict[choice]
... except: print 'Invalid input.  Please try again.'
```

If the user's choice reconciles with `item_dict`, then we get the name of the table to search. We can then ask MySQL for Python to return the column headings of that table.

```
>>> statement = """DESCRIBE %s""" %item_dict[choice]
>>> command = cur.execute(statement)
>>> results = cur.fetchall()
>>> column_list = []
>>> for record in results:
...     column_list.append(record[0])
```

With the column names in a list, we can offer them to the user in the same way as the table names.

```
>>> for i in xrange(0, len(column_list)):
...     print "%s.  %s" %(i+1, column_list[i])
...
1.  id
2.  name
3.  price
>>> table_choice = input("Please input the number of the table you wish
to query. ")
```

Once again, we would check that the value entered is an integer within the range offered. This can be affected with a `try-except-else` statement:

```
while True:
    try:
        if column_choice > 0:
            if column_choice < len(column_list):
                continue
            else:
                break
        else:
            break
    except:
        print "Invalid input. Please try again."
    else:
        break
```

From here one would then solicit the search query from the user and submit it to MySQL.

Changing queries dynamically

But what if the user does not want to submit a precise query but needs a list of the possibilities? There are a couple of ways to clarify the search. We could first keep a list of the common search queries. This is something done often by the likes of Google and Yahoo!. This works very well with large datasets served through web servers because it uses a static list of terms and simply culls them out. For more dedicated applications, one can use MySQL's pattern matching ability to present known options on-the-fly.

Pattern matching in MySQL queries

Where Python's regular expression engine is very robust, MySQL supports the two following metacharacters for forming regular expressions:

- %: Zero or more characters matched in aggregate
- _: Any single character matched individually

Pattern matching is always a matter of comparison. Therefore, with either of these, never use operators of equality.

```
SELECT * FROM menu WHERE name = 's%';          WRONG
SELECT * FROM menu WHERE name <> 's%';          WRONG
```

Instead, use the keywords LIKE and NOT LIKE.

```
SELECT * FROM menu WHERE name LIKE 's%';          RIGHT
SELECT * FROM menu WHERE name NOT LIKE 's%';      RIGHT
```

Using metacharacters, one can match records using very irregular terms. Some of the possible combinations follow below:

- s%: A value that begins with the letter *s*
- %s: A value that ends with the letter *s*
- %s%: A value that contains the letter *s*
- s%l: A value that begins with *s* and ends with *l*
- s%l%: A value that begins with *s* and contains at least one instance of the letter *l*
- s_l%: A value that begins with *s* and whose third letter is *l*
- _____: A five letter value (that is five underscore characters in succession)
- __%: A value with at least two characters

Putting it into practice

For a smaller dataset or even larger datasets served over low-contest or no-contest connections (for example local servers or dedicated LAN connections), there is the option of running a live query to present the user with the possible options. If the user has specified the database and table to be used, as in the example seen previously, then it is a small matter to match patterns in a column using LIKE and a regular expression.

The MySQL sentence for what we are doing, along with its results, is as follows:

```
mysql> SELECT name FROM menu WHERE name LIKE 's%';
+--------+
| name   |
+--------+
| salmon |
| sole   |
+--------+
2 rows in set (0.00 sec)
```

It is important to phrase the query in such a way as to narrow the returned values as much as possible.

Here, instead of returning whole records, we tell MySQL to return only the namecolumn. This natural reduction in the data reduces processing time for both MySQL and Python. This saving is then passed on to your server in the form of more sessions able to be run at one time.

In Python, the preceding statement would look like this:

```
column = 'name'
term = 's%'
statement = """select %s from menu where name like '%s'""" % (column,
term)
```

Using the conversion specifier (%s), this code can easily be adapted for more dynamic uses.

Having restricted the parameters of the search, we are in greater control of the results and can therefore anticipate the number of fields in each record returned. We then have to execute the query and tell the cursor to fetch all of the records. To process the records, we iterate over them using a pattern similar to what we used previously:

```
command = cur.execute(statement)
results = cur.fetchall()

column_list = []
for record in results:
    column_list.append(record[0])

print "Did you mean:"
for i in xrange(0, len(column_list)):
    print "%s.   %s" % (i+1, column_list[i])
option = raw_input ('Number:')
intoption = int(option)
```

The results for this code are:

```
Did you mean:
1.   salmon
2.   sole
Number:
```

Naturally, we must then test the user input. After that, we can process the query and return the results.

This example is shown using terminal options so we do not use any JavaScript to transfer the options. However, in modern day reality, any application that relies on a web browser—either for background processing or for a primary interface, can use this code with minor modifications.

Project: A command-line search utility

This chapter has been about querying MySQL from Python. As a project to finish it out, we will build a command-line search utility. Rather than ask the user for the search term, we will expect the user to state the term as an argument for the command-line invocation.

 With a bit more code for this project, we could create a GUI for this program. GUI programming increases the complexity of the code. How much more complex it gets depends on the library being used, but it is nonetheless unnecessary for what we need to illustrate in this project. Until we are certain that we have a database and can connect to it, it is best to keep it simple.

Now, it is true that we could simply take input and feed it through MySQL for Python as a generic SELECT * statement. The logic for this bare bones implementation has been illustrated previously to a great extent. We can create something a bit more sophisticated.

The following characteristics should apply to our search utility:

- The user calls it from the command line (that is, shell prompt)
- The search term is defined at the time of calling
- If the -t flag is issued, the following term is the table to be used; default is to search all tables
- If the -f flag is issued, the output is formatted by table
- If the -o flag is issued, the output is written to the given file

To illustrate, calling the application searchme.py, one should be able to call the application as follows:

```
./searchme.py -t menu -f -o output.txt query
```

This should search the table menu from the database fish for the term query, format the output, and write it to a file called output.txt. You may need to nuance this statement depending on your operating system's requirements. For example, Windows users should not include ./ before the program call. For more help with calling Python on Windows, see the Python Windows FAQ at the following URL: http://www.python.org/doc/faq/windows/.

Preparing a database for searching

For this project, however, we will leave behind the fish database for the moment and use the world sample database available from MySQL. For users of Linux, Unix, and Mac OS X, download the database from the following URL:

http://downloads.mysql.com/docs/world.sql.gz

To unpack this archive, simply issue the appropriate unpacking command:

```
gunzip world.sql.gz
```

Windows users, or users without the utility gunzip, should use the ZIP file:

http://downloads.mysql.com/docs/world.sql.zip

Then use an archive manager to unpack the ZIP file.

Regardless of your platform, you should then be left with a file world.sql. From the directory in which that file resides, log into MySQL. You first need to create a database world and then import the file.

1   To create the database, type the following at the prompt:
    ```
    CREATE world;
    ```

2   Then tell MySQL to use that database:
    ```
    USE world;
    ```

3   Import the file with the following MySQL command:
    ```
    SOURCE world.sql;
    ```

MySQL will then populate the database world with three tables of data: City, Country, and CountryLanguage.

Planning your work, then working your plan

All of the flags mentioned as characteristics previously are nothing more than added functionality to the core function of searching. Our first order of business should therefore be to create well-abstracted search functionality. Then we can build on it to allow for the functionality of each of the given flags. So our plan of development may be summarized as follows:

- Develop a well-abstracted search functionality.
- Implement specification of the search term from the command-line.
- Implement and incorporate the functionality of each flag in turn:
  -t, -f, and -o.

Develop a well-abstracted search functionality

Abstraction is the secret of all computer programming. It is what enables computer programs to be run for more than one single task. In the early days of computing, programs were written with very narrow applications. This was usually due to limits in the technology involved. In the modern day, the obtuseness of some languages still keeps them from being applied beyond certain domains (for example, BIOS systems). Even then, languages such as **Forth** are so difficult to follow that they are largely viewed as write-once-and-forget-about-it. Fortunately, Python offers us significant flexibility, and this flexibility is carried through in MySQL for Python. This allows us to create the infrastructure of a search while allowing us to specify select parts of it.

In this project, we will specify the host, database, and user information for the database connection. The rest of the query information, however, will be open to the user. First, however, we begin our program with a shebang (line):

```
#!/usr/bin/env python
```

This is a Linux shebang line that calls whichever Python interpreter is set for general use in the environmental variables of the shell. If we want a specific interpreter, we can naturally edit this and call the other interpreter directly. This format will also work on newer versions of Mac OS. If you are on Windows, you will naturally have to modify this line according to the directory structure of your Windows installation. A common Windows shebang line is:

```
#!c:/Python/python.exe -u
```

Ensure that you do not forget the trailing -u flag. This puts Python into an unbuffered mode on Windows systems.

Next, we import MySQL for Python. Until we are ready to add more functionality beyond a hard-coded search query, we should hold off on importing more modules.

```
import MySQLdb
```

Now we are ready to create a database connection. You will recall from the first chapter that the format for creating a database connection is:

```
[variable] = MySQLdb.connect(host="[hostname]",
                             user="[username]",
                             passwd="[password]",
                             db="[database name]")
```

For the `world` database, using user `user` and password `p4ssw0rd` on the localhost, the invocation for the connection is:

```
mydb = MySQLdb.connect(host = 'localhost',
                       user = 'user',
                       passwd = 'p4ssw0rd',
                       db = 'world')
```

We then must create the cursor:

```
cur = mydb.cursor()
```

We are then ready to construct a query infrastructure. To ensure as much flexibility as possible, we simply pull all of the variables out of the MySQL SELECT syntax and define them separately.

```
table =    'City'

column = 'Name'

term = 's%'

statement = """select * from %s where %s like '%s'""" %(table, column,
term
```

This hardwiring of the search query allows us to test the connection before coding the rest of the function. By defining the variables discretely, we make it easier to change them to user-determined variables later.

There may be a tendency here to insert user-determined variables immediately. With experience, it is possible to do this. However, if there are any doubts about the availability of the database, your best fallback position is to keep it simple and hardwired. This reduces the number of variables in making a connection and helps one to blackbox the situation, making troubleshooting much easier.

With the query constructed, we can execute it and get the results:

```
command = cur.execute(statement)
results = cur.fetchall()
```

You can then test the connection with the following code:

```
record_list = []
for record in results:
        record_list.append(record[0])


for i in xrange(0, len(record_list)):
      print "%s.  %s" %(i+1, record_list[i])
```

The logic of this code is discussed previously in this chapter so we will pass over it here as understood.

If you execute the program, the output should scroll off the screen and you should get a list of 431 cities. The last entry should read as follows:

```
431.  Santa Monica
```

Knowing that we can interact with the database, we can now go to the next step, specifying the search term from the command-line.

Specifying the search term from the command-line

Python allows you to receive a command-line argument using the sys module. If the only argument expected on the command-line is the name of the query, we could get by with code like this:

```
    import sys
    ...
    query = sys.argv[1]
```

Alas, life is seldom so simple. If we were to follow this route of development, all the flags mentioned previously for this program would be mandatory and have to be submitted every time the program ran. So, for the sample call on page 24, we would have to program for six fixed arguments everytime the program is called. Recall that the command read:

```
./searchme.py -t menu -f -o output.txt query
```

The arguments for `sys.argv` that would be required are:

- 0 the command itself, naturally
- 1 the flag `-t`
- 2 the table name
- 3 the `-f` flag
- 4 the flag `-o`
- 5 the output file name
- 6 the search string for the query

If we pulled all the flags and left only the arguments in a set order, we would still have three arguments. This makes the program cumbersome and makes calls to it error-prone.

By far, the better way forward is to use the module `optparse`. Importing `optparse` incorporates high-level support for processing arguments at runtime. Another alternative is the `getopt` module, but this is not as robust or as easy to use.

For consistency's sake, let's edit the preamble of our Python program to import the module.

```
import optparse
```

The `optparse` module provides an `OptionParser` class that handles both option processing and error handling. It also provides a standardized interface similar to other programs (for example, `-h` for help). All for the meager cost of a module import.

To access all this option parsing goodness, we need to instantiate an object of the `OptionParser` class.

```
opt = optparse.OptionParser()
```

Adding arguments then is simply a matter of adding options using the `add_option()` method of the object. For our purposes, we need to follow a straightforward syntactic formula:

```
object.add_option("-[short flag option]", "--[long flag option]",
action="store", type="string", dest = "[variable name under which to
store the option]"
```

We will keep to this formula for the sake of simplicity even when other options might seem more logical.

The optparse module is a very robust kit for option parsing, and the full syntax of it is beyond the scope of this book. A fuller discussion can be found in the online help() function or the Python documentation.

So to add an option for the query, we include this:

```
opt.add_option("-q", "--query", action="store", type="string",
dest="term")
```

After all the options are assigned in the code, we then have to compile them.

```
opt, args = opt.parse_args()
```

The parse_args() method returns a tuple. The first of the two values, opt, is an object containing the values of all the options passed to the program. The second value, args, is a list of any remaining arguments.

These last three lines should precede the MySQLdb call to connect to the database. You may then change the assignment of the variable term.

```
term = opt.term
```

Whatever value is given in the dest argument of the add_option() method becomes an attribute of the OptionParser object. Therefore, you could also delete the term assignment line and edit the statement value to reflect opt.term. However, this makes the code more difficult to read by someone else or even by yourself six months down the line. Remember the second line of the Zen of Python:

Explicit is better than implicit

With that code written, you should be able to call the program with a -q flag and set the query from the command-line. If the program is called searchme.py, a sample query would be:

```
./searchme.py -q 'dubai'
```

The results should be singular:

1. Dubai

Knowing that it is a MySQL database, you could also pass MySQL metacharacters.

```
./project-ch2.py -q 'm%i'
```

and get multiple hits in return:

1. `Mallawi`
2. `Makati`
3. `Marawi`
4. `Malasiqui`
5. `Mati`
6. `Madurai`
7. `Malkajgiri`
8. `Morvi`
9. `Miyazaki`
10. `Maebashi`
11. `Moriguchi`
12. `Manzhouli`
13. `Moroni`
14. `Mbuji-Mayi`
15. `Matadi`
16. `Mexicali`
17. `Maradi`
18. `Maiduguri`
19. `Makurdi`
20. `Miaoli`
21. `Moshi`
22. `Mytiti`
23. `Miami`

Note that your search will complete and return the same regardless of whether you use `-q` or `--query`.

Implementing and incorporating the other functions: -t, -f, and -o

Now we can add the other options to the program. Like the `-q` flag for preceding query, we can use `-t` to assign values for the table.

```
opt.add_option("-t", "--table", action="store", type="string",
dest="table")
```

Unless you want to support multiple formats for the output, the format flag should be a Boolean value.

```
opt.add_option("-f", "--format", action="store_true", dest="format")
```

In order to store a Boolean variable, we set the default action as either `store_true` or `store_false`. The former is for setting the value to `True` when the flag is present; the converse is true for the latter. Because of the type of action applied to the option, the Boolean type of the variable is understood by Python.

We then assign the value of `opt.table` to `table` and `opt.format` to the variable `format`.

For formatting, we then set up a conditional clause that runs if the format flag is present. Given that we are formatting the output on one level, we can also revise the code so that the default is raw. The following code snippet should follow from where the value of `record[0]` is appended to `column_list`, taking the place of that loop as well as the `for` loop discussed in the section *Planning your work, then working your plan* (earlier in this chapter).

```
column_list = []
for record in results:
    column_list.append(record[0:])

if form is True:
    columns_query = """DESCRIBE %s""" % (table)
    columns_command = cur.execute(columns_query)
    headers = cur.fetchall()
    column_list = []
    for record in headers:
            column_list.append(record[0])

    output=""
    for record in results:
            output = output + "=========================\n\n"
            for field_no in xrange(0, len(column_list)):
                    output = output + column_list[field_no]+ ": " +
str(record[field_no]) + "\n"
            output = output + "\n"

else:
    output=[]
    for record in xrange(0, len(results)):

            output.append(results[record])
    output = ''.join(output)
```

Note that the subscript for `record` in the third line has been broadened to include the rest of the record.

At this stage, you can append an output statement at the end of the program to see its results.

```
print output
```

We are not yet at the end for this program as we also need to include facility for writing the output to a file of the user's choice.

Including an option for an output file

At this point, including an option for an output file is simply a matter of inserting the option into the list at the beginning of the program and then testing for it once output is finally saved. To add the option to the list managed by optparse, we simply insert this line after the last option:

```
opt.add_option("-o", "--output", action="store", type="string",
dest="outfile")
```

Note that the output variable is not a requirement in our program. Therefore, one cannot assign it as automatically as the other variables were assigned. Instead, one must test for it, prefixing the object handle to its attribute. If a value has been assigned, then write the file. Otherwise, default output is STDOUT.

```
if opt.outfile:
    outfile = opt.outfile
    out = open(outfile, w)
    out.write(output)

else:
    print output
```

Room to grow

While the projection specification that we set for ourselves is fulfilled, there is more that can be done on this program to make it more serviceable in a production environment. Some areas that you might look at for further practice are:

- Set the host, database, username, and password from command-line options. You will naturally need to error-check each of them. You will probably want to use the getpass module to accept the password in production environments.
- Set an option for the column variable and testing whether that column exists in the chosen database.
- Set up error-checking for the results itself.

The `world` database has a few other tables besides `City`. Can you aggregate their records in Python without using a `JOIN` statement?

Summary

It almost goes without saying that querying and data retrieval is the bread and butter of database programming. In this chapter, we have covered the formation of a MySQL query and how to pass it from Python. We also saw how to use user-defined variables to allow dynamic formation of statements rather than pre-configured queries. In order to adjust our program flow, we also saw how to determine the characteristics of a database and its tables from within Python. Finally, we programmed a command-line search utility that returns data of the user's choice in two different formats.

In the next chapter, we will look at the flipside of the `SELECT` command, `INSERT`.

3
Simple Insertion

The obvious complement to record retrieval is the insertion of data into a MySQL database. Data insertion is a matter of learning the syntax of the MySQL keyword for the task and applying it through MySQL for Python.

As with retrieval, MySQL functions on the basis of parameter-based invocation and the returning of results in accordance with those parameters. All of this is again based on using MySQL for Python as an intermediary to that process to invoke MySQL, to log in, and to connect to our chosen database.

You will recall that, in *Chapter 2, Simple Querying*, we needed to validate user input consistently. Malformed input would have caused our program to throw an error without it. That caution goes doubly for insertion. Unqualified user input can corrupt a database and even give the malicious user access to all traffic on the server by granting him or her unwarranted administrative privileges.

In this chapter, we will look at the following:

- Forming an insertion statement in MySQL
- Passing an insertion to MySQL
- User-defined variables in a MySQL insertion
- Passing metadata between databases
- Changing insertion statements dynamically, without user input

Each of these sections will be built into the project at the end of this chapter: Inserting user input into MySQL from the command-line without using the MySQL shell.

Forming a MySQL insertion statement

As with record retrieval in the previous chapter, inserting data into MySQL through Python relies on understanding data insertion in MySQL itself. You will recall that the requirements of a computing language necessitate the use of as few words as possible to do anything. Ideally, there should be only one word as the Zen of Python reads:

> *There should be one — and preferably only one — obvious way to do it.*

For retrieval, we used the SELECT command. For putting data into the database, we use INSERT. So instead of saying "Put everything on the far table!" or "Stick everything over there!", MySQL needs specification such as:

```
INSERT INTO far VALUES("everything");
```

This is perhaps the most basic insertion statement that one can make for MySQL. You can tell from it that the basic syntax of MySQL's INSERT statement is as follows:

```
INSERT INTO <some table> (<some column names>) VALUES("<some
values>");
```

Now let's take this skeleton of a statement apart and see how MySQL compares to what we might use in English.

INSERT

It should be clear by now that the use of INSERT is for our benefit as humans. There is nothing special about the word other than the fact that the MySQL programmer used it. It is easier to remember, closer to being standard throughout English, and better reflects the action being called than, say, STICK. As you may know, *put* is currently used in other programming languages for much the same kind of functionality (for example, fputs in PHP, C, C++). The keyword consequently could have been PAPAYA if the MySQL programmers coded the database system to use that word instead of INSERT (of course, the usability of the system would have taken a sharp drop at that point). All that matters is that we use the word that the system requires in order to do the action that we desire.

It is worth noting that there is one other keyword that can be used for placing data into a MySQL database. REPLACE uses much the same syntax as INSERT.

```
REPLACE INTO <some table> SET("<some column name>" = "<some value>");
```

As it is formed on analogy with SELECT, we will not discuss REPLACE much. However, you can read more about it on the MySQL manual page at: http://dev.mysql.com/doc/refman/5.1/en/replace.html

INTO

In a lot of ways, the MySQL database handles insertion like a postmaster. It will put mail anywhere you tell it as long as the box exists. So if we are going to tell MySQL to INSERT something, we must tell it where that something must go. To do that we use the complementary keyword INTO. This is the natural complement to the commands INSERT and REPLACE.

If you are new to computer programming, it may still seem reasonable to ask a computer to just do something. But computers are ultimately just machines, exceedingly fast and dumb. They will not reason unless they are explicitly, painstakingly, told how to reason by the programmer. They cannot guess unless told *how*. In the early days of modern computing, the 1970s and early 1980s, programmers would describe this dynamic of computing with the acronym **GIGO**—*garbage in, garbage out*. If you as the programmer don't tell it what to do, it won't know how to do it.

Table name

Python helps with this process by offering high-level handles for a lot of common functionality, but there are still limits to that automation and elements of programming for which one must assume responsibility. Where MySQL sticks your data is one of them. The table value is yours to define. If you tell MySQL the correct place to put information, all is well. If it puts it in the wrong place, chances are you are to blame (unless someone is holding a strong magnet next to the CPU at the time). If MySQL does not know what to do with your data, it will throw an error—as we will see in the next chapter.

Column names

In this part of the statement, you indicate to MySQL the order in which you will pass the values later in the statement. These are dealt with like variable names and so are not set in quotes, single or double.

The column names that you must address here and in the value section of the statement are determined by the nature of the database. If we use the `fish` database from the previous chapter, we have the following dataset:

```
mysql> select * from menu;
```

```
+----+----------------+-------+
| id | name           | price |
+----+----------------+-------+
|  1 | tuna           |  7.50 |
|  2 | bass           |  6.75 |
|  3 | salmon         |  9.50 |
|  4 | catfish        |  5.00 |
|  5 | trout          |  6.00 |
|  6 | haddock        |  6.50 |
|  7 | yellowfin tuna | 12.00 |
|  8 | sole           |  7.75 |
+----+----------------+-------+
8 rows in set (0.00 sec)
```

The definitions for this dataset are purposely poor for illustrative reasons.

```
mysql> describe menu;
```

```
+-------+--------------+------+-----+---------+----------------+
| Field | Type         | Null | Key | Default | Extra          |
+-------+--------------+------+-----+---------+----------------+
| id    | int(11)      | NO   | PRI | NULL    | auto_increment |
| name  | varchar(30)  | YES  |     | NULL    |                |
| price | decimal(6,2) | YES  |     | NULL    |                |
+-------+--------------+------+-----+---------+----------------+
3 rows in set (0.00 sec)
```

As such, the only value that is required, 'that cannot be left blank', is the value for `id`, the primary key. This is already set by the system because it is automatically incremented. Therefore, we can get away with the following statement:

```
mysql> insert into menu(name) values("shark");
```

You will notice that we have left off the value for the price column. The effect is that it is now set to a NULL value:

```
mysql> select * from menu;
+----+---------------+-------+
| id | name          | price |
+----+---------------+-------+
|  1 | tuna          |  7.50 |
|  2 | bass          |  6.75 |
|  3 | salmon        |  9.50 |
|  4 | catfish       |  5.00 |
|  5 | trout         |  6.00 |
|  6 | haddock       |  6.50 |
|  7 | yellowfin tuna| 12.00 |
|  8 | sole          |  7.75 |
|  9 | shark         |  NULL |
+----+---------------+-------+
9 rows in set (0.00 sec)
```

NULL values in themselves are not bad. All computing is data and code, but both code and data must be controlled by the programmer to affect a desired, controlled result. Otherwise, errors are sure to creep in along with aberrations, and compromises in security and effectiveness will be the result.

Any data on which a program depends for its execution should be required. If this were an enterprise database, you would probably want this hole closed and so would define the table differently. You would want to require a non-NULL value for as many columns as are necessary to ensure the security and serviceability of your database.

VALUES

There are two keywords that you can use to introduce the data to be inserted at this point in the INSERT statement: VALUE or VALUES. Either one is correct; both can be used with either a single value or multiple values. There needs to be no consonance between the number of values being inserted and the number aspect of the keyword.

```
VALUES("<some values>", "<some more values>", "<some other values>");
```

is to MySQL the same as:

```
VALUE("<some values>", "<some more values>", "<some other values>");
```

just like the following two phrases of an `INSERT` statement are the same:

```
VALUE("<some values>");
VALUES("<some values>");
```

All this keyword slot does is introduces the values in parentheses.

<some values>

The values that follow the `VALUES` keyword must appear in the same order as the column names. Otherwise, MySQL will try to place the data in the wrong location. If you do not verify the integrity of the data passed to MySQL, the data can quickly get out of hand. Consider the effect of this statement on the table menu.

```
mysql> INSERT INTO menu(name, price) VALUES("13.00", "shark");
```

Because of the discord between the order of column names and the order of values, this statement tells MySQL to insert the fields `name` and `price` with the following values:

- name = 13.00
- price = shark

The problem is that these values are not allowed by the definition of the table:

```
mysql> describe menu;
```

Field	Type	Null	Key	Default	Extra
id	int(11)	NO	PRI	NULL	auto_increment
name	varchar(30)	YES		NULL	
price	decimal(6,2)	YES		NULL	

```
3 rows in set (0.00 sec)
```

The field `name` is supposed to be a thirty character string. The field `price` is supposed to be a decimal value with up to six numbers to the left of the decimal point and up to two to the right. So what happens when the two are mixed up to the point of utter confusion? Disaster.

```
mysql> select * from menu;
+----+---------------+-------+
| id | name          | price |
+----+---------------+-------+
|  1 | tuna          |  7.50 |
|  2 | bass          |  6.75 |
|  3 | salmon        |  9.50 |
|  4 | catfish       |  5.00 |
|  5 | trout         |  6.00 |
|  6 | haddock       |  6.50 |
|  7 | yellowfin tuna| 12.00 |
|  8 | sole          |  7.75 |
|  9 | shark         |  NULL |
| 10 | 13.00         |  0.00 |
+----+---------------+-------+
10 rows in set (0.00 sec)
```

We get a fish called `13.00` that costs nothing! The value `13.00` can be a `varchar` string and is so interpreted by MySQL. However, `shark` cannot be interpreted as a decimal value in this context.

It is worth noting that the reason `shark` cannot be a decimal value is because it is not defined as such. By passing it in double quotes, we indicate that it is a value, not a variable name. If, however, we had previously defined a variable `shark` as a decimal value, then we could use it accordingly.

Such a definition could be done in either MySQL or Python. In Python, we would use a simple variable assignment statement:

```
shark = 13.00
```

This would be truncated by Python to `13.00`, but it would nonetheless preserve the integrity of the datatype (to insert `13.00`, we would need to use a `DECIMAL` type for the column when we create the table). The second zero could later be reclaimed with a formatting convention.

In MySQL, we would use the SET command. See the MySQL manual Section 8.4, for more:

```
http://dev.mysql.com/doc/refman/5.1/en/user-variables.html
```

; (semicolon)

As noted in the previous chapter, the semicolon is the line delimiter in MySQL. While necessary to indicate the end of any MySQL statement, it is not used when passing commands through MySQL for Python.

Helpful ways to nuance an INSERT statement

Like `SELECT` has other helpful quantifiers to weed through the data being returned, `INSERT` has ways of nuancing the origin of the data to be inserted as well as the timing and conditions of the insertion. The three most common ways of altering the way MySQL processes an `INSERT` statement are:

- `INSERT...SELECT...`
- `INSERT DELAYED...`
- `INSERT...ON DUPLICATE KEY UPDATE...`

In the following section, we take each one in turn.

INSERT...SELECT...

Using `INSERT...SELECT...` we can tell MySQL to draw from different tables without having to draw them into Python or to set a variable in MySQL. It functions on the following syntactic template:

```
INSERT INTO <target table>(target column name) SELECT <source column
name> FROM <source table>;
```

By default, the SELECT phrase of the sentence is greedy and will return as many hits as it can. As with a generic SELECT statement, however, we can restrict the hits returned using WHERE. See the *Other helpful quantifiers* section in the previous chapter for more on this critical argument to SELECT.

To understand how to use this technique well, let us switch to the world database from MySQL that was mentioned in the previous chapter.

```
USE world;
```

The database has three tables. If you forget what they are, simply type:

```
SHOW TABLES;
```

You will then be rewarded with the following output:

```
mysql> show tables;
+-----------------+
| Tables_in_world |
+-----------------+
| City            |
| Country         |
| CountryLanguage |
+-----------------+
3 rows in set (0.00 sec)
```

In order to affect a statement using INSERT...SELECT..., it is necessary to understand the make-up of each database. Use DESCRIBE to get the definitions on each.

```
mysql> describe City;
+-------------+----------+------+-----+---------+----------------+
| Field       | Type     | Null | Key | Default | Extra          |
+-------------+----------+------+-----+---------+----------------+
| ID          | int(11)  | NO   | PRI | NULL    | auto_increment |
| Name        | char(35) | NO   |     |         |                |
| CountryCode | char(3)  | NO   |     |         |                |
| District    | char(20) | NO   |     |         |                |
| Population  | int(11)  | NO   |     | 0       |                |
+-------------+----------+------+-----+---------+----------------+
5 rows in set (0.00 sec)
```

```
mysql> describe Country;
```

Field	Type	Null	Key	Default	Extra
Code	char(3)	NO	PRI		
Name	char(52)	NO			
Continent	enum('Asia','Europe','North America','Africa','Oceania','Antarctica','South America')	NO		Asia	
Region	char(26)	NO			
SurfaceArea	float(10,2)	NO		0.00	
IndepYear	smallint(6)	YES		NULL	
Population	int(11)	NO		0	
LifeExpectancy	float(3,1)	YES		NULL	
GNP	float(10,2)	YES		NULL	
GNPOld	float(10,2)	YES		NULL	
LocalName	char(45)	NO			
GovernmentForm	char(45)	NO			
HeadOfState	char(60)	YES		NULL	
Capital	int(11)	YES		NULL	
Code2	char(2)	NO			

```
15 rows in set (0.01 sec)
```

```
mysql> describe CountryLanguage;
```

Field	Type	Null	Key	Default	Extra
CountryCode	char(3)	NO	PRI		
Language	char(30)	NO	PRI		
IsOfficial	enum('T','F')	NO		F	
Percentage	float(4,1)	NO		0.0	

```
4 rows in set (0.01 sec)
```

INSERT...SELECT... allows us to draw from each of the tables to form a new one. Let's say we wanted a table Combo that operated off the same identifier as City and incorporated the names for the first 999 countries listed in that database. We would begin by creating a MySQL table for the task. Creating a MySQL table is addressed in a later chapter, so here we assume the existence of a table Combo with the following definition:

Field	Type	Null	Key	Default	Extra
ID	int(11)	NO	PRI	NULL	auto_increment
Name	char(35)	NO		NULL	
CountryCode	char(3)	NO		NULL	

Having done that we can insert the desired data from City into Combo using the following INSERT command:

```
INSERT INTO Combo(ID, Name, CountryCode) SELECT ID, Name, CountryCode
FROM City WHERE ID < 1000;
```

A SELECT command to the database then shows the effect. For the sake of space, let's restrict ID to 10.

```
mysql> SELECT * FROM Combo WHERE ID<=10;
+----+----------------+-------------+
| ID | Name           | CountryCode |
+----+----------------+-------------+
|  1 | Kabul          | AFG         |
|  2 | Qandahar       | AFG         |
|  3 | Herat          | AFG         |
|  4 | Mazar-e-Sharif | AFG         |
|  5 | Amsterdam      | NLD         |
|  6 | Rotterdam      | NLD         |
|  7 | Haag           | NLD         |
|  8 | Utrecht        | NLD         |
|  9 | Eindhoven      | NLD         |
| 10 | Tilburg        | NLD         |
+----+----------------+-------------+
10 rows in set (0.00 sec)
```

This significantly cuts down on I/O and therefore dramatically reduces processing time—whether perceived or real. It lightens the load on the network and makes it appear more responsive and able to handle more requests (all other dynamics being equal).

Note that even if your program is run on the same system as the database being queried, you will still have the dynamics of a network and therefore suffer lag if your program passes too many requests to MySQL too quickly.

Sluggishness on many systems is due to excessive data transfer between processes, not because of the speed at which those processes are executed.

More information on the INSERT...SELECT... functionality can be found in the MySQL manual at:

http://dev.mysql.com/doc/refman/5.1/en/insert-select.html

INSERT DELAYED...

The DELAYED argument to INSERT causes MySQL to handle the insertion in deference to other MySQL processes. When the server is sufficiently quiet, the INSERT command is executed. Until then, MySQL keeps it on hold.

The DELAYED argument simply follows the INSERT command. Otherwise, the syntax is the same:

```
INSERT DELAYED INTO <some table> (<some column names>) VALUES("<some
values>");
```

For finer details on the DELAYED argument to INSERT, see the MySQL manual at http://dev.mysql.com/doc/refman/5.1/en/insert-delayed.html

INSERT...ON DUPLICATE KEY UPDATE...

Whenever you insert a record into a large table, there is a chance of creating an identical record. If your INSERT statement would result in two identical records, MySQL will throw an error and refuse to create the record. The error you get will look something like this:

```
ERROR 1062 (23000): Duplicate entry '1' for key 'PRIMARY'
```

To mitigate against this error and the chance of submitted data not being inserted properly, MySQL offers this further argument to the INSERT command. The syntax is as follows:

```
INSERT INTO <some table>(<some column names>) VALUES ("<some values>")
ON DUPLICATE KEY UPDATE <change to make the data unique>
```

After UPDATE, simply include what you have MySQL do to the record that you would insert in order to ensure that it is no longer a duplicate. In practice, this means incrementing the Primary key identifier. So where we get an error with one statement, we can adapt the statement. In the following statement, we get an error due to a duplicate ID number:

```
mysql> INSERT INTO Combo(ID, Name, CountryCode) VALUES ("27",
"Singapore", "SGP");
ERROR 1062 (23000): Duplicate entry '27' for key 'PRIMARY'
```

Using the ON DUPLICATE KEY UPDATE... argument, we can insert the value and ensure that the record is unique:

```
mysql> INSERT INTO Combo(ID, Name, CountryCode) VALUES ("4078",
"Singapore", "SGP") ON DUPLICATE KEY UPDATE ID=ID+1;
Query OK, 1 row affected (0.00 sec)
```

Note that if there is no conflict in values, MySQL will process the statement as if you did not include the ON DUPLICATE KEY UPDATE... clause.

If we then run a quantified SELECT statement against the table, we see that we now have two unique records for Singapore:

```
mysql> select * from Combo WHERE Name="Singapore";
+------+-----------+-------------+
| ID   | Name      | CountryCode |
+------+-----------+-------------+
| 3208 | Singapore | SGP         |
| 4078 | Singapore | SGP         |
+------+-----------+-------------+
2 rows in set (0.00 sec)
```

Passing an insertion through MySQL for Python

As you can see, inserting data into MySQL is a straightforward process that is largely based around ensuring that the database daemon knows where you want your data placed. Inserting data into MySQL may seem a bit more complicated than retrieving it but the previous discussion shows it is still logical, but just requires a few more keywords in order to be useful.

Setting up the preliminaries

Using INSERT with MySQL for Python is just as easy as using SELECT. As we saw in the previous chapter, we pass the command to MySQL using the execute() method of the database cursor object.

We will again use the fish database and the menu table as follows:

```
+----+----------------+-------+
| id | name           | price |
+----+----------------+-------+
|  1 | tuna           |  7.50 |
|  2 | bass           |  6.75 |
|  3 | salmon         |  9.50 |
|  4 | catfish        |  5.00 |
|  5 | trout          |  6.00 |
|  6 | haddock        |  6.50 |
|  7 | yellowfin tuna | 12.00 |
+----+----------------+-------+
```

Once again, we need to set up the database objects in our Python session. If you are using the same Python terminal session as you did for the previous chapter, you may want to go through this process anyway to ensure that all names are set for the examples to come. Alternatively, close the session by pressing *Ctrl+D* and initiate a new one. Then import MySQL for Python, tend to the database login and create the cursor object as follows:

```
import MySQLdb
mydb = MySQLdb.connect(host = 'localhost',
                       user = 'skipper',
                       passwd = 'mysecret',
                       db = 'fish')
   cur = mydb.cursor()
```

Now we are ready to insert data using Python.

A simple INSERT statement

Inserting data through MySQL for Python uses the same method as retrieving it using `execute()`. You will recall that data retrieval using MySQL for Python follows this formula:

```
results_variable = cursor_handle.execute('MySQL SELECT statement')
```

And so one gets a Python statement that looks like the following:

```
command = cur.execute('SELECT * FROM menu')
```

The main difference in data insertion is that no values are being returned. Therefore, because we are not retrieving any data, we do not need to assign the value of returning data to a variable. Instead, we pass the insertion command as a stand-alone command.

The basic system call for the insertion command would follow this template:

```
cursor_handle.execute('MySQL INSERT statement')
```

Using this template, we can pass the following MySQL INSERT statement:

```
INSERT INTO menu(name, price) VALUES("shark", "13.00");
```

Without worrying about validating the integrity of the data for the moment, we insert this statement through MySQL for Python as follows (using the cursor object cur as defined previously):

```
cur.execute("""INSERT INTO menu(name, price) VALUES("shark",
"13.00")""")
```

Of course, as with the `SELECT` statement in the previous chapter, this statement can become difficult to control rather quickly because of the number of quotation marks and parentheses. If this proves difficult to follow for you, simply break the statement down by defining the argument for `execute()`, the actual MySQL statement, in a separate line. As with elsewhere in Python, you can use triple quotes to assign a value verbatim. The preceding call could then be rewritten as follows:

```
statement = """INSERT INTO menu(name, price) VALUES("shark",
"13.00")"""
cur.execute(statement)
```

Using triple quotes is also helpful for handling more complex statements as they can bridge multiple lines. This makes it easier to format statements in a way that humans can read more easily. Therefore, to use the `ON DUPLICATE KEY UPDATE...` example from earlier in this chapter, we can define the statement:

```
INSERT INTO Combo(ID, Name, CountryCode) VALUES ("4078", "Singapore",
"SGP") ON DUPLICATE KEY UPDATE ID=ID+1;
```

As follows for better readability:

```
statement = """INSERT INTO Combo(ID, Name, CountryCode)
                         VALUES ("4078", "Singapore", "SGP")
                         ON DUPLICATE KEY UPDATE ID=ID+1;"""
```

As the Zen of Python reads:

Readability counts

The virtue of readability in programming is often couched in terms of being kind to the next developer who works on your code. There is more at stake, however. With readability comes not only maintainability but control.. If it takes you too much effort to understand the code you have written, you will have a harder time controlling the program's flow and this will result in unintended behavior. The natural consequence of unintended program behavior is the compromising of process stability and system security.

If this is still too complex for you to follow with ease, it may be advisable to rework the value of `statement` by employing string formatting techniques as shown later in the chapter under the heading *Using user-defined variables*.

More complex INSERT commands

To pass the INSERT command with any of its optional arguments, simply include them in the statement. For example, where we had the following INSERT... SELECT... command:

```
INSERT INTO Combo(ID, Name, CountryCode) SELECT ID, Name, CountryCode
FROM City WHERE ID < 1000;
```

One can simply pack all of that into the value of statement:

```
statement = """INSERT INTO Combo(ID, Name, CountryCode) SELECT ID,
Name, CountryCode FROM City WHERE ID < 1000;"""
```

The DELAYED argument can be passed similarly. The previous statement passed through execute() would look like this:

```
cur.execute("""INSERT DELAYED INTO Combo(ID, Name, CountryCode) SELECT
ID, Name, CountryCode FROM City WHERE ID < 1000;""")
```

Likewise, we could include the INSERT...ON DUPLICATE KEY UPDATE... argument as follows:

```
cur.execute("""INSERT INTO Combo(ID, Name, CountryCode) VALUES
("4078", "Singapore", "SGP") ON DUPLICATE KEY UPDATE ID=ID+1""")
```

It is not necessary to use triple quote marks when assigning the MySQL sentence to statement or when passing it to execute(). However, if you used only a single pair of either double or single quotes, it would be necessary to escape every similar quote mark. As a stylistic rule, it is typically best to switch to verbatim mode with the triple quote marks in order to ensure the readability of your code.

Using user-defined variables

Just as in data retrieval, it is inevitable that you will want to utilize user input when inserting data into MySQL. MySQL for Python provides a consistent, Pythonic interface for this.

We use the same string conversion specifier as we did when incorporating user input into our SELECT statements in the previous chapter. Using the fish database, if we assume that the user gives us the name of the fish and the cost, we can code a user-defined INSERT statement as follows:

```
import MySQLdb, sys

mydb = MySQLdb.connect(host = 'localhost',
                       user = 'skipper',
                       passwd = 'secret',
                       db = 'fish')
cur = mydb.cursor()

fish = sys.argv[1]
price = sys.argv[2]

statement = """INSERT INTO menu(name, price) VALUES(%s, %s)""" % (fish,
price)
cur.execute(statement)
```

An alternative way of rendering the last two lines is to leave the value insertion to the execute() function. Instead of using % (fish, price) at the end of the first of the two lines, we can include the fish and price values as a second argument to execute():

```
statement = "INSERT INTO menu(name, price) VALUES (%s, %s)"

cur.execute(statement, (fish, price))
```

To make this program executable, you can preface this code with a shebang line, make the file executable (by changing the permissions on the file), and then call it as you would any other local executable that is not in your execution path. Alternatively, you can call it from the command-line by prefacing it with a call to your local Python interpreter. In either case, don't forget to supply the arguments for sys.argv[]. Here I have run it using the latter method:

```
python ./user-defined-data.py angel 7.00
```

This then appends the data to the database in real time.

```
mysql> SELECT * FROM menu;
+----+----------------+-------+
| id | name           | price |
+----+----------------+-------+
|  1 | tuna           |  7.50 |
|  2 | bass           |  6.75 |
|  3 | salmon         |  9.50 |
|  4 | catfish        |  5.00 |
|  5 | trout          |  6.00 |
|  6 | haddock        |  6.50 |
|  7 | yellowfin tuna | 12.00 |
|  8 | sole           |  7.75 |
|  9 | angel          |  7.00 |
+----+----------------+-------+
9 rows in set (0.01 sec)
```

As this is all within the Python API, you are not limited merely to `%s`, but can use the same string formatting techniques as you would anywhere else in Python.

Using metadata

On February 23, 2006, an American B-2 bomber crashed shortly after take-off in Guam due to bad data being fed to the airplane's flight control computers. A lack of data checking resulted in the loss of a $2.1 billion plane. As with any user interaction in programming, it is foolish to trust data without validating its integrity first.

One of the main ways of validating user input is to verify the data definition for the database. More often than not, the database definition will be known at the time of application development. You can then verify user input against a known specification. However, if you do not have this luxury, you will need to query the database for its definition and ensure the user's data does not run afoul of it.

Querying the database for its structure

If we are completely ignorant of a database's structure, we need to first retrieve a table listing. To affect that, we use SHOW TABLES.

```
statement = """SHOW TABLES"""
command = cur.execute(statement)
```

Be sure to follow the execute() call with fetchall() assigned to a variable to hold the tuple that is returned.

```
results = cur.fetchall()
```

The tuple results can then be accessed to give the user a choice.

```
print "Which table would you like to use?"
for i in xrange(0, len(results)): print i+1, results[i][0]
choice = input("Input number:")
```

As fish only has one table, the output of the for loop would simply be:

1 menu

But if we do the same for the world database, we get a more realistic selection:

1 City

2 Combo

3 Country

4 CountryLanguage

The user can then choose from the list. If we want to verify the user's data, we need to verify three things:

1. The value input by the user is only a number.
2. The numeric value is not outside the offered range.
3. The value is a whole number.

To validate the input as a number, we need to import the string module and use the isdigit() method of string objects.

```
import string
```

We would then use an if statement along the following lines:

```
if choice.isdigit() is True:
    print "We have a number!" ## or do further checking
```

We then need to confirm that the input is within the given range. To verify that the value of `results` is greater than `0` but not greater than the number of given options:

```
if (choice<0) or (choice>len(results)):
    print "We need a new number!" ## or do further checking
```

Within the previous range, however, we still run into problems with decimals. We currently have no protection against `choice` being equal to *3.5*, for example. There are a couple of ways that we can protect against this at the validation stage:

- By checking the length of the input and telling the user that we need a single digit within the given range
- By stripping out all but the first digit and returning the results to the user for confirmation

To check the length of the input, we simply use Python's built-in `len()` function in a conditional loop:

```
if len(choicea) != 1:
    print "We need a single digit within the given range, please."
```

This, however, is not the most user-friendly way to handle the data. In cases where there are a lot of choices, it can even leave the user confused. Better is to offer an alternative by way of confirmation. To do this, we convert the input to a string using Python's built-in `str()` function and then present the first element of the indexed string to the user for confirmation.

```
choice_string = str(choice)
confirm = input("Did you mean %s?" %(choice_string[0]))
```

If `confirm` is assigned a positive value by the user—whether it is `yes`, `true`, or just `1`, we should then convert the value of `choice_string[0]` to an integer. We do this with Python's built-in `int()` function.

```
real_choice = int(choice_string[0])
```

This has the benefit of handling input from users who either have poor typing skills or who may otherwise input gobbledygook after their initial, valid selection.

Retrieving the table structure

After validating the user's input, we have the choice of database to be used. We now need to give the user details on the fields being used by that table. Again, we use DESCRIBE.

```
table_statement = """DESCRIBE %s""" %(results[real_choice-1][0])
cur.execute(table_statement)
table_desc = cur.fetchall()
```

It is worth noting here that indices start at 0 but our choices to the user started at 1. Therefore, whatever choice the user makes must be reduced by one in order to synchronize it with the index of results.

Also, we do not want to pass the value of the entire tuple in the statement. We just want the value of the table to be queried. Therefore, we must subscript the results record with a 0.

In MySQL, the DESCRIBE statement returns a table. In MySQL for Python, we get another tuple. Each element in that tuple is a row in the table returned by MySQL. So where MySQL would return the following.

```
mysql> DESCRIBE CountryLanguage;
```

Field	Type	Null	Key	Default	Extra
CountryCode	char(3)	NO	PRI		
Language	char(30)	NO	PRI		
IsOfficial	enum('T','F')	NO		F	
Percentage	float(4,1)	NO		0.0	

```
4 rows in set (0.00 sec)
```

A prettified version of what Python returns is the following:

```
>>> for i in xrange(0, len(table_desc)): print table_desc[i]
...
('CountryCode', 'char(3)', 'NO', 'PRI', '', '')
('Language', 'char(30)', 'NO', 'PRI', '', '')
('IsOfficial', "enum('T','F')", 'NO', '', 'F', '')
('Percentage', 'float(4,1)', 'NO', '', '0.0', '')
```

The differences between xrange() and range() are often overlooked or even ignored. Both count through the same values, but they do it differently. Where range() calculates a list the first time it is called and then stores it in memory, xrange() creates an immutable sequence that returns the next in the series each time it is called. As a consequence, xrange() is much more memory efficient than range(), especially when dealing with large groups of integers. As a consequence of its memory efficiency, however, it does not support functionality such as slicing, which range() does, because the series is not yet fully determined.

Each element of each row is then available by a further subscript for the column that you want to access:

```
>>> print table_desc[0][0]
CountryCode
>>> print table_desc[0][1]
char(3)
>>> print table_desc[1][3]
PRI
```

So to offer the user the format of the table columns, we could use the following code:

```
print "The records of table %s follow this format:" % (results[choice-
1][0])
for i in xrange(0, len(table_desc)):
    print table_desc[i][0]
```

The output is as follows:

```
The records of table CountryLanguage follow this format:
CountryCode
Language
IsOfficial
Percentage
```

We can also walk through this data to give the user the format of each field for each record in the table. The fields of information for each field in any MySQL table remains constant and follow this order:

- **Field**: The name of the column
- **Type**: The data type allowed in that column, along with its length
- **Null**: Whether a null value is allowed
- **Key**: Whether this value is a primary key for the table
- **Default**: What the default value is, if no value is entered as input for this column
- **Extra**: Any additional information about this column

To access a particular column, one simply appends the appropriate column number as a subscript, as shown previously.

Knowing this, one can code in helps options for each field in turn. This can be a JavaScript pop-up or a manual page for each column. For the sake of space, however, this is left here as an exercise for yourself.

Changing insertion values dynamically

Just because user input is not valid, it does not mean we should scrap it and ask the user for a new input. Rather, we can accept an entire statement, assign what values will fit and come back to the user to correct data that will not.

To do this, we need to import the string module and define three functions to do the following:

1. Validate the `name` column.
2. Validate the `price` column.
3. Query the user for a correction.

After defining the functions, we pass the user values to the first two functions, we then pass the user values in turn to the first two functions which then calls the third function only if the data does not check out.

Simply append `string` to the import line for the program or add the following line below it:

```
import string
```

Now, let's define the three functions.

Validating the value of name

This function needs to do the following:

1. Receive the value of the name column.
2. Check whether it is all letters—for example, no fish has numbers in its market name.
3. Call query() if necessary.
4. Return the name value to the main program, corrected if necessary.

The first is accomplished with the definition line:

```
def valid_name(name):
```

We then accomplish the rest of the specified functionality with an if...else statement:

```
if name.isalpha() is False:
    fish = query("name", name, "alpha")
else:
    fish = name
```

Finally, we return the value of fish to the main program:

```
return(fish)
```

Validating the value of price

Validating the value of price requires similar functionality. Here is the function that we need for the task:

```
def valid_price(price):
    if price.isdigit() is False:
        price = query("price", price, "digit")
    else:
        price = price
    return(price)
```

Querying the user for a correction

As you can tell from the calls in the preceding functions, this function will take three arguments and query the user for a correction according to them. Our definition thus begins:

```
def query(column, value, kind):
```

For `kind`, we will use two different possible values: alpha and digit. Depending on which one is used, this function will behave differently. For validating the alpha character of name value, we use the following `if...` clause:

```
    if kind == "alpha":
        print "For %s, you input %s.  This is not a valid value for
column %s.  Please enter the name of the fish in the appropriate
format." %(column, value, column)
        new_value = raw_input("New name: ")
        new_value = valid_name(new_value)
        return (new_value)
```

If type is not alpha but digit, we use an `elif` clause to continue with the user query:

```
    elif kind == "digit":
        print "For %s, you input %s.  This is not a valid price.
Please enter the price in the appropriate format." %(column, value)
        new_price = raw_input("New price: ")
        new_price = valid_price(new_price)
        return (new_price)
```

Finally, because this function interacts with the user, we want to ensure that it cannot be called from another program or with any other values for type other than alpha or digital. To affect this in the shortest amount of code possible, we use a simple `else` statement.

```
    else:
        return -1
```

We return the value `-1` here, in an effort to ensure that the erroneous call does not go unnoticed.

Passing fish and price for validation

Having defined the three functions, we now need to call them and to pass to them the values for fish and price. We therefore put this code just after assigning the values of `sys.argv[1]` and `sys.argv[2]` to `fish` and `price`, respectively.

```
fish = valid_name(fish)
price = valid_price(price)
```

Essentials: close and commit

In programs that interface with multiple databases or otherwise persist beyond the database connection that you have initiated, you will find a need to use a couple of MySQL commands that we have not yet discussed: `close` and `commit`.

In need of some closure

When one is finished with a database, it is good practice to close the cursor proxy. This ensures the cursor is not used again to refer to that database connection and also frees up resources. To close a cursor connection in MySQL for Python, simply issue the method call to your cursor object:

```
cur.close()
```

What happened to commit?

If you are experienced with using the MySQL shell or perhaps programming interfaces with MySQL using different APIs, you may wonder what has happened to the `commit` call that one normally would make at the end of every transaction to render changes permanent.

MySQL for Python ships with an autocommit feature. Therefore, when the connection is closed, the changes are committed. However, if you are programming to several databases and want to ensure one is closed before another is opened, MySQL for Python still supports a `commit()` function. You simply call it with the handle of the database.

```
mydb.commit()
```

After committing the changes to the database, one typically closes the database connection. To do this, use the database object's `close()` method:

```
mydb.close()
```

Why are these essentials non-essential?

Unless you are running several database threads at a time or have to deal with similar complexity, MySQL for Python does not require you to use either `commit()` or `close()`. Generally speaking, MySQL for Python installs with an autocommit feature switched on. It thus takes care of committing the changes for you when the cursor object is destroyed.

Similarly, when the program terminates, Python tends to close the cursor and database connection as it destroys both objects.

Project: A command-line insertion utility

We can now put together the elements of database programming that we have covered in this chapter to form a robust command-line insertion utility. For this project we want to create a program with the following functionality:

- Runs from the command-line
- Uses a flag system allowing for the `-h` flag for help
- Allows the user to define the database being used
- Allows the user to designate which user and password combination to use
- Allows the user to ask for the tables available in a given database
- Provides the user with the column structure of the table on demand
- Validates user input for the given table of the selected database
- Builds the database `INSERT` statement on-the-fly
- Inserts the user input into the chosen table of the selected database

The necessary modules

Before we jump into coding, let us first assess which modules we need to import. The modules we need are listed next to our required functionality as follows. The need for `MySQLdb` is understood.

- Flag system: `optparse`
- Login details: `getpass`
- Build the `INSERT` statement: `string`

Our `import` statement thus looks like this:

```
import getpass, MySQLdb, optparse, string
```

In addition to these, we will also use the `PrettyTable` module to provide the user with the column structure of the table in a neat format. This module is not part of the **standard library**, but is easily installed using the following invocation from the command-line:

```
easy_install prettytable
```

If this does not work for you or you prefer to install the module manually, you will benefit from the instructions at the PrettyTable site: `http://code.google.com/p/prettytable/wiki/Installation`

If you prefer not to install PrettyTable, you will obviously want to modify the code according to your preferences when we get to printing out the database definition table to the user.

The main() thing

In this project, we will have several functions. In order to ensure that we can call those functions from other programs, we will code this project using a `main` function. The other functions will be inserted before the `main()` function in the program, but starting with the `main()` function and coding the others as needed helps us to keep from losing the plot of the program. So let's define `main()`:

```
def main():
```

> In any size of program, using a `main()` function is good practice and results in a high degree of readability. Ideally, `main()` should be among the smallest of the functions in a program. The point is that `main()` should be the brains of the program that coordinates the activity of the classes and functions.

From here, the flow of the `main()` function will follow this logic:

1. Set up the flag system.
2. Test the values passed by the user.
3. Try to establish a database connection.
4. If successful, show the user the tables of the designated database.
5. Offer to show the table structure, and then do so.
6. Accept user input for the INSERT statement, column-by-column.
7. Build the INSERT statement from the user input and execute it.
8. Print the INSERT statement to the user for feedback.
9. Commit changes and close all connections.

Coding the flag system

As we did in the previous chapter, we need to tell Python which flags should be supported and to which variables the values should be assigned. The code looks like this:

```
opt = optparse.OptionParser()
opt.add_option("-d", "--database", action="store", type="string",
dest="database")
opt.add_option("-p", "--passwd", action="store", type="string",
dest="passwd")
opt.add_option("-u", "--user", action="store", type="string",
dest="user")
opt, args = opt.parse_args()
```

If you don't understand this, see the relevant section under the project listing from the previous chapter. For simplicity's sake, we then pass the values to simpler variable names:

```
database = opt.database
passwd = opt.passwd
user = opt.user
```

If you have trouble with the program after you code it, here is a point for blackboxing. Simply insert the following loop to show what the computer is thinking at this point:

```
for i in (database, passwd, user): print "'%s'" %(i)
```

Blackboxing is jargon in the IT industry and simply means to isolate the parts of a problem so that each piece can be tested separately of the others. With this `for` loop, we can ensure that Python has properly assimilated the flagged input from the user.

Testing the values passed by the user

Next, we need to ensure that the user has not passed us empty or no data. If the user has, we need to ask for a new value.

```
while (user == "") or (user == None):
    print "This system is secured against anonymous logins."
    user = getpass.getuser()

while (passwd == "") or (passwd == None):
    print "You must have a valid password to log into the
database."
```

```
        passwd = getpass.getpass()

    while (database == "") or (database == None):
        database = raw_input("We need the name of an existing database
to proceed.  Please enter it here:  ")
```

Note that we are not using `if`. If we had, we would have needed to set up a loop to consistently check the value of the data. Using `while` saves us the trouble.

Try to establish a database connection

Having checked the login data, we can now attempt a connection. Just because the user data has checked out does not mean that the data is valid. It merely means that it fits with our expectations. The data is not valid until the database connection is made. Until then, there is a chance of failure. We therefore should use a `try...` `except...` structure.

```
    try:
        mydb = MySQLdb.connect(host = 'localhost',
                               user = user,
                               passwd = passwd,
                               db = database)
        cur = mydb.cursor()
        quit = 1
    except:
        print "The login credentials you entered are not valid for
the database you indicated.  Please check your login details and try
again."
        quit = 0
```

Here we use `quit` as a token to indicate the success of the `connection`. One could just as easily use `connected` or `is_connected`. A successful connection is not made until a cursor object is created.

Within the `except` clause, it is important to tell the user why the program is going to terminate. Otherwise, he or she is left in the dark, and the program can effectively become useless to them.

Showing the tables

Next, we cull out the tables from the database and show them to the user. We only do this if a successful connection has been made.

```
if quit == 1:
    get_tables_statement = """SHOW TABLES"""
    cur.execute(get_tables_statement)
    tables = cur.fetchall()

    print "The tables available for database %s follow below:"
%(database)
    for i in xrange(0, len(tables)):
        print "%s. %s" %(i+1, tables[i])
    table_choice = raw_input("Please enter the number of the table
into which you would like to insert data.  ")
```

For the sake of formatting, we increment the number of the table by one in order to use the natural number system when presenting the options to the user.

Upon receiving the number of `table_choice` from the user, we must validate it. To do so, we stringify the number and pass it to a function `valid_table()`, which we will create later in the development process. For now, it is enough to know that the function needs the user's choice and the number of tables in the designated database. For simplicity, we pass the list of tables.

```
table_choice = str(table_choice)
table_no = valid_table(table_choice, tables)
```

Once the number chosen is validated, we must decrement the number to synchronise it with the whole number system used by Python.

```
table = tables[table_no-1][0]
```

Showing the table structure, if desired

The next step is to show the user the data structure of the table, if desired. We affect this with a `raw_input` statement and an `if...` clause:

```
show_def = raw_input("Would you like to see the database
structure of the table '%s'? (y/n) " %(table))
```

Before launching into the `if...` statement, , we can economize on our code. Regardless of whether the user wants to see the table format, we will need the column headers later to affect the insertion. We can take care of retrieving them now so that the information is available in the `if...` statement as well as out, both for the price of one MySQL statement.

```
def_statement = """DESCRIBE %s""" % (table)
cur.execute(def_statement)
definition = cur.fetchall()
```

If the user chooses `y` to the input at `show_def`, then we run the following `if` loop:

```
if show_def == "y":
    from prettytable import PrettyTable
    tabledef = PrettyTable()
    tabledef.set_field_names(["Field", "Type", "Null", "Key",
"Default", "Extra"])
    for j in xrange(0, len(definition)):
        tabledef.add_row([definition[j][0], definition[j][1],
definition[j][2], definition[j][3], definition[j][4],
definition[j][5]])
    tabledef.printt()
```

As mentioned when discussing the modules for this project, here we import `PrettyTable` from the module `prettytable`. This merely allows us to output a nicely formatted table similar to MySQL's own. It is not required for the program to work as long as you convey the value of the six tabular fields for each row. While this example is quite serviceable, you can find more information on how to use the PrettyTable module at: `http://code.google.com/p/prettytable/`

Note that, if `show_def` equals anything other than a simple `y`, the `if` loop will not execute.

Accepting user input for the INSERT statement

We next need to ask the user for the values to be inserted. To guide the user, we will prompt them for the value of each column in turn:

```
print "Please enter the data you would like to insert into
table %s" % (table)

columns = []
values = []
for j in xrange(0, len(definition)):
    column = definition[j][0]
```

```
                    value = raw_input("Value to insert for column '%s'?"
      % (definition[j][0]))
            columns.append(str(column))
            values.append('"' + str(value) + '"')
        columns = ','.join(columns)
        values = ','.join(values)
        print columns
        print values
```

The lists `columns` and `values` obviously correspond to the respective parts of the MySQL `INSERT` statement. It is important to remember that the column headers in a MySQL statement are not set in quotes, but that the values are. Therefore, we must format the two lists differently. In either case, however, the items need to be separated by commas. This will make it easier when building the next `INSERT` statement.

If you encounter difficulty in coding this project, this is another good point for blackboxing. Simply print the value of each list after the close of the `for` loop to see the value of each at this point.

Building the INSERT statement from the user input and executing it

Having the user's values for insertion, we are now at a point where we can build the MySQL statement. We do this with string formatting characters.

```
        statement = """INSERT INTO %s(%s) VALUES(%s)""" % (table,
    columns, values)
```

We then execute the statement. For extra security against malformed data, you could couch this in a `try...except...` structure.

```
        cur.execute(statement)
```

If the execute statement was processed without a problem, it is a good idea to give the user some feedback. An appropriate output here would be the statement that was processed.

```
        print "Data has been inserted using the following statement:
    \n", statement
```

Committing changes and closing the connection

Finally, we can commit the changes and close the connection. This is not typically necessary for a single run database program such as this, but it is not a bad habit to maintain.

```
cur.close()
mydb.commit()
mydb.close()
```

It is worth noting that committing before closing is not wholly necessary. The one implies the other. However, `commit()` allows us to commit changes to the database without closing the database connection, so we can commit changes at regular intervals.

Coding the other functions

We are not done yet. With `main()` finished, we now have to fill out the program with the auxiliary functions that were called in the course of `main()`.

- `valid_digit()`
- `valid_string()`
- `valid_table()`
- `query()`

 The other functions must be inserted before the `main()` function is called, otherwise Python will throw a `NameError`.

valid_digit() and valid_string()

The first three functions should validate input as: digital, alpha character string, or as a valid number on the table menu presented to the user. If the input does not check out, then each should call `query()` to ask the user for new input, providing the type of valid input required as an argument with the value input by the user. The first two require only the value to be validated. They therefore look like this:

```
def valid_digit(value):
    if value.isdigit() is not True:
        value = query(value, "digit")
    else:
        value = value
    return value
```

```
def valid_string(value):
    if value.isalpha() is not True:
        value = query(name, "alpha")
    else:
        value = value
    return value
```

valid_table()

To validate the table selection, you will remember that we passed the number of
the user's selection and the table names to valid_table(). This function compares
the user's selection to the number of tables available and calls query() if there is a
problem. The function is therefore coded as follows:

```
def valid_table(choice, tables):
    valid_choice = valid_digit(choice) # Check whether the choice is a
valid number
    valid_choice = int(valid_choice)
    while 0 <= valid_choice <= len(tables) :    # Ensure the choice is
among the valid options
        print "Your selection is outside the bounds of possible
choices."
        valid_choice = query(valid_choice, "digit")
    return valid_choice
```

query()

The function query() uses an if...elif...else structure to alert the user
to the malformed data, asks for new input, and validates it. It therefore calls
valid_digit() and valid_string() as necessary for the last task. Querying
and testing is of two kinds: digit and alpha. Within the present program, only
these two are called, but there is a chance that this function could be called wrongly
from another Python program. Therefore, we try to fail softly by returning 1 if the
wrong argument is passed for type.

```
def query(value, type):
    if type == "alpha":
        print "The value you entered ('%s') is not correct.  Please
enter a valid value." %(value)
        new_value = raw_input("New value: ")
        valid_string(new_value)
        return new_value

    elif type == "digit":
```

```
        print "The value you entered ('%s') is not correct.  Please
enter a valid value." %(value)
        new_value = raw_input("New value: ")
        valid_digit(new_value)
        return new_value

    else:
## if type is neither "alpha" nor "digit"
        return 1
```

Calling main()

As the program stands now, it does nothing. It is simply a bunch of functions. While they call each other, there is nothing that instigates the execution process if the file is fed to the Python interpreter. We need to call main().

As every Python program can also function as a module, it is necessary for us to ensure that main() is only executed if the program is called directly. Now that all the functions are defined, we can use an if statement to verify how the program is called and to launch main() accordingly.

```
if __name__ == '__main__':
    main()
```

 Calling main() as a result of this if statement at the very end of the program is like not connecting the power to an electric circuit until you are ready to test it. It helps us to avoid lots of possible problems.

Now the program can be called at the command-line. You can either give it a shebang line at the top and ensure the file is set for execution, or call it as an argument to the Python interpreter:

python ./project-ch3.py -d world -u skipper -p secret

For reference, the full code of the program to follow is here. First, the shebang line and the imported modules:

```
#!/usr/bin/env python

import getpass, MySQLdb, optparse, string
```

Next, we define all supporting functions:

```
def valid_digit(value):
    if value.isdigit() is not True:
        value = query(value, "digit")
    else:
        value = value
    return value

def valid_string(value):
    if value.isalpha() is not True:
        value = query(name, "alpha")
    else:
        value = value
    return value

def query(value, type):
    if type == "alpha":
        print "The value you entered ('%s') is not correct.  Please
enter a valid value." %(value)
        new_value = raw_input("New value: ")
        valid_string(new_value)
        return new_value

    elif type == "digit":
        print "The value you entered ('%s') is not correct.  Please
enter a valid value." %(value)
        new_value = raw_input("New value: ")
        valid_digit(new_value)
        return new_value

    else:
    ## if type != "alpha" and type != "digit":
        return 1

def valid_table(choice, tables):
    valid_choice = valid_digit(choice) # Check whether the choice is a
valid number
    valid_choice = int(valid_choice)
    while (valid_choice <= 0) or (valid_choice > len(tables)):   #
Ensure the choice is among the valid options
        print "Your selection is outside the bounds of possible
choices."
        valid_choice = query(valid_choice, "digit")
    return valid_choice
```

We then need to define `main()`, the master function. First we parse the options and assign their values:

```
def main():
    opt = optparse.OptionParser()
    opt.add_option("-d", "--database", action="store", type="string",
dest="database")
    opt.add_option("-p", "--passwd", action="store", type="string",
dest="passwd")
    opt.add_option("-u", "--user", action="store", type="string",
dest="user")
    opt, args = opt.parse_args()

    database = opt.database
    passwd = opt.passwd
    user = opt.user
```

Next, we validate the input, asking the user for clarification as necessary:

```
    while (user == "") or (user == None):
        print "This system is secured against anonymous logins."
        user = getpass.getuser()

    while (passwd == "") or (passwd == None):
        print "You must have a valid password to log into the
database."
        passwd = getpass.getpass()

    while (database == "") or (database == None):
        database = raw_input("We need the name of an existing database
to proceed.  Please enter it here:  ")
```

Then we try to connect to the database with the credentials that the user passed to the program. If we fail, we print a simple error message:

```
    try:
        mydb = MySQLdb.connect(host = 'localhost',
                               user = user,
                               passwd = passwd,
                               db = database)
        cur = mydb.cursor()
        quit = 1

    except:
        print "The login credentials you entered are not valid for
the database you indicated.  Please check your login details and try
again."
        quit = 0
```

If we successfully make a connection, we carry on showing the tables of the database and further interacting with the user to form the INSERT statement:

```
if quit == 1:
    get_tables_statement = """SHOW TABLES"""
    cur.execute(get_tables_statement)
    tables = cur.fetchall()

    print "The tables available for database %s follow below:"
%(database)
    for i in xrange(0, len(tables)):
        print "%s. %s" % (i+1, tables[i])
    table_choice = input("Please enter the number of the table
into which you would like to insert data.  ")
    table_choice = str(table_choice)
    table_no = valid_table(table_choice, tables)
    table = tables[table_no-1][0]

    show_def = raw_input("Would you like to see the database
structure of the table '%s'? (y/n) " %(table))

    def_statement = """DESCRIBE %s""" %(table)
    cur.execute(def_statement)
    definition = cur.fetchall()
    if show_def == "y":
        from prettytable import PrettyTable
        tabledef = PrettyTable()
        tabledef.set_field_names(["Field", "Type", "Null", "Key",
"Default", "Extra"])
        for j in xrange(0, len(definition)):
            tabledef.add_row([definition[j][0], definition[j][1],
definition[j][2], definition[j][3], definition[j][4],
definition[j][5]])
        tabledef.printt()

    print "Please enter the data you would like to insert into
table %s" %(table)
    columns = ''
    values = '"'
    for j in xrange(0, len(definition)):
        column = definition[j][0]
        value = raw_input("Value to insert for column '%s'?"
%(definition[j][0]))
        columns = columns + str(column)
        values = values + str(value)
```

```
            if j < len(definition)-1:
                columns = columns + ", "
                values = values + '", "'
            else:
                values = values + '"'
```

We then form the `INSERT` statement and execute it. It is always a good idea to give the user feedback about what data has just been processed:

```
        statement = """INSERT INTO %s(%s) VALUES(%s)""" %(table,
columns, values)
        cur.execute(statement)
        print "Data has been inserted using the following statement:
\n", statement
```

The next bit of code is necessary only if you have switched off auto-commit in MySQL for Python. Otherwise, you can skip this part.

```
        cur.close()
        mydb.commit()
        mydb.close()
```

Finally, we need to check whether the program has been called directly. If the program is imported as a module into another Python program, `main()` is never run.

```
if __name__ == '__main__':
    main()
```

Room to grow

We have fulfilled the specification we set out for this project. However, there are several points that you might consider for further development:

- Set the host name dynamically while validating the data. This will require you either to create a **whitelist** of hosts or to do some network programming in order to validate the existence not just of the host, but of a running MySQL server on it.

- Validate the success of the `INSERT` statement by running a `SELECT` statement afterward. Ideally, you will need to close one connection and open another one to be sure that the data is there.

- Validate the user's data more fully than we have here.

- Abstract the database connection and/or the table selection to a function. See how small you can make `main()`.

Summary

In this chapter, we have covered the MySQL INSERT command and how to implement it in Python. In particular, we have seen how to form INSERT statements and pass them to MySQL through MySQLdb. Using Python, we also looked at how to use user-defined variables in MySQL statements, changing the INSERT statement dynamically. In the next chapter, we will look at how to handle MySQL errors.

4

Exception Handling

Any application that is used by multiple users in a production environment should have some level of exception handling implemented.

In this chapter, we will look at the following:

- Why errors and warnings are a programmer's friend
- The difference between errors and warnings
- The two main kinds of errors passed by MySQL for Python
- The six kinds of `DatabaseError`
- How to handle errors passed to Python from MySQL
- Creating a feedback loop for the user, based on the errors passed

At the end of this chapter, we will use this information along with the knowledge from the preceding chapters to build a command-line program to insert, update, and retrieve information from MySQL and to handle any exceptions that arise while doing so.

Why errors and warnings are good for you

The value of rigorous error checking is exemplified in any of the several catastrophes arising from poor software engineering. Examples abound, but a few are particularly illustrative of what happens when bad data and design go unchallenged.

On 4 June 1996, the first test flight of the Ariane 5 rocket self-destructed 37 seconds after its launch. The navigation code from Ariane 4 was reused in Ariane 5. The faster processing speed on the newer rocket caused an operand error. The conversion of a 64-bit floating-point value resulted in a larger-than-expected and unsupported 16-bit signed integer. The result was an overflow that scrambled the flight's computer, causing too much thrust to be passed by the rocket itself, resulting in the crash of US$370 million worth of technology. Widely considered to be one of the most expensive computer bugs in history, the crash arose due to mistakes in design and in subsequent error checking.

On 15 January 1990, the American telecommunications company AT&T installed a new system on the switches that controlled their long-distance service. A bug in the software caused the computers to crash every time they received a message from one of their neighboring switches. The message in question just happened to be the same one that the switches send out when they recover from a system crash. The result: Within a short time, 114 switches across New York City were rebooting every six seconds, leaving around 60,000 people without long distance service for nine hours. The system ultimately had to be fixed by reinstalling the old software.

On the Internet, a lack of proper error-checking still makes it possible for a malformed ping request to crash a server anywhere in the world. The **Computer Emergency Response Team** (**CERT**) Advisory on this bug, CA-1996-26, was released in 1996, but the bug persists. The original denial-of-service attack has thus evolved into the distributed denial-of-service attack employing botnets of zombie machines worldwide.

More than any other part of a computing system, errors cost significantly more to fix later than if they were resolved earlier in the development process. It is specifically for this reason that Python outputs error messages to the screen, unless such errors are explicitly handled otherwise.

A basic dynamic of computing is that the computer does not let anyone know what is happening inside itself. A simple illustration of this dynamic is as follows:

```
x = 2
if x == 2:
    x = x + x
```

Knowing Python and reading the code, we understand that the value of x is now 4. But the computer has provided us no indication of the value of x. What's more, it will not tell us anything unless we explicitly tell it to do so. Generally speaking, there are two ways you can ask Python to tell you what it's thinking:

- By outputting values to the screen
- By writing them to a file

Here, a simple print statement would tell us the value of x.

Output displayed on the screen or saved to a file are the most common ways for programs to report their status to users. However, the similar effect is done by indicator lights and other non-verbal forms of communication. The type of output is necessarily dependent on the hardware being used.

By default, Python outputs all errors and warnings to the screen. As MySQL for Python is interpreted by Python, errors passed by MySQLdb are no different. This naturally gives the debugging programmer information for ironing out the performance of the program—whether determining why a program is not executing as planned or how to make it execute faster or more reliably. However, it also means that any information needed for tracing the error, along with parts of the code, is passed to the user, whoever they may be.

This is great for debugging, but makes for terrible security. That is why the Zen of Python reads:

Errors should never pass silently.

Unless explicitly silenced.

One needs the error messages to know why the program fails, but it is a security hazard to pass raw error messages to the user. If one wants the user to handle an error message, it should be sanitized of information that may compromise the security of the system.

Handling exceptions correctly takes a lot of code. At the risk of sounding like a hypocrite, it should be noted that the exigencies of a printed book do not allow for the reproduction of constant, rigorous error-handling in the code examples such as this chapter espouses. Therefore, while I state this principle, the programming examples included in this book do not always illustrate it as they should. If they did, the book would be significantly thicker and heavier (and probably cost more too!).

Further, the more complicated an application, the more robust the error-handling should be. Ultimately, every kind of error is covered by one of the several types that can be thrown by MySQL for Python. Each one of them allows for customized error messages to be passed to the user.

With a bit of further coding, one can check the authentication level of the user and pass error messages according to their level of authorization. This can be done through a flag system or by using modules from the Python library. If the former is used, one must ensure that knowledge of the flag(s) used is guarded from unauthorized users. Alternatively, one can employ both systems by checking the authentication level of users or programs that pass a particular flag to the program.

Errors versus warnings: There's a big difference

As with Python in general, the main difference between errors and warnings is that warnings do not cause a program to terminate. Errors do. Warnings provide notice of something we should note; errors indicate the reason the program cannot continue. If not handled appropriately, warnings therefore pass process information to the user without interrupting the execution of the program. This lack of detectability makes warnings more dangerous to the security of an application, and the system in general, than errors. Consequently, the error-handling process of an application must account for both errors and warnings.

While Python handles warnings and exceptions differently by default, especially with regard to program execution, both are written to `stderr`. Therefore, one handles them the same way that one handles standard errors (see *Handling exceptions passed from MySQL* in the later sections).

Additionally, one can set warnings to be silenced altogether or to carry the same gravity as an error. This level of functionality was introduced in Python 2.1. We will discuss this more later.

The two main errors in MySQLdb

Python generally supports several kinds of errors, and MySQL for Python is no different. The obvious difference between the two is that `MySQLdb`'s errors deal exclusively with the database connection. Where `MySQLdb` passes warnings that are not MySQL-specific, all exceptions are related to MySQL.

The MySQL-specific exceptions are then classified as either warnings or errors. There is only one kind of warning, but `MySQLdb` allows two categories of errors— `DatabaseError` and `InterfaceError`. Of the former, there are six types that we will discuss here.

DatabaseError

When there is a problem with the MySQL database itself, a DatabaseError is thrown. This is an intermediate catch-all category of exceptions that deal with everything from how the data is processed (for example, errors arising from division by zero), to problems in the SQL syntax, to internal problems within MySQL itself. Essentially, if a connection is made and a problem arises, the DatabaseError will catch it.

Several types of exceptions are contained by the DatabaseError type. We look at each of these in the section *Handling exceptions passed from MySQL.*

InterfaceError

When the database connection fails for some reason, MySQLdb will raise an InterfaceError. This may be caused from problems in the interface anywhere in the connection process.

Warnings in MySQL for Python

In addition to errors, MySQL for Python also supports a Warning class. This exception is raised for warnings like data truncation when executing an INSERT statement. It may be caught just like an error, but otherwise will not interrupt the flow of a program.

Handling exceptions passed from MySQL

MySQL for Python takes care of the nitty-gritty of communication between your program and MySQL. As a result, handling exceptions passed from MySQL is as straightforward as handling exceptions passed from any other Python module.

Python exception-handling

Python error-handling uses a try...except...else code structure to handle exceptions. It then uses raise to generate the error.

```
while True:
    try:
        x = int(raw_input("Please enter a number: "))
        break
    except:
        print "That is not a valid number.  Please try again..."
```

While this is the textbook example for raising an error, there are a few points to keep in mind.

```
while True:
```

This sets up a loop with a condition that applies as long as there are no exceptions raised.

```
try...break
```

Python then tries to execute whatever follows. If successful, the program terminates with break. If not, an exception is registered, but not raised.

```
except
```

The use of except tells Python what to do in the event of an exception. In this case it prints a message to the screen, but it does not raise an exception. Instead, the while loop remains unbroken and another number is requested.

Catching an exception from MySQLdb

All exceptions in MySQL for Python are accessed as part of MySQLdb. Therefore, one cannot reference them directly. Using the fish database, execute the following code:

```python
#!/usr/bin/env python

import MySQLdb

mydb = MySQLdb.connect(host ='localhost',
                       user = 'skipper',
                       passwd = 'secret',
                       db = 'fish'
cur = mydb.cursor()

# Note the use of '7a' instead of '7'
statement = """SELECT * FROM menu WHERE id=7a"""

try:
    cur.execute(statement)
    results = cur.fetchall()
    print results
except Error:
    print "An error has been passed."
```

The preceding code will return a `NameError` from Python itself. For Python to recognize the exception from `MySQLdb`, change each instance of `Error` to read `MySQLdb.Error`. The `except` clause then reads as follows:

```
except MySQLdb.Error:
    print "An error has been passed."
```

The resulting output will be from the `print` statement.

An error has been passed.

Raising an error or a warning

An exception is only explicitly registered when `raise` is used. Instead of the `print` statement used in the `except` clause previously, we can `raise` an error and update the `print` statement with the following line of code:

```
raise MySQLdb.Error
```

Instead of the friendly statement about an error passing, we get a stack trace that ends as follows:

```
_mysql_exceptions.Error
```

> Remember that `MySQLdb` is a macro system for interfacing with `_mysql_` and, subsequently, with the C API for MySQL. Any errors that pass from MySQL come through each of those before reaching the Python interpreter and your program.

Instead of raising an actual error, we can raise our own error message. After the `MySQLdb.Error` in the raise line, simply place your error message in parentheses and quotes.

```
raise MySQLdb.Error("An error has been passed.  Please contact your
system administrator.")
```

As shown here, the exact error message is customizable. If `raise` is simply appended to the preceding code as part of the `except` clause, the usual stack trace will be printed to `stdout` whenever the `except` clause is run. Note also that the flow of the program is interrupted whenever `raise` is executed.

The same process applies when raising a warning. Simply use `MySQLdb.Warning` and, if necessary, also use a suitable warning message.

Making exceptions less intimidating

For many users, program exceptions are a sign on par with Armageddon and tend to elicit the anxiety and mystery that accompany the usual view of that occasion. In order to be more helpful to users and to help users be more helpful to their IT support staff, it is good practice to give error messages that are explanatory rather than merely cryptic. Consider the following two error messages:

- Exception: `NameError` in line 256 of `someprogram.py`.

- The value you passed is not of the correct format. The program needs an integer value and you passed a character of the alphabet. Please contact a member of IT staff if you need further clarification on this error and tell them the error message is: "Unknown column '7a' in 'where clause' on line 256 of `someprogram.py`".

Admittedly, the first takes up less space and takes less time to type. But it also is guaranteed to compromise the usefulness of your program for the user and to increase the number of phone calls to the IT helpdesk. While the second may be a bit longer than necessary, the user and helpdesk will benefit from a helpful message, regardless of its verbosity, more than an overly technical and terse one.

To accomplish a user-friendly error message that nonetheless provides the technical information necessary, catch the exception that Python passes. Using the previous `if...except` loop, we can catch the error without the traceback as follows:

```
#!/usr/bin/env python


import MySQLdb

mydb = MySQLdb.connect(host ='localhost',
                       user = 'skipper',
                       passwd = 'secret',
                       db = 'fish')
cur = mydb.cursor()

statement = """SELECT * FROM menu WHERE id=7a"""

try:
    cur.execute(statement)
    results = cur.fetchall()
    print results
except MySQLdb.Error, e:
    print "An error has been passed. %s" %e
```

Now when the program is executed, we receive the following output:

```
An error has been passed. (1054, "Unknown column '7a' in 'where clause'")
```

This could easily be revised to similar wording as the second of the two error examples seen just now.

Catching different types of exceptions

It is typically best practice to process different types of exceptions with different policies. This applies not only to database programming, but to software development in general. Exceptions can be caught with a generic except clause for simpler implementations, but more complex programs should process exceptions by type.

In Python, there are 36 built-in exceptions and 9 built-in warnings. It is beyond the scope of this book to go into them in detail, but further discussion on them can be found online.

For exceptions see:

```
http://python.about.com/od/pythonstandardlibrary/a/
lib_exceptions.htm
```

For warnings visit:

```
http://python.about.com/od/pythonstandardlibrary/a/
lib_warnings.htm
```

The Python documentation also covers them at:

```
http://docs.python.org/library/exceptions.html
```

Types of errors

The following are the six different error types supported by MySQL for Python. These are all caught when raising an error of the respective type, but their specification also allows for customized handling.

- DataError
- IntegrityError
- InternalError
- NotSupportedError
- OperationalError
- ProgrammingError

Each of these will be caught by using `DatabaseError` in conjunction with an `except` clause. But this leads to ambiguous error-handling and makes debugging difficult both for the programmer(s) who work on the application as well as the network and system administrators who will need to support the program once it is installed on the end user's machine.

DataError

This exception is raised due to problems with the processed data (for example, numeric value out of range, division by zero, and so on).

IntegrityError

If the relational integrity of the database is involved (for example a foreign key check fails, duplicate key, and so on), this exception is raised. To illustrate this, save the following code into a file for inserting data into the `fish` database that we have used in previous chapters:

```
#!/usr/bin/env python

import MySQLdb, sys

mydb = MySQLdb.connect(host ='localhost',
                       user = 'skipper',
                       passwd = 'secret',
                       db = 'fish')
cur = mydb.cursor()

ident = sys.argv[1]
fish = sys.argv[2]
price = sys.argv[3]

statement = """INSERT INTO menu(id, name, price) VALUES ("%s", "%s",
"%s")""" % (ident, fish, price)
print "Data has been inserted using the following statement: \n",
statement
cur.execute(statement)
```

Change the database login information as necessary. Then call it with an existent value for the identifier. For example:

```
> python temp.py 2 swordfish 23
```

The type of error follows a multiple line traceback:

```
_mysql_exceptions.IntegrityError: (1062, "Duplicate entry '2' for key
'PRIMARY'")
```

InternalError

This exception is raised when there is an internal error in the MySQL database itself (for example, an invalid cursor, the transaction is out of sync, and so on). This is usually an issue of timing out or otherwise being perceived by MySQL as having lost connectivity with a cursor.

NotSupportedError

MySQL for Python raises this exception when a method or database API that is not supported is used (for example, requesting a transaction-oriented function when transactions are not available. They also can arise in conjunction with setting characters sets, SQL modes, and when using MySQL in conjunction with **Secure Socket Layer (SSL)**.

OperationalError

Exception raised for operational errors that are not necessarily under the control of the programmer (for example, an unexpected disconnect, the data source name is not found, a transaction could not be processed, a memory allocation error occurrs, and so on.). For example, when the following code is run against the fish database, MySQL will throw an OperationalError:

```python
#!/usr/bin/env python


import MySQLdb, sys
mydb = MySQLdb.connect(host = 'localhost',
                        user = 'skipper',
                        passwd = 'secret',
                        db = 'fish')
cur = mydb.cursor()

statement = """SELECT * FROM menu WHERE id=7a"""
cur.execute(statement)
results = cur.fetchall()
print results
```

The error message reads as follows:

```
SELECT * FROM menu WHERE id=7a
Traceback (most recent call last):
  File "temp.py", line 54, in <module>
    cur.execute(statement)
  File "/usr/local/lib/python2.6/dist-packages/MySQL_python-1.2.3c1-
py2.6-linux-i686.egg/MySQLdb/cursors.py", line 173, in execute
  File "/usr/local/lib/python2.6/dist-packages/MySQL_python-
1.2.3c1-py2.6-linux-i686.egg/MySQLdb/connections.py", line 36, in
defaulterrorhandler
_mysql_exceptions.OperationalError: (1054, "Unknown column '7a' in 'where
clause'")
```

ProgrammingError

Exception raised for actual programming errors (for example, a table is not found or already exists, there is a syntax error in the MySQL statement, a wrong number of parameters is specified, and so on.). For instance, run the following code against the fish database:

```python
#!/usr/bin/env python

import MySQLdb

mydb = MySQLdb.connect(host ='localhost',
                       user = 'skipper',
                       passwd = 'secret',
                       db = 'fish')
cur = mydb.cursor()
fish = sys.argv[1]
price = sys.argv[2]
statement = """INSERTINTO menu(name, price) VALUES("%s", "%s")"""
% (fish, price)
print "Data has been inserted using the following statement: \n",
statement
cur.execute(statement)
```

The values you pass as arguments do not matter. The syntactic problem in the MySQL statement will cause a ProgrammingError to be raised:

```
_mysql_exceptions.ProgrammingError: (1064, 'You have an error in your
SQL syntax; check the manual that corresponds to your MySQL server
version for the right syntax to use near \'INSERTINTO menu(name, price)
VALUES("jellyfish", "27")\' at line 1')
```

Customizing for catching

Each of the previous types can be caught with the `DatabaseError` type. However, catching them separately allows you to customize responses. For example, you may want the application to fail softly for the user when a `ProgrammingError` is raised but nonetheless want the exception to be reported to the development team. You can do that with customized exception handling.

Catching one type of exception

To catch a particular type of exception, we simply include that type of exception with the `except` clause. For example, to change the code used for the `OperationalError` in order to catch that exception, we would use the following:

```
#!/usr/bin/env python


import MySQLdb, sys
mydb = MySQLdb.connect(host = 'localhost',
                       user = 'skipper',
                       passwd = 'r00tp4ss',
                       db = 'fish')
cur = mydb.cursor()

statement = """SELECT * FROM menu WHERE id=7a"""

try:
    cur.execute(statement)
    results = cur.fetchall()
    print results
except MySQLdb.OperationalError, e:
    raise e
```

After the traceback, we get the following output:

```
_mysql_exceptions.OperationalError: (1054, "Unknown column '7a' in 'where
clause'")
```

You can similarly catch any of MySQL for Python's `error` types or its `warning`. This allows much greater flexibility in exception-handling. We will see more of this in the project at the end of the chapter.

Catching different exceptions

To customize which error is caught, we need different `except` clauses. The basic structure of this strategy is as follows:

```
try:
    <do something>
except ErrorType1:
    <do something>
except ErrorType2:
    <do something else>
```

To combine the examples for the `OperationalError` and `ProgrammingError` that we just saw, we would code as follows:

```
#!/usr/bin/env python


import MySQLdb, sys
mydb = MySQLdb.connect(host ='localhost',
                       user = 'skipper',
                       passwd = 'secret',
                       db = 'fish')
cur = mydb.cursor()

identifier = sys.argv[1]

statement = """SELECT * FROM menu WHERE id=%s""" %(identifier)

try:
    cur.execute(statement)
    results = cur.fetchall()
    print results
except MySQLdb.OperationalError, e:
    raise e
except MySQLdb.ProgrammingError, e:
    raise e
```

After writing this into a file, execute the program with different arguments. A definite way to trigger the `OperationalError` is by passing a bad value like 7a. For the `ProgrammingError`, try an equals sign.

One can do more than simply `print` and `raise` exceptions in the except clause. One can also pass system calls as necessary. So, for example, one could pass programming variables to a function to send all errors to a set address by a protocol of your choosing (SMTP, HTTP, FTP, and so on.). This is essentially how programs such as Windows Explorer, Mozilla Firefox and Google's Chrome browsers send feedback to their respective developers.

Combined catching of exceptions

It is not uncommon to want to handle different errors in the same way. To do this, one simply separates the errors by a comma and includes them within parentheses after except. For example, the preceding program could be rewritten as follows:

```
#!/usr/bin/env python


import MySQLdb, sys
mydb = MySQLdb.connect(host ='localhost',
                       user = 'skipper',
                       passwd = 'secret',
                       db = 'fish'))
cur = mydb.cursor()

identifier = sys.argv[1]

statement = """SELECT * FROM menu WHERE id=%s""" %(identifier)

try:
    cur.execute(statement)
    results = cur.fetchall()
    print results
except (MySQLdb.OperationalError, MySQLdb.ProgrammingError), e:
    raise e
```

As with most parts of Python, enclosing the two error types in parentheses tells Python to accept either one as the error type. However, only one will be output when e is raised.

Raising different exceptions

Python will raise whatever valid type of error you pass to the raise statement. It is not particularly helpful to raise the wrong exceptions. However, particularly when debugging or auditing code that has been copied from another project, one should be aware that it can be done (as in the story of Ariane 5, at the beginning of this chapter).

To illustrate this using the code listing previously, change the except clause to read as follows:

```
except (MySQLdb.OperationalError, MySQLdb.ProgrammingError), e:
    raise ValueError
```

Then pass bad arguments to the program like 7a or ?.

Note that any use of `raise` will provide a stack trace. If you do not want a stack trace printed, then you should simply use a `print` statement to output the error message, as shown earlier in this chapter.

Creating a feedback loop

Being able to follow different courses of action based on different exceptions allows us to tailor our programs. For a `DataError` or even a `ProgrammingError`, we may want to handle the exception behind the scenes, hiding it from the user, but passing critical information to the development team. For `Warning` or non-critical errors, we may choose to pause execution of the program and solicit more information from the user. To do this, we would use a `raw_input` statement as part of the `except` clause. In order to be concise, the following program treats errors and warnings the same way, but they could easily be separated and treated with greater granularity.

```python
#!/usr/bin/env python


import MySQLdb, sys

mydb = MySQLdb.connect(host ='localhost',
                       user = 'skipper',
                       passwd = 'secret',
                       db = 'world')
cur = mydb.cursor()

identifier = sys.argv[1]
statement = """SELECT * FROM City WHERE ID=%s""" %(identifier)

while True:
    try:
        print "\nTrying SQL statement: %s" %(statement)
        cur.execute(statement)
        results = cur.fetchall()
        print "The results of the query are:"
        print results
        break
    except (MySQLdb.Error, MySQLdb.Warning):
        new_id = raw_input("The city ID you entered is not valid.
Please enter a valid city ID:   ")
        print "Using the new city ID value '%s'" %(new_id)
        statement = """SELECT * FROM City WHERE ID=%s""" %(new_id)
```

Project: Bad apples

Bad apples come in all shapes and sizes. Some are users; some are staff. Either is capable of giving the computer bad data or the wrong commands. MySQL, on the other hand, validates all data against the database description. As mentioned earlier in this book, all statements have to be made according to a set syntax. If there is a mismatch along the way, an exception is thrown.

For this project, therefore, we will implement a program to do the following:

- Insert and/or update a value in a MySQL database table
- Retrieve data from the same table
- Handle MySQL errors and warnings
- Notify the appropriate staff

Exactly how these elements are implemented will naturally differ depending on your local dynamics. Further, there are plenty of other checks beyond these that one could include. For example, if you have a whitelist or blacklist against which you can check input data, it would follow to include that check with what we implement here. The point of this project is to handle any error that MySQL can throw and to do so appropriately without resorting to generic exception-handling. Depending on how you code it, not all errors need to be handled because not all of them will ever be thrown. However, here we aim for comprehensiveness if merely for the exercise.

For this project, we will use the following functions:

- `connection()`: To create the database connection
- `sendmail()`: To send error messages to different maintainers (for example, database administrator)

Additionally, we will have a class `MySQLStatement` with the following methods and attributes (`__init__` naturally being assumed):

- `type`: Attribute of the instance to indicate what kind of statement is being processed
- `form()`: Method to form the MySQL statement
- `execute()`: Sends the SQL statement to MySQL and receives any exceptions

All of these will once again be controlled by `main()`.

The preamble

Before coding the functionality mentioned, we need to attend to the basics of the shebang line and import statements. We therefore start with the following code:

```
#!/usr/bin/env python

import MySQLdb
import optparse
import sys
```

After this, we need to include support for options:

```
# Get options
opt = optparse.OptionParser()
opt.add_option("-i", "--insert", action="store_true", help="flag
request for insertion - only ONE of insert, update, or select can be
used at a time", dest="insert")
opt.add_option("-u", "--update", action="store_true", help="flag
request as an update", dest="update")
opt.add_option("-s", "--select", action="store_true", help="flag
request as a selection", dest="select")
opt.add_option("-d", "--database", action="store", type="string",
help="name of the local database", dest="database")
opt.add_option("-t", "--table", action="store", type="string",
help="table in the indicated database", dest="table")
opt.add_option("-c", "--columns", action="store", type="string",
help="column(s) of the indicated table", dest="columns")
opt.add_option("-v", "--values", action="store", type="string",
help="values to be processed", dest="values")
opt, args = opt.parse_args()

# Only one kind of statement type is allowed.  If more than one is
indicated, the priority of assignment is SELECT -> UPDATE -> INSERT.
if opt.select is True:
    statement_type = "select"
elif opt.update is True:
    statement_type = "update"
elif opt.insert is True:
    statement_type = "insert"
```

Then, as a matter of style, we assign the option values to more generic variable names for ease of handling:

```
database = opt.database
table = opt.table
columns = opt.columns
values = opt.values
```

Making the connection

The first function we define is `connection()`. This is called with the name of the database as specified by the user. For security reasons, we do not allow the user to specify the host. Also, for reasons of simplicity, we will hardwire the login credentials into the function.

```
def connection(database):
    """Creates a database connection and returns the cursor.  Host is
hardwired to 'localhost'."""
    try:
        mydb = MySQLdb.connect(host ='localhost',
                               user = 'skipper',
                               passwd = 'secret',
                               db = 'database')
        cur = mydb.cursor()
        return cur
    except MySQLdb.Error:
        print "There was a problem in connecting to the database.
Please ensure that the database exists on the local host system."
        raise MySQLdb.Error
    except MySQLdb.Warning:
        pass
```

If the connection is made successfully, the function returns the cursor to the calling function. All errors at this point are fatal. We print a message to guide the user and then exit. All warnings are passed silently.

Sending error messages

Next is a very simple SMTP server that we use to send messages through localhost. To our import statements at the beginning of the program file, we need to add:

```
import smtplib
```

Then we can call it in a function as follows:

```
def sendmail(message, recipient):
    """Sends mail through localhost.  Takes error message and intended
recipient as arguments."""


    fromaddr = "pythonprogram@someaddress.com"
    toaddrs  = recipient + "@someaddress.com"

    # Add the From: and To: headers at the start!
    msg = ("From: %s\r\nTo: %s\r\n\r\n" %(fromaddr,toaddrs)
```

```
        msg = msg + str(message[0]) + message[1]

        server = smtplib.SMTP('localhost')
        server.set_debuglevel(1)
        server.sendmail(fromaddr, toaddrs, msg)
        server.quit()
```

Before running this code, you will naturally want to change the value of the SMTP server to be used from `localhost` if you do not have a mail server on your local system. Also note that many ISPs verify the existence of domains prior to forwarding a message, so you should also check your values in that regard before using this function.

By allowing the function to receive both the message and the recipient, we can reuse this code for different exceptions. As noted in the Python documentation on `smtplib`, this is a simple example and does not handle all of the dynamics of RFC822. For more on RFC822, see: `http://www.faqs.org/rfcs/rfc822.html`.

This code is derived from the documentation on `smtplib`, which can be found at `http://www.python.org/doc/2.5.2/lib/SMTP-example.html`

This example assumes that you are running an SMTP server on your local machine and so directs `smtplib`'s `SMTP` class to use `localhost`. However, you can easily adapt this to any SMTP server by using the `login` method of the `SMTP` class. For example, the function could read:

```
        fromaddr = "me@example.com"
        toaddr = "you@example.com"
        msg = ("From: %s\r\nTo: %s\r\b\r\n From me to you" %(fromaddr,
        toaddr))

        server = smtplib.SMTP('mail.example.com')
        server.login('me@example.com', 'secretpass')
        server.set_debuglevel(0)
        server.sendmail(fromaddr, toaddr, msg)
        server.quit()
```

If you need to use a particular port on the server, simply append it to the server address you use to instantiate the SMTP object:

```
        server = smtplib.SMTP('mail.example.com:587')
```

An example of how to do this with Google's email service can be found at `http://www.nixtutor.com/linux/send-mail-through-gmail-with-python/`.

For reasons of spam and other security issues, you will want to hardwire as many variables as is reasonably possible into this function. For example, you would not want to allow the domain name of either the recipient or the sender to be dynamically set. If you had to send an error message to someone who is not on the domain, it is better to set up mail-forwarding from an address on that domain than to allow anyone with access to the module to send messages to and from random domains while using your server.

Finally, while you are developing the program, it is helpful to keep `server.set_debuglevel` switched on and set to 1. When the program is moved into regular use, however, you will want to change it to 0, so the user does not see the debugging messages output by the server.

The statement class

Next we need to write the `MySQLStatement` class. Instances of this class will have as an attribute what kind of class they are. Further, they will have methods to form and execute an SQL statement that incorporates the user's input in the appropriate kind of statement.

The __init__ method

First, we need to give the class a conscience. We do this with the `__init__()` method:

```
class MySQLStatement:
    def __init__(self):
        """Creates an instance to form and execute a MySQL
statement."""
        self.Statement = []
```

You will notice that we are starting to use **docstrings**. As the code gets more complex and there is an increased likelihood that we will reuse it, we will start using docstrings with greater frequency.

> If you are unclear on what docstrings are and why you should use them, see this rationale for their use: `http://www.python.org/dev/peps/pep-0257/#rationale`.

We have no need to specify otherwise, so every instance of MySQLStatement will inherit the generic characteristics of a Python object.

Storing the statement type

The `statement` type is the only attribute that we will have in this class. Simply put, it stores the value that we pass to it. We could store the same value in a variable within the `main()` function and pass it as an argument to the object methods, but that would not leave us with re-usable code. Having the type as an attribute of the object ensures that we can access this same object as a module import instead of calling the entire program directly.

The code is as follows:

```
def type(self, kind):
    """Indicates the type of statement that the instance is.
Supported types are select, insert, and update.  This must be set
before using any of the object methods."""
    self.type = kind
```

Here we do not challenge the value of kind when this attribute is invoked. Rather, we allow any value to be passed to the `main()` function. We will talk more about verifying the type in *Room to grow*, later in this chapter.

Forming the statement

The first method that we will code forms the SQL statement from the user's data. The code for this method is as follows:

```
def form(self, table, column, info):
    """Forms the MySQL statement according to the type of
statement, using table as the tablename, column for the fields, and
info for values"""

    data = info.split(',')
    value = "'" + data[0]
    for i in xrange(1, len(data)):
        value = value + "', '" + data[i]
    value = value + "'"

    if self.type == "select":
        statement = """SELECT * FROM %s WHERE %s=%s""" %(table,
column, value)
        return statement
    elif self.type == "insert":
        statement = """INSERT INTO %s(%s) VALUES(%s)""" %(table,
column, value)
        return statement
    elif self.type == "update":
        statement = """UPDATE %s SET %s=%s WHERE %s=%s""" %(table,
column, data[0], column, data[1])
        return statement
```

If the same value is given for the two columns, the update will effectively be a replacement. If they differ, the first will be where the update is applied and the second will indicate the condition under which it is to be affected.

As usual in MySQL for Python, we leave off the semicolon at the end of the statement.

Different MySQL statements allow for comma-delimited values to be passed. Some don't. While comma-separated values without quotes are fine for the column names, the values must have quotes to have meaning (otherwise, they are read as variable names).

Even if we insisted the user pass values in quotes, we would still have the problem of getting the `optparse` module to recognize all of them as such. Therefore, we create a small routine to split the user's values on the comma and to insert quotes around each value.

Depending on which type of statement is held in the type attribute, we either form a SELECT, INSERT, or UPDATE statement. To process these options, we use a series of `if...elif...elif`.

Up to now, we have not covered the MySQL UPDATE statement. Up to now, we have not covered the MySQL UPDATE statement. UPDATE is similar to REPLACE in that it changes values that are already entered into the database. Where REPLACE affects changes in old rows and otherwise functions like INSERT, UPDATE impacts multiple rows at a time, wherever the given condition is met. As seen here, the basic syntax of UPDATE is:

```
UPDATE <table> SET <column>='<new value>' WHERE <column>='<old
value>';
```

Execute the MySQL statement

The final method of the class is `execute()`. As the name implies, this method accepts the statement to be processed. It also includes the table of the database specified by the user as well as the cursor returned by `connection()`. Here we include the majority of our exception-handling:

```
def execute(self, statement, table, cursor):
    """Attempts execution of the statement resulting from
MySQLStatement.form()."""
    while True:
        try:
            print "\nTrying SQL statement: %s\n\n" %(statement)
            cursor.execute(statement)

            if self.type == "select":
                # Run query
```

```
output = cursor.fetchall()

results = ""
data = ""
for record in output:
    for entry in record:
        data = data + '\t' + str(entry)
    data = data + "\n"
results = results + data + "\n"
return results


elif self.type == "insert":
    results = "Your information was inserted with the
following SQL statement: %s" % (statement)
    return results
elif self.type == "update":
    results = "You updated information in the database
with the following SQL statement: %s" % (statement)
    return results
```

Handling any fallout

If there is a failure along the way in the process, we need to handle the exceptions that are raised. To do so, we use a series of except clauses to process the different exceptions accordingly. In the following code, where the different exceptions are noted is indicated by comments:

```
# OperationalError
except MySQLdb.OperationalError, e :
    sendmail(e, "pythondevelopers")
    print "Some of the information you have passed is not
valid.  Please check it before trying to use this program again.  You
may also use '-h' to see the options available."
    print "The exact error information reads as follows:
%s" % (e)
    raise


# DataError
# ProgrammingError
except (MySQLdb.DataError, MySQLdb.ProgrammingError), e:
    sendmail(e, "pythondevelopers")
    print "An irrecoverable error has occured in the way
your data was to be processed.  This application must now close.  An
error message describing the fault has been sent to the development
team.  Apologies for any inconvenience."
    raise
```

```
        # IntegrityError
        except MySQLdb.IntegrityError, e:
            sendmail(e, "dba")
            print "An irrecoverable database error has occurred
and this process must now end.  An error message describing the fault
has been sent to the database administrator.  Apologies for any
inconvenience."
            raise

        # InternalError
        # NotSupportedError
        except (MySQLdb.InternalError, MySQLdb.NotSupportedError),
e:
            sendmail(e, "dba")
            sendmail(e, "pythondevelopers")
            print "An irrecoverable error has occurred and this
process must now end.  An error message describing the fault has been
sent to the appropriate staff.  Apologies for any inconvenience."
            raise

        except MySQLdb.Warning:
            pass
```

Some errors can be handled more or less the same way. Instead of creating separate `except` clauses for each, we group them. Similarly, different exceptions may require addressing by more than one team. So in the last `except` clause, processing internal and not supported errors, we send the error message to both the database administrator as well as the team who maintains the program. Finally, warnings are passed over.

The main() thing

As usual, the `main()` function is the brains of our program. As options are set earlier in the program, `main()` is left to instantiate the `MySQLStatement` object and pull the puppet strings to get the functions and methods to form the appropriate statement and execute it. If there is a failure along the way, we want to field it accordingly.

Try, try again

The main actions of `main()` begin as follows:

```
request = MySQLStatement()
try:
    request.type(statement_type)
    phrase = request.form(table, columns, values)
    cur = connection(database)
    results = request.execute(phrase, table, cur)
    print "Results:\n", results
    cur.close()
```

We first create an object `request`. This is the only part of `main()` that is definite; the rest is performed under the caveat of `try`. If there is a failure along the way, the process is scrubbed and an exception is processed.

Within the `try` clause, we first set the type of statement to be formed. Note that the way we coded the `type` attribute, allows any value to be set. Similarly here, the value of `type` is not validated.

Following on from setting `type`, we pass the table name, the column(s), and value(s) to be used to the `form()` method. Depending on the value of type, `form()` will return one of the three supported statements. This is stored in `phrase`.

Next, we need a cursor. For this, we call the `connection()` function. The cursor is then returned and given the rubric `cur`.

We then pass `phrase` and `cur`, along with the name of the table in question, to the execute method of our object. `MySQLStatement.execute()` returns the output of a selection or otherwise returns a positive statement if the process has been successful. The results are then printed to screen.

If all else fails

If there should be a failure and the `try` statement does not succeed, we can pick up the pieces and move on with the following `except` clauses:

```
except MySQLdb.Error, e:
    sendmail(e, "pythondevelopers")
    print "The values you entered are not valid.  Please check the
information you are using before trying again."
    print "The SQL statement that was tried reads as follows: %s"
% (statement)
    raise MySQLdb.Error

except MySQLdb.Warning:
    pass
```

Room to grow

The program discussed previously will process data given in a set format and do one of three things with it (SELECT information from the fish database, INSERT new data, or UPDATE old data to new.). Using various forms of exception-handling, it also process any error that MySQL throws.

Despite all this code, however, there is quite a bit that it does not do. Some points for you to consider when further developing this code are as follows:

- How would you implement handling of Python-specific exceptions (for example, NameErrors, KeyErrors, and so on)?

- Should you modify the type attribute to be self-validating? If so, how would you do it?

- Currently, warnings are passed silently; how would you handle them more securely?

- How would you change the UPDATE feature to handle more than one column at a time (that is, change the value in column price according to the value of column name)?

- How would you implement new features such as support for REPLACE or DELETE?

- The e-mail messages can serve as a makeshift log of the different errors, but there is currently no central listing. How would you implement a database for logging exceptions and their given messages?

- Currently, the error messages that are sent are still pretty vague. What kind of information would you want to pass if this were a web application? What if it were a desktop application? How would you gather that information and send it in a feedback message?

- The program currently prints the results of a SELECT query to the screen without column headers. How would you affect them using the PrettyTable module mentioned in the previous chapter?

Summary

In this chapter, we have covered how to handle errors and warnings that are passed from MySQL for Python and the differences between them. We have also looked at how to pass errors silently and when, the several types of errors supported by MySQL for Python, and how to handle errors properly.

In the next chapter, we will look at how to retrieve single and multiple records efficiently, ensuring we do not use resources needlessly or for longer than necessary.

5
Results Record-by-Record

As seen earlier, MySQL's SELECT statement can be very greedy. Using fetchall() processes all hits in one go. However, as we will see in this chapter, there are times when you should avoid this.

In this chapter, we will look at the following:

- Certain circumstances under which record-by-record processing is desirable
- How iteration helps us get each record in turn
- Using custom-created Python iterators for record-by-record processing
- Using fetchone() to process one record at a time
- Using fetchmany() to retrieve data in small chunks
- How to use loops to walk through a series of records

At the end of the chapter, we will put these lessons to use for writing a program that works with returned data record-by-record.

The problem

You have set up your database program as a **daemon,** so it runs persistently and can be called by users throughout the network. Based on what we have covered in earlier chapters, it retrieves all the records into the application process itself before processing each one as a list. You have debugged it thoroughly and so you know it works. Still, within a week of deployment, the service is jamming up and colleagues are drawing comparisons between your program's processing time and the speed of molasses in January. What happened?

To understand the problem, it is worth revisiting the process by which a query is processed in MySQLdb. After making the connection, one passes an execute() call according to the cursor object— cursor.execute() for an instance of MySQLdb. Cursor that is named cursor. When that execute() call is passed, MySQLdb does not return the results, but returns the number of rows affected by the query (the results are retrieved, but not immediately returned). Consider the code for the execute() method, part of the docstring and the exception-handling clauses have been removed for this snippet and replaced with an ellipsis(   ).

```
def execute(self, query, args=None):
        """Execute a query.
        query -- string, query to execute on server
        args -- optional sequence or mapping, parameters to use with
query.
...
        Returns long integer rows affected, if any
        """

        from types import ListType, TupleType
        from sys import exc_info
        del self.messages[:]
        db = self._get_db()
        charset = db.character_set_name()
        if isinstance(query, unicode):
            query = query.encode(charset)
        if args is not None:
            query = query % db.literal(args)
        try:
            r = self._query(query)
...

        self._executed = query
...
        return r
```

To get the results, we have previously used fetchall(). For most applications, this is tantamount to cracking a nut with a sledgehammer. Whenever you use fetchall(), MySQLdb returns all affected rows to your program in one go. This is typically unnecessary for user interaction. Further, being used simultaneously by multiple users, the multiple instances of the application then consume system resources like a sinkhole, causing the server to slow or, worse, to crash.

 It is worth noting that MySQL for Python supports a rowcount attribute of cursor and this is the preferred way of accessing the total of affected rows. One simply references the attribute as follows:

rows = cursor.rowcount

The problem would be resolved by regulating the rate at which one draws down the information to the user. This results in greater user satisfaction.

Why?

There are a number of reasons why one might opt to process records individually or at least in smaller chunks. Three of the most compelling reasons are:

- Limits of computing resources
- Network latency
- Pareto's principle

From the perspective of efficiency, any one of these reasons is good enough to warrant retrieval of smaller amounts of data. We look at each in greater detail in the following section.

Computing resources

Despite Moore's law holding true for many years now, it is coming under increasing pressure as a trend and cannot be presumed to hold true indefinitely. While one may have a budget with numbers so big that it looks like a phone directory, one's resources are only faster or more powerful on a comparative scale.

Moore's law states that the number of transistors that one is able to fit on an integrated circuit will double every two years.

This law is not much of a natural law as a business observation was made by Gordon Moore, co-founder of Intel. He did not state in such absolute terms, but wrote of the trend in the 19 April 1965 edition of *Electronics* magazine (*Volume 38, Number 8*):

> *The complexity for minimum component costs has increased at a rate of roughly a factor of two per year. Certainly over the short term this rate can be expected to continue, if not to increase.*

Moore has since gone on record saying that the trend cannot continue forever, but can be expected to break within the next twenty years. His paper is available for download on the following Intel website:

`ftp://download.intel.com/museum/Moores_Law/`

Click on `Articles-Press_Releases` and then on `Gordon_Moore_1965_Article.pdf`

It therefore behooves one as the developer or project manager to continue prudent use of one's resources. Especially, there are two conditions where this applies, which we will look at now.

Local resources

In the largest economies of the world, the majority of businesses have a relatively small operating budget. In the United Kingdom, for example, 97 percent of businesses employ fewer than 20 employees. In the United States, this figure is 89 percent. Australian small businesses account for 96 percent of the corporate economic system. The dynamics are the same across Canada, New Zealand, and the rest of the English-speaking world and are not likely to change significantly in other countries. Most applications, therefore, will be used by small businesses that typically have restricted budgets for computing resources.

In such a limited computing environment, performing and returning an exhaustive search can slow the system for other purposes. This applies to a single host or a local area network. One must keep in mind that most small businesses will run one MySQL server with several databases on it. Therefore, even if the application is not using the same database, it can overload the server, resulting in lag or latency, and loss of productivity.

It is worth noting that querying in large blocks to the point of locking up a system is a mistake that has been made even by professionals. One is reminded of earlier versions of **Filemaker Pro**—a database application for the Mac OS used widely in small business situations. When more than one large-ish query was passed to the server at one time, it became overloaded. It would then change the cursor to a teacup as if to tell the user, "Come back later. It might be a while."

The problem of resource scarcity is compounded by even good service administration. By their nature, the policies of system and network administrators tend to be at odds with the business cycle and therefore require constant revision and maintenance. Best practice says to design minimal resources than necessary for a task or for a project. However, the project requirement needs of a growing business will repeatedly push the resources toward breaking point. We thus need to make our software sufficiently robust to handle the tension, which ensues from that pushing. For Filemaker Pro, the system was pushed to its limit and therefore brought up a **teacup**.

This problem of anticipating how the user is going to push the system to its limits is as old as software engineering. Many modern methods of software development are designed to liaise with the end users throughout the development process; examples include evolutionary process systems (incremental and concurrent process models), component-based systems, and iterative models such as agile development. The point of this is not only to ensure a good fit for the software to the user's problems but, as part of that fit, to employ metrics in order to see how the system will be used most heavily in the target environment, and to ensure a reasonable amount of scalability.

Web applications

Perhaps the most common illustration of limited resources currently is the web application. Whether your site serves up a simple web page or a full service Web 2.0 application, you cannot escape the fundamental limits of the CPU to perform a given number of **flops** per second.

Combined with other system dynamics such as **input and output (I/O)**, **cache coherence**, **memory management**, and **interprocessor communication**, the capabilities of the server are finite and measurable. This mandates a cap on the amount throughout from disk to port and subsequently limits the number of users that any service can support.

The common, non-technical view is that servers can process requests from multiple users at one time. This is erroneous. Servers process requests quickly using a **first-in first-out (FIFO)** queue system. Therefore, the greater the number of users requesting a page, the longer the time between the processing of the first request and the second for each user. If that delay becomes sufficiently long, the server and the client will lose contact with each other. Because **HTTP persistent connections** do not require the client to issue an **end-of-request signal**, the server will interpret this lack of communication as an end of request and close the connection. The user will then receive a message that the connection has timed out. Refreshing the page then opens a new connection and starts the process again.

Examples of such events abound. Perhaps the most common form is the so-called **Slashdot effect**, named after the Slashdot website, but the same dynamics are at play whenever a site gets more traffic than it is built to withstand. Barring a misconfiguration of either the server or the networks used along the way, a time out arises from the server becoming overwhelmed and unable to maintain communication with user clients. Of the variables located on the host machine, the primary reason for the server becoming overwhelmed is inefficiency in the way dynamic content is generated.

Network latency

Beyond problems on the server itself, retrieving results by individual records is also advisable under certain network conditions. One needs to compare only the response times of a web application at times of peak and trough, to see how **network latency** impacts on the apparent responsiveness of an application. This latency is not always on any one network. Rather it is more often than not a negative synergy arising from small amounts of latency in networks on the route, from the browser to the server.

Server-client communications

The latency that occurs, impacts on the client-server communication and the timing of the *TCP/IP* dialogue that normally occurs. As this is disrupted, client requests can be dropped and it consequently appears to the server as if the client has closed the connection. The result is the same as the time out mentioned previously.

Apparent responsiveness

Network latency — whether on a LAN, WAN, or external network like the Internet, necessarily impinges upon the apparent responsiveness of the server and any application being served to the user. Even if it does not cause a timing out of the connection, latency slows down the entire communication process. The result is sluggishness in the application.

With the increasing ubiquity of *AJAX calls*, this sluggishness will become even more pronounced. A case in point; users of mainstream search engines or fully-featured web suites such as *2easy Office* will be used to suggestions in completing forms. These suggestion lists are usually generated through an AJAX-like call to the server. Such calls necessarily increase the amount of traffic between server and client. When combined with other user traffic at a given time, the user's receipt of the system's recommendations can be delayed increasingly.

Pareto's Principle

Pareto's Principle is a commonly applied rule of thumb: 80 percent of anything is trivial and that 20 percent is critical. It has been further extended to say that 20 percent of any process produces 80 percent of the output. The observation has been demonstrated in order to apply the rule from its origins in Italian land ownership to the solving of business problems to combat trends in trench warfare in the Second World War. It also applies, with some qualification, to user queries in an application.

Vilfredo Pareto was an Italian microeconomist who did most of his work in the 19th century. One of his most famous contributions is the observation that 80% of the land in his native Italy was owned by 20% of the population. This observation was later noted by Joseph Juran, an American management consultant, who observed that 80% of a business problem results from 20% of the apparent causes.

The Pareto Principle is alternatively known as the 80/20 rule or the law of the vital few. The point is that the major part of any situation, process, or thing results from and is largely controlled by a very significant minority. The percentages involved sometimes change depending on the milieu and can be 70/30 (search engine indexing), 90/10 (worldwide health expenditure), or even 95/5 (fundraising for charities).

Assuming the query is formed well by the user, the majority of user queries that are not exhaustive in nature will be resolved by a minority of the available data. Therefore, unless the query mandates an exhaustive query, one would do well to avoid being greedy in results to be returned. As the main overhead in most computing processes is **I/O**, it is best to let MySQL and MySQLdb handle filtering. Otherwise, you are left to return all results to your process and mill through them. This has its place, as we shall see, but it is not usually the best route to the desired results.

How?

As we have seen, record-by-record retrieval can save a lot of overhead. To retrieve a data piecemeal using MySQL for Python, one can call one of two methods of the Cursor object: fetchone() or fetchmany().

The fetchone() method

The fetchone() method of a cursor object returns exactly one row of results. If the query affects no rows, None is returned. Consider the following code:

```
import MySQLdb

mydb = MySQLdb.connect(host = 'localhost',
                       user = 'skipper',
                       passwd = 'secret',
                       db = 'fish')
cur = mydb.cursor()
statement = "SELECT * FROM menu WHERE name='shark'"
cur.execute(statement)
result = cur.fetchone()
print result
```

The outcome will be a raw form of the first record that matches the query.

```
(11L, 'shark', Decimal('13.00')
```

Note that only the first result will be printed using the preceding code. As the query leaves us vulnerable if there is more than one result, this is undesirable. If we are only going to process one record, we should nuance the SELECT statement, so that as few matches as possible will be returned. The more criteria one applies to the query, the fewer the records that will be returned.

For example, let's say we had a database of students at a university. Retrieving all records from a database of students will necessarily return a very large set of records. Retrieving those of a particular discipline will return fewer. Retrieving those who studied that discipline and another, denominated one will return still fewer. Limiting the query by year of graduation or year of birth will return even fewer. Even with limiting the query, we are likely to get more than one result. In such circumstances, one will find the second method of the Cursor class to be helpful.

The fetchmany() method

The fetchmany() method returns blocks of results according to a set limit. Where fetchone() was simply a method of the cursor object, fetchmany() requires the desired number of records to be passed as an argument. The basic syntax of the call is as follows:

```
<variable name> = <cursor name>.fetchmany(<number of records to
retrieve>)
```

An example of its use in reducing how much data is returned is as follows. Our SQL statement is very greedy, but the fetchmany() method keeps the results manageable.

```
#!/usr/bin/env python

import MySQLdb

mydb = MySQLdb.connect(host = 'localhost',
                       user = 'skipper',
                       passwd = 'secret',
                       db = 'world')
cur = mydb.cursor()
statement = "SELECT * FROM City"
cur.execute(statement)

results = cur.fetchmany(10)
for result in results:
    print result
```

The output of this program is as follows. Recall that we are leaving the data raw for the moment.

```
(1L, 'Kabul', 'AFG', 'Kabol', 1780000L)

(2L, 'Qandahar', 'AFG', 'Qandahar', 237500L)

(3L, 'Herat', 'AFG', 'Herat', 186800L)

(4L, 'Mazar-e-Sharif', 'AFG', 'Balkh', 127800L)

(5L, 'Amsterdam', 'NLD', 'Noord-Holland', 731200L)

(6L, 'Rotterdam', 'NLD', 'Zuid-Holland', 593321L)

(7L, 'Haag', 'NLD', 'Zuid-Holland', 440900L)

(8L, 'Utrecht', 'NLD', 'Utrecht', 234323L)

(9L, 'Eindhoven', 'NLD', 'Noord-Brabant', 201843L)

(10L, 'Tilburg', 'NLD', 'Noord-Brabant', 193238L)
```

This code returns only the first ten rows and then exits. We can return more with another `fetchmany()` call. Assuming a cursor `cur` for an established database connection and the importing of the `time` module, we can run:

```
cur.execute("SHOW TABLES")
time.sleep(20)
print cur.fetchmany(10)
time.sleep(20)
print cur.fetchmany(10)
```

Using `time.sleep()`, we suspend execution of the program for a few seconds between retrievals. This does not shut the MySQL server down, but plays nicely with other processes that might issue a query, thus avoiding the problem in FileMaker Pro that was mentioned earlier.

Naturally, in the real world, you would normally want to work through all of the data. To do that, we need some iteration.

Iteration: What is it?

Unless we know that our `fetchone()` call by design will return a single record or that our `fetchmany()` call will return all results, it is necessary to retrieve the next record or set of records through an iterative cycle. How we implement that, however, depends on the conditions of our programming.

In its simplest form, **iteration** is the repetition of a process in order to progress through a series. The series may be data to be processed (the returned results of a database query) or a series of events to be performed (the calls necessary to retrieve records individually).

As we shall see, Python allows for the creation of iterative loops as well as iterator objects. Which one you use and when, naturally depends on the other dynamics of your application.

Generating loops

Iterating through results is done with one of two control flow tools: `while` or `for`.

while...if loops

The use of `while...if` for generating and controlling iteration is a combination of the two control-flow tools used elsewhere in generic Python. One initiates a recurring retrieval cycle that continues while there is valid data to process, but is broken if there is no data to process. If there is no data returned, `fetchone()` returns a value of `None`. This is therefore the value for which the `if` statement checks.

In using `while`-based controls, one does not always use `if` to check the data. Rather, as we have seen in previous chapters, one can simply allow an error to arise and thus break out of the loop.

Using the previous example of `fetchone()`, we can use the following nested loop to walk through the records:

```
import MySQLdb

mydb = MySQLdb.connect(host = 'localhost',
                       user = 'skipper',
                       passwd = 'secret',
                       db = 'fish')
cur = mydb.cursor()
statement = "SELECT * FROM menu WHERE name='shark'"
cur.execute(statement)
    while 1:
        result = cur.fetchone()
        if result == None:
            break
        print result
```

Running the preceding code produced the following raw results:

```
(11L, 'shark', Decimal('13.00'))
```

As seen in earlier chapters, you can make this more useful to the user with a bit more code.

It is important to note that `while` creates the recurring retrieval of data that is checked by the `if` statement. Without `while`, only attempt at retrieval is made and the results only printed if not equal to `None`. Without the `if` statement, an infinite loop is created.

The for loop

Recall from the beginning of the chapter that the `execute()` method of the `Cursor` class returns the number of records affected by the query. That number is also stored in the `rowcount` attribute of the `cursor` object. Using that attribute, we can create a `for` loop to walk through the results individually:

```
import MySQLdb
import time

mydb = MySQLdb.connect(host = 'localhost',
                       user = 'skipper',
                       passwd = 'secret',
                       db = 'fish')
cur = mydb.cursor()
statement = "SELECT * FROM menu WHERE name='tuna'"
cur.execute(statement)
numrows = int(cursor.rowcount)
for x in xrange(0,numrows):
        row = cursor.fetchone()
          print row

        time.sleep(5)
```

If one is seeking to optimize one's memory usage, use `xrange()` instead of `range()` for large series or for series accessed infrequently. Using `range()` causes Python to store the entire series at once, where `xrange()` creates series items on demand. You can learn more about `xrange()` in the Python documentation at `http://docs.python.org/library/functions.html`.

The output of this program will be the same as the previously discussed `while` loop.

As indicated previously, one uses a `for` loop to walk through the return of `fetchmany()`. One could rewrite the last code from just after the `execute()` call with the following:

```
numtakes = int(cur.rowcount)/5
for x in range(0,numtakes+1):
    result = cur.fetchmany(5)
    for row in result:
        print row
```

Unless you know that the number of rows being returned is divisible by the size you give `fetchmany()`, you need to account for the remainder. To accomplish this, we add one to the iteration count.

Iterators

Since Version 2.2, Python has supported the use of iterators. Iteration in its simplest form can be seen whenever one works through a list one-by-one, usually with a `for` loop. For example, assume a list of objects:

```
alist = ['chihuahua', 'boxer', 'greyhound']
```

We iterate through the list with a `for` loop:

```
for i in alist:
    print i
```

The results are the list printed in order. Wherever and whenever you use a `for` loop to work through a series, you employ iteration (for example, lists by item, files by line, and so on).

As the name implies, iterators are objects used to iterate over a set of values. By definition, an iterator is an object that has a next method to return the next item in a series.

 More information on iterators is available in the Python documentation by following the links at:

`http://docs.python.org/glossary.html#term-iterator`

One creates an iterator using the `iter()` function. One passes the set to `iter()` as an argument.

```
iterator = iter(<name of set>)
```

This creates an iterator object that is normally named with an assignment statement. One then simply requests items in the series one-by-one with the `next()` method of the object just created.

```
idem = iterator.next()
```

This assigns the next item in the series to the variable `idem`.

Illustrative iteration

The function of iterators can be seen in an example using the `fetchall()` method:

```
#!/usr/bin/env python


import MySQLdb

mydb = MySQLdb.connect(host = 'localhost',
                       user = 'skipper',
                       passwd = 'secret',
                       db = 'fish')
cur = mydb.cursor()
statement = "SELECT * FROM menu WHERE name='shark'"
cur.execute(statement)
result = cur.fetchall()

series = iter(result)

for i in xrange(0, cur.rowcount):
    print series.next()
```

In this instance, we create an iterator out of the series of records returned by `fetchall()`. We then iterate through the series according to the number of rows returned, calling the next method of the iterator object series whenever we needed another record.

One can use `while` with an iterator object. In doing so, however, one must make allowances for either the point at which the returned data ends or the point where the iterator object raises a `StopIteration` exception.

 A `StopIteration` exception is always raised by an iterator at the end of a series. Using a `for` loop usually avoids having to handle it.

Iteration and MySQL for Python

MySQL for Python's `Cursor` class supports two methods that are primarily used in iteration: `fetchone()` and `fetchmany()`. As shown in the previous sections, it is possible to use within the main flow of a program. While this gets the job done, the better way is to abstract the iteration into a function or method.

Generators

Functions and methods that contain loops for controlling iteration are usually **generators**. By definition, generators are functions or methods that contain the keyword `yield`.

The term `yield` was introduced in Python 2.2 as a special keyword. Its sole purpose was to indicate that a function is a generator. Whenever a function contains the keyword `yield`, Python's byte code compiler would compile it as a result. (see *PEP 255* for more on this).

The net effect is that `yield` causes two main results:

- The function does not return a single value, but a generator object for the iterator defined within it
- The dynamics of the function are suspended after each iteration until the next method is called

What this means for us as programmers is that we never get the full series from a generator, but the ability to access the series in a resource-sensitive way. The data is generated only when we ask for it. In the context of a generator, `yield` functions like `return`. The function that includes `yield` returns a generator object, not a particular value.

Using fetchone() in a generator

Creating a generator using `fetchone()` is simply a matter of incorporating the method into an iterative function. `MySQLdb` cursors are iterators themselves, but the following code illustrates how to include them in other iterative structures:

```
#!/usr/bin/env python

import MySQLdb

mydb = MySQLdb.connect(host = 'localhost',
                       user = 'skipper',
                       passwd = 'secret',
                       db = 'world')
cur = mydb.cursor()
statement = "SELECT * FROM City"
cur.execute(statement)


def iter_results(cursor, recordnum):
    for x in xrange(0,recordnum):
```

```
        result = cursor.fetchone()
        if not result:
            break
        else:
            yield result

myresults = iter_results(cur, 5)
for item in myresults:
    print item
```

Using the world database, we can pass a statement to select every city, but then take only the first three. When dealing with the potential return of large amounts of data, generators allow us to deal with the data in chunks. In this instance, the iterator that is returned will return only the first five rows of those affected by the SQL statement.

Using fetchmany() in a generator

Similarly to fetchone(), the fetchmany() method can be incorporated into a generator to return an iterator. As with fetchone(), MySQLdb cursors are iterators themselves. The following code illustrates how to include fetchmany() into another iterative structure. The following code returns all results, but in blocks set by the program call:

```
#!/usr/bin/env python

import MySQLdb

mydb = MySQLdb.connect(host = 'localhost',
                       user = 'skipper',
                       passwd = 'secret',
                       db = 'world')
cur = mydb.cursor()
statement = "SELECT * FROM City"
cur.execute(statement)

def iter_results(cursor, recordnum):
    while 1:
        result = cursor.fetchmany(recordnum)
        if result == None:

            break
        for item in result:
            yield item

myresults = iter_results(cur, 5)
for idem in myresults:
    print idem
```

Currently, the preceding code retrieves results in batches of five rows. But it does so with such speed that it might as well be all at once. The savings here are in memory usage—more or less the same system resources are allotted for each iteration and then released back to the system to be allotted again. So memory usage does not ramp up with each iteration.

If we wanted to affect the same results as we did for the function written for `fetchone()`, previously, we need to limit the iteration of the generator. We do not need to change the generator. Instead, we need to change the `for` loop by which we walk through the results. Change the last loop to read as follows:

```
for span in xrange(0,5):
    print myresults.next()
```

This treats `IterResults()` as the generator that it is and simply calls the next function of the generator object named `myresults`.

The output will be the return of the first five records of affected rows.

```
(1L, 'Kabul', 'AFG', 'Kabol', 1780000L)
(2L, 'Qandahar', 'AFG', 'Qandahar', 237500L)
(3L, 'Herat', 'AFG', 'Herat', 186800L)
(4L, 'Mazar-e-Sharif', 'AFG', 'Balkh', 127800L)
(5L, 'Amsterdam', 'NLD', 'Noord-Holland', 731200L)
```

Project: A movie database

The project for this chapter involves querying the **Sakila** database from MySQL.

 Sakila is a database of fictitious movies and films.

For this project, we will write a program with the following features:

- Accepts user input for the name of either a film or an actor
- Returns the first record for confirmation by the user
- If the first set of data is confirmed as being what the user wants, the entire set is returned
- All errors are fatal and result in error messages being passed to the user
- All warnings are explicitly silenced

Getting Sakila

The Sakila sample database represents the possible tables for a DVD rental store. It is available for download from the MySQL website:

```
http://downloads.mysql.com/docs/sakila-db.zip
```

Once you have downloaded the file, unpack it into a temporary directory. Then you are ready to create the database.

Creating the Sakila database

To create the Sakila database, one follows similar steps to what we did for the world database. Where the world database came in a single *.sql file dump and so required a single source command, Sakila comes in two files and requires them to be sourced in a specific order.

In a terminal session, enter the sakila-db directory (that is, the directory created when you unzip the sakila-db.zip file). Then log into MySQL.

Once logged into MySQL, we may need to create the database itself.

```
mysql> CREATE DATABASE sakila;
```

This is not necessary with Sakila as the file will include the CREATE statement. We do not need to tell MySQL the names and structures for the tables explicitly. Instead, we source the schema file:

```
mysql> source sakila-schema.sql
```

This creates the structure of the database tables. Next, fill the tables with data by source-ing the data file:

```
mysql> source sakila-data.sql
```

Then, having created the database, its tables, and its data, we can look around in the database by use-ing it.

```
mysql> use sakila;
```

Further information on installing the Sakila database can be found at
http://dev.mysql.com/doc/sakila/en/sakila.html#sakila-installation.

The structure of Sakila

The Sakila database is intended to represent the tables that would drive a DVD rental database application. As such, it has several more tables than world:

```
mysql> show tables;
+----------------------------+
| Tables_in_sakila           |
+----------------------------+
| actor                      |
| actor_info                 |
| address                    |
| category                   |
| city                       |
| country                    |
| customer                   |
| customer_list              |
| film                       |
| film_actor                 |
| film_category              |
| film_list                  |
| film_text                  |
| inventory                  |
| language                   |
| nicer_but_slower_film_list |
| payment                    |
| rental                     |
| sales_by_film_category     |
| sales_by_store             |
| staff                      |
| staff_list                 |
| store                      |
+----------------------------+
```

Of all of these tables now available, we shall use two for this project: `actor_info` and `film_list`. The first contains the names and films of the actors in the database and has the following structure:

```
mysql> describe actor_info;
```

Field	Type	Null	Key	Default	Extra
actor_id	smallint(5) unsigned	NO		0	
first_name	varchar(45)	NO		NULL	
last_name	varchar(45)	NO		NULL	
film_info	varchar(341)	YES		NULL	

The `film_list` table contains all of the films and their respective actors:

```
mysql> describe film_list;
```

Field	Type	Null	Key	Default	Extra
FID	smallint(5) unsigned	YES		0	
title	varchar(255)	YES		NULL	
description	text	YES		NULL	
category	varchar(25)	NO		NULL	
price	decimal(4,2)	YES		4.99	
length	smallint(5) unsigned	YES		NULL	
rating	enum('G','PG','PG-13','R','NC-17')	YES		G	
actors	varchar(341)	YES		NULL	

Planning it out

Knowing a bit more about the `Sakila` database, we can take another look at our planned functionality and consider what we will need to do.

- Accept user input for the name of either a film or a thespian

This will entail use of the `optparse` module again. Depending on which is flagged, we will need one of two possible MySQL statements.

- Return the first record for confirmation by the user

We will rely on `fetchone()` to do this. This gives the user a preview of the data so we don't waste resources fetching unwanted data.

- If the first set of data is confirmed as being what the user wants, the entire set is returned

This will require `fetchmany()` to cut down on system resources.

- All errors are fatal and result in error messages being passed to the user
- All warnings are explicitly silenced to the user (they are, however, logged to `stderr`)

This requires explicit exception-handling as detailed in the previous chapter. Errors and warnings will be explicitly handled in a `try...except` structure.

The SQL statements to be used

To create the functionality we detailed just now, we will need two MySQL statements. One returns the films of an actor or actress. The other returns the actors for a particular film.

Returning the films of an actor

The first query uses the `actor_info` table to return the movies in which an actor has appeared. Because we ask the user only for the surname of the actor or actress, we need to fetch the first name from the database, along with the list of film titles in which the thespian has appeared. For simplicity's sake, we will return the last name of the actor, as well, in order to keep all of the data in a neat bundle for processing. The template for this MySQL query is thus:

```
SELECT first_name,last_name,film_info FROM actor_info WHERE last_name
= '<a value>';
```

Note that we require the user to specify the surname specifically. We will see in the following section how to allow the user to enter partial data.

Returning the actors of a film

The second query uses the `film_list` table and returns the actors for a given film. To make troubleshooting easier by keeping all results in a single returned value, we will also ask for the `title` field of the record. A first go at a template for this MySQL query therefore looks like this:

```
SELECT title,actors FROM film_list WHERE title = '<a value>';
```

But this is not satisfactory for our program in terms of usability. The main problem is that this statement requires the user to remember the name of the film in its entirety. But most people do not do that. Usually, the title of a film gets abbreviated to the first few words. Therefore, we need to use a special MySQL keyword: LIKE. To use LIKE in the previous statement, we substitute it for the **equals sign** =:

```
SELECT title,actors FROM film_list WHERE title LIKE '<a value>';
```

LIKE allows us to use **wildcard characters** and **regular expressions**. If we simply gave MySQL a value in the preceding template, the results would tend to be the same as using a symbol of equality. For our purposes, we should anticipate a lack of specificity on the part of the user and allow him or her to input the first words, or even just the first letter of a title. We then rely on MySQL to sort out which titles match. To do this we use the percentage symbol %.

```
SELECT title,actors FROM film_list WHERE title LIKE '<a value>%';
```

The % symbol in MySQL comparisons is similar to the use of an asterisk (*) in Python's regular expressions.

Note that % is a **universal quantifier** and matches any number of any characters—even zero occurrences of characters. Therefore, ZERO% will match ZEROS, ZERO TOLERANCE, and ZERO alone. If you only want to match one character, use the **underscore** wildcard (_) as an **existential quantifier**. The string ZERO_ would then match ZEROS but not ZERO TOLERANCE or ZERO itself.

To match a value that incorporates one of the wildcards, escape from the wildcard with the **backslash** (\)like you do in Python. So to match ZERO_ we would use ZERO_.

Accepting user data

To accept the user data, we have two options. We can either generate a dialogue that walks the user through a series of questions and assigns values within the program as appropriate. Or we can use the optparse module and rely on the user to indicate their preference at runtime. We shall leave the former as an exercise and implement the latter. The beginning of the preamble to this program thus reads:

```
#!/usr/bin/env python

import MySQLdb
import optparse
```

We then need to parse the options:

```
opt = optparse.OptionParser()
opt.add_option("-a", "--actor", action="store", help="denotes the
lastname/surname of the actor for search - only ONE of actor or film
can be used at a time", dest="actor")
opt.add_option("-f", "--film", action="store", help="denotes film for
search", dest="film")
opt, args = opt.parse_args()
```

As our specification is only for one type of data at a time, we need to ensure that the user does not ask for both actor and film simultaneously. We do this with a simple while test.

```
badoptions = 0
while opt.film and opt.actor:
    print "Please indicate either an actor or a film for which you
would like to search.  This program does not support search for both
in tandem."
    badoptions = 1
    break
```

The value of status will indicate the overall status of the program—whether it should still be executed. As we shall see, by setting status to 1 we ensure the program does not execute if the user asks for both kinds of searches.

A MySQL query with class

For the rest of the features, we will implement a class called MySQLQuery. This class will have the following methods and attributes:

- **__init__**: To create an instance of the class.
- **Type**: The type of statement required—whether actor or film.

- **Connection**: To create the database `connection` and to return the cursor for data retrieval.

- **Query**: To create the appropriate type of SQL query. Passes a statement to `execute()` and passes the results along.

- **Execute**: To execute the statement formed by `query()`, retrieve the data as appropriate, and then pass it along to `format()` for formatting. It then receives the results back from `format()` and passes it up the chain to `query()`.

- **Format**: To receive output from `execute()`, parse it and repackage it appropriately, and pass it back to execute for further returning.

The __init__ method: The consciousness of the class

The first method of the class is, of course, __init__. As discussed in previous chapters, an __init__ method is customary for the proper functioning of a class. It is not necessary; the class can function without it. However, using one allows us to customize the nature of the object being initiated.

> More on Python classes and the use of __init__ can be found in the Python documentation:
>
> `http://docs.python.org/tutorial/classes.html#class-objects`

For this project, the __init__ method looks like this:

```
def __init__(self):
    """Creates an instance to form and execute a MySQL
statement."""
    self.Statement = []
```

Setting the query's type

Once the object is instantiated, we need to set the `type` of the query. This is critical to the smooth running of the rest of the program as follows:

```
def type(self, kind):
    """Indicates the type of statement that the instance is.
Supported types are select, insert, and update.  This must be set
before using any of the object methods."""
    self.type = kind
```

As in the project from last chapter, we simply assign the value of `kind` to `self.type`.

Creating the cursor

Naturally, in order to query the database, we must have a cursor by which we execute a query and fetch results. Rather than code this into the main () function or into the preamble, we put it here in a function on its own:

```
def connection(self):
    """
    Creates a database connection and returns the cursor.  All login
information is hardwired.
    HOST = localhost
    USER = skipper
    DATABASE = sakila
    """
    try:
        mydb = MySQLdb.connect(host = 'localhost',
                               user = 'skipper',
                               passwd = 'secret',
                               db = "sakila")
        cur = mydb.cursor()
        return cur
```

Obviously, this implementation can be called from any other Python program that can import it. You therefore want to be careful about permissions and other security issues. While this can be a trajectory by which a login is leaked, hardwiring the login ensures that a rogue user cannot exceed the permissions of the given user.

It is worth noting that any Python program that can import a module can also read that module's code by using the inspect module.

To illustrate, name the program as moviesearch.py. Then open a Python shell in the directory that holds the file. In the shell, type the following:

```
>>> import moviesearch, inspect
```

```
>>> inspect.getsource(moviesearch)
```

You will then be treated to a full printout of the code for this program. Any user on a network can do the same thing if they have access to the module.

Naturally, we need to handle any fallout from a failed connection. Here we handle exceptions in a blanket manner, but one can (and should) implement appropriate rules for each possible exception.

```
except MySQLdb.Error:
     print "There was a problem in connecting to the database.
Please ensure that the 'sakila' database exists on the local host
system."
     raise
except MySQLdb.Warning:
     pass
```

Forming the query

The next step requires us to form the query. To do this, we will use the templates discussed previously and insert them appropriately into the method. The user's input will be received as value.

This function will be used to handle all queries. So we must be able to toggle between the initial sample and a fuller query. To do this, we will use a sample switch. The opening line of the definition thus reads:

```
def query(self, value, sample):
```

We then start by testing the value of sample. If it is 1, we return a sample of the data.

```
if sample == 1:
    if self.type == 'actor':
        statement = """SELECT first_name,last_name,film_info
FROM actor_info WHERE last_name = '%s'""" %(value)
    else:
        statement = """SELECT title,actors FROM film_list
WHERE title LIKE '%s'""" %("%" + value + "%"
    returnself.execute(statement, sample)
```

Otherwise, we retrieve all records that match.

```
else:
    if self.type == 'actor':
        statement = """SELECT first_name,last_name,film_info
FROM actor_info WHERE last_name = '%s'""" %(value)
    else:
        statement = """SELECT title,actors FROM film_list
WHERE title LIKE '%s'""" %("%" + value + "%")
    results = self.execute(statement, sample)
    return results
```

In either case, we check the value of `self.type`, form the appropriate query, and pass the resulting `statement` and the value of `sample` to the `execute()` method. When results are received from `execute()` we pass them back to the calling process.

Executing the query

The `execute()` method calls the `connection()` method and uses the returned `cursor` to execute the statement received from `query()` because its behavior still relies on the value of `sample`, its structure is similar to `query()`.

```
def execute(self, statement, sample):
    """Attempts execution of the statement resulting from
MYSQLQuery.form()."""
    while True:
        try:
            cursor = self.connection()
            cursor.execute(statement)
            if cursor.rowcount == 0:
                print "No results found for your query."
                break

            elif sample == 1:
                output = cursor.fetchone()
                results = self.format(output, sample)
                return results

            else:
                output = cursor.fetchmany(1000)
                results = self.format(output, sample)
                return results
```

Note that the argument to `fetchmany()` is the total number of records in Sakila. In real-life situations where multiple users are working against much larger databases, you would do well to iterate through the records.

Since the statement does not have to come from `query()`, but can be passed by a calling module, we again should be ready to handle any fallout from a failed query.

```
        except MySQLdb.Error:
            raise MySQLdb.Error

        except MySQLdb.Warning:
            pass
```

Here as we handle exceptions in a blanket fashion, it is advisable to handle exceptions in greater detail.

Formatting the results

As seen previously, the `output` of the search is passed to `format()` in order to be repackaged for the user. The value of `output` is a tuple and must be processed accordingly. Once again, how the data is processed is determined by whether it is a sample or not. The definition declaration thus reads:

```
def format(self, output, sample):
```

In the course of this method, we will use iteration often. Therefore, we create a blank object called `results` onto which we can add the parsed data.

```
results = ""
```

Formatting a sample

If a sample is needed, we then use an `if...else` loop to control program flow according to whether the user is searching for a drama or a film.

```
if sample == 1:
    if self.type == "actor":
        data = output[0] + " " + output[1] + ": "
        titles = output[2]
        entry = titles.split(';')
        data = data + entry[0].split(':')[1]
        results = results + data + "\n"
        return results


    else:
        data = output[0] + ": "
        actors = output[1]
        data = data + output[1]
        results = results + data + "\n"
        return results
```

If an actor is sought, the output will follow this template:

`<first_name> <last_name>: <first few titles>`

For a film, the results would be:

`<title>: <list of actors in a comma-delimited series>`

Formatting a larger set of results

If a sample is not required, it is safe to assume that the full amount of results are to be processed. This forms the else part of the greater `if...else` loop of this method. Within it, we have another `if...else` loop to process the data by actor or title, as we did with the previous sample `return`.

```
else:
    if self.type == "actor":
        for record in output:
            actor = record[0] + " " + record[1] + ": "
            for item in xrange(2,len(record)):
                names = record[item].split(';')
                for i in xrange(0, len(names)):
                    if i == 0:
                        titles = "\n " + names[i]
                    else:
                        titles = titles + '\n' + names[i]
            data = actor + titles + '\n'
            results = results + data + "\n"

    else:
        for record in output:
            title = record[0] + ": "
            for item in xrange(1, len(record)):
                names = record[item].split(',')
                for i in xrange(0, len(names)):
                    if i == 0:
                        actor = "\n " + names[i]
                    else:
                        actor = actor + '\n' + names[i]
            data = title + actor + '\n'
            results = results + data + '\n'
    return results
```

The results of either part of the loop will be in this format:

```
<full name of film or thespian>:
<list of actors in the film or films of the thespian>
```

If any part of a program's execution is unclear, the best way to figure out what's going on is to use `print`. Use it not only to print out values at different points of execution, but also the types of different variables. For example, if one inserts `print output` on the line after assigning results, Python will output that value. But if one inserts `print type(output)`, Python tells us that the variable `output` is a **tuple**.

The main() thing

Having coded the `MySQLQuery` class, we can now write the `main()` function of the program. The first thing to do in `main()` is to test the value of `status`. We do this with a while loop that continues as long as `status` is equal to `0` (and `break` is not called).

```
while status == 0:
```

We then need to create an instance of `MySQLQuery` and try to execute the operational part of `main()`. This includes first assigning the type of query to `MySQLQuery.type`.

```
while status == 0:
    request = MySQLQuery()
    try:
        if opt.actor:
            request.type("actor")
            value = opt.actor
        elif opt.film:
            request.type("film")
            value = opt.film
```

Next, we query the database by calling the `query()` method. You will recall that `query()` passes the MySQL statement to `execute()`, which then passes the results to `format()`. The results are then returned down the chain. If you want to ensure that resources are relinquished before the next method is called, simply return the output of each method back to `main()` before calling the next one.

```
results = request.query(value, 1)
```

Here we pass the value to `query()` as well as a `1` to indicate the need for a sample. If results are returned, the sample should be output to the user for confirmation.

```
if results:
    print "Sample returns for the search you requested are
as follows."
    print results
    confirm = raw_input("Are these the kind of data that
you are seeking? (Y/N) ")
    confirm = confirm.strip()
```

The confirm variable should ideally begin with either a Y or an N. To ensure that the user has not accidentally hit the space bar before entering his or her response, we strip the whitespace out of the input value. If the answer is yes, we expect the first character then to be a capital Y, as indicated. If it is not, we default to a fatal break.

```
        if confirm[0] != 'Y':   # if confirmation is not given,
then break.
            print "\n\nSuitable results were not found.
Please reconsider your selection of %s and try again.\n" %(request.
type)
            break
```

If confirmation is given, we then use the same object and send a second query call for the full listing of records.

```
        if confirm[0] == 'Y':
            results = request.query(value, 0)
            print "\n\nResults for your query are as follows:\n\n"
            print results
            break
```

If there are no results, execute() tells the user so. We can therefore simply break.

```
        else:
            break
```

Finally, if trying to run the core of the main() method fails, we need to handle the fallout. Here we implement some general exception-handling that should be more robust in most applications of any size.

```
    except MySQLdb.Error:
        raise MySQL.Error

    except MySQLdb.Warning:
        pass
```

Calling main()

Finally, we call main() only if the program is called directly.

```
if __name__ == '__main__':
    main()
```

Running it

If you save the file now as `moviesearch.py`, you can call it from the command-line with either an `-a` or `-f` flag for actor or film, respectively. Of course, there is also the helpful `-h` flag to explain the syntax.

Room to grow

The results of this project may appear to be marginally more complex than the example on retrieving from earlier in this book. However, this project can easily be extended and applied in several ways to form the basis of a fully-functional program. Some points for extension are as follows:

- Step through the results one-by-one, waiting for the user to indicate when to proceed to the next record

- Create a menu from the results returned and allow the user to select which record to return

- Allow the user to select multiple records to be either returned to the screen or output to a file

- Using the other tables in the database, develop reports of customer trends by actor and genre

- Create a web-based, point-of-sale (POS) interface that would allow users to input the DVDs being rented and register how much was being received from which customer

- For that same POS interface, write the necessary code for the program to recommend movies for the customer based upon the actors and genres of their past rentals

Summary

In this chapter, we have covered how to retrieve different sets of data using MySQL for Python. We have seen:

- Situations in which record-by-record retrieval is desirable
- How to use iteration to retrieve sets of records in smaller blocks
- How to create iterators and generators in Python
- When to use `fetchone()` and when to use `fetchmany()`

In the next chapter, we will look at how to handle multiple MySQL inserts.

6
Inserting Multiple Entries

When we deal with large amounts of data that are all going into the same database, running single instances of individual INSERT commands can take a ridiculous amount of time and waste a considerable amount of I/O. What we need is a way to insert multiple items in one go.

In this chapter, we will look at the following:

- How iteration can help us execute several individual INSERT statements rapidly
- Using executemany() to submit several INSERT statements in one go
- When not to use executemany()
- Throttling how much data is inserted at a time

At the end of the chapter, we will put these lessons to use in writing a conversion program that inserts the contents of a **comma-separated value (CSV)** file into MySQL.

The problem

You need to collate and rearrange the contents of several databases into one table whenever a given indicator is achieved (the indicator may be, among other things, a stock price, a value in one of the databases, or the flight pattern of African swallows). The format and length of the tables are predictable. There are 5,000 records in each table so manually running a separate INSERT statement for each record is not a viable option even with the programs used in earlier chapters. The problem calls for a means of iterating through a series and changing the INSERT statement automatically. Using what we have covered in previous chapters, we could pursue one of the following two ways to do this:

- Write a MySQL script to insert the data in batch mode
- Iterate over the data to form and execute a MySQL INSERT statement accordingly

None of these are a very good solution to the present problem.

Why not a MySQL script?

As we have seen when we created the `world` and `Sakila` databases, a MySQL script can contain the schema of a database, the values of the database tables, or both. To create data quickly, there is nothing better. However, following are the several drawbacks to using a script in this scenario:

- Lack of automation
- Debugging the process
- Inefficient I/O

Lack of automation

Barring the use of an automation daemon (for example, cron) to run a cron job or a similar scheduled task, a DBA or their designate would have to run the script. This unnecessarily consumes time. It is comparable to swapping tape backups when automated backup services are available and proven.

 Most modern computing systems support automatic task scheduling. On Unix-based systems like Linux and Mac OS X, one can schedule processes to be run at set times and on a regular rotation. One of the most widely used programs for such scheduling is **cron**. A single scheduled task in cron has thus come to be known as a **cron job**.

Debugging the process

Creating a MySQL script can be a very tedious task, and the slightest error or oversight can ruin the entire process. Using the `--force` flag causes MySQL to ignore errors in the source file. It is therefore not something that should be used regularly if one values the integrity of data. If the script is malformed for any reason, a two minute data insertion job can quickly become a two hour (at least!), unscheduled debugging process.

Inefficient I/O

Dumping large amounts of data on MySQL can create latency across the network. If the script were run by a DBA or similar, that person should rightly evaluate the state of the network before running it. Regardless of experience and training, judgment calls naturally require estimation and can result in ambiguous decision-making. While this is unavoidable, it should be minimized where possible.

If the server is experiencing high traffic, the DBA would need to find something else to do and reschedule the running of the script. This randomly postpones the time of execution and the availability of the results. Also, it runs the risk of the DBA forgetting to execute the script.

If the script is automated with a cron job or similar, we risk dumping a lot of data onto MySQL at a time when others are doing more time sensitive tasks. On most servers, we can background the process, so it does not adversely impact the client processes. This, however, only ensures that the process will be run. It does not guarantee that the process will be finished by a particular time.

Why not iterate?

Every time a program iterates to read or insert data, it creates a certain amount of I/O processing. Depending on how a program is written will determine how much I/O is included in each loop.

A test sample: Generating primes

To illustrate this, consider a program that accepts a series of numbers, generates the prime numbers that are equal to or less than each of those numbers and inserts those numbers into a database called `primes` with a table of the same name. The table has the following description:

```
mysql> describe primes;
```

Field	Type	Null	Key	Default	Extra
ID	int(11)	NO	PRI	NULL	auto_increment
NUMBER	int(11)	NO		0	
PRIMES	varchar(300)	NO		0	

and can be created with the following statement:

```
CREATE TABLE `primes` (`ID` int(11) NOT NULL auto_increment, `NUMBER`
int(11) NOT NULL default '0', `PRIMES` varchar(300) NOT NULL default
'0', PRIMARY KEY (`ID`))  ENGINE=MyISAM DEFAULT CHARSET=latin1;
```

Using the `sys` module to handle user input, the `string` module to split the series of entries, and `MySQLdb` to handle the database connection, we get the following preamble:

```
#!/usr/bin/env python
import MySQLdb, string, sys
```

Next, we need a function that will generate the prime numbers to a certain limit called n.

```
def primes(n):
    """Returns a list of prime numbers up to n using an algorithm
based on
the Sieve of Eratosthenes."""
    if n < 2: return ['A number less than two is not prime by
definition.']
    else:
        s = range(3,n+1,2)
        maxfactor = n ** 0.5
        half = (n+1)/2-1
        i = 0
        m = 3
        while m <= maxfactor:
            if s[i]:
                j = (m*m-3)/2
                s[j] = 0
                while j < half:
                    s[j] = 0
                    j += m
            i = i + 1
            m = 2 * i + 3
        return str([2] + [x for x in s if x])
```

This algorithm is based on the **Sieve of Eratosthenes**, one of the simplest ways of generating prime numbers. It uses the following steps:

1. Generate a list of integers from 2 to n.
2. Discount the multiples of each number that remains and that has a square less than or equal to n; this leaves all the prime factors of n.
3. Stop when the square of the number in the series is greater than n.

Prime numbers by definition have no other factor, but themselves and one. The lowest prime number is therefore 2. For this reason, we check whether n is less than 2 and return a message accordingly.

For this program, we want a string returned so we convert the results before we return them.

For more on the Sieve of Eratosthenes and how it works, see the entry on Wikipedia:

`http://en.wikipedia.org/wiki/Sieve_of_Eratosthenes`

The previous algorithm can be found in many forms and in many languages on the Internet. Two of the best that informed this discussion are as follows:

`http://www.maths.abdn.ac.uk/~igc/tch/mx3015/notes/node79.html`

`http://code.activestate.com/recipes/366178/`

Next, we create a function to form and execute the INSERT statement.

```
def insert(n, p, cur):
    statement = """INSERT INTO primes(number, primes) VALUES("%s",
"%s")""" % (n\
, p)
    cur.execute(statement)
    return statement
```

This function takes the number, the primes, and the cursor object handle as arguments.

Finally, our `main()` function looks like this:

```
def main():
    numbers = sys.argv[1]
    iterations = numbers.split(',')
    for n in iterations:
        mydb = MySQLdb.connect(host = 'localhost',
                               user = 'skipper',
                               passwd = 'secret',
                               db = 'primes')
        cur = mydb.cursor()

        n = int(n)
        try:
            p =  primes(n)
            if p.isalpha():
                raise ValueError
            else:
                statement = insert(n, p, cur)
                print "Data entered with the following statement:\n",
statement
        except:
            raise
```

We split the values passed by the user and iterate through them with a `for` loop. Note that we include the database connection and cursor object creation as part of the iteration.

We then include the usual `if` clause to call `main()`:

```
if __name__ == '__main__':
    main()
```

Comparing execution speeds

We can test the speed of this program by giving it a series of simple primes to generate—even of the same number. Here we call it with a series of sevens to process and with the Unix command `time` to measure its speed.

```
time ./primes.py "7, 7, 7, 7, 7, 7, 7, 7, 7, 7, 7, 7, 7, 7, 7, 7, 7,
7, 7, 7, 7, 7, 7, 7"
```

Given this series of sevens, we get a real execution time of 0.175 seconds for the previously discussed implementation.

If we rearrange the program by moving the `mydb` and `cur` assignment lines to follow immediately after the preamble (remembering to adjust the indentation), we get an execution speed of 0.138 seconds. This difference in speed (0.037 seconds) is not particularly significant on a local system with a single user, but it would be magnified synergistically on a server with hundreds or thousands of users.

So, we see that, if the connection and cursor is created each time, the program will be less efficient than if the loop contained only the execution of the statement and the connection and cursor were persistent in the cycle of the program. However, even just passing a series of single statements to MySQL through `Cursor.execute()` will consume more in protocol than necessary. Excessive iteration consumes resources needlessly.

Introducing the executemany() method

As seen in previous chapters, `MySQLdb` provides multiple ways to retrieve data such as: `fetchall()`, `fetchmany()`, and `fetchone()`. These allow us to use different strategies for processing data according to how many records we have to process and the environment in which we are working. `MySQLdb` also provides more than one way to insert information.

Up to now, we have used `Cursor.execute()` whenever we needed to insert data. As shown previously, however, executing single statements in iteration greatly increases the processing requirements of the program. For this reason, MySQL for Python provides another method for `Cursor` objects—`executemany()`.

To be sure, `executemany()` is effectively the same as simple iteration. However, it is typically faster. It provides an optimized means of affecting `INSERT` and `REPLACE` across multiple rows.

executemany(): Basic syntax

The `executemany()` call has the following basic syntax:

```
<cursor object handle>.executemany(<statement>, <arguments>)
```

Note that neither the `statement` to be processed nor its `arguments` is optional. Both are required; otherwise, a `TypeError` will be thrown by Python.

The data type of each argument to `executemany()` should be noted as:

- `statement`: A string containing the query to execute
- `arguments`: A sequence containing parameters to use within the statement

Using any other type for `statements` or `arguments` will result in Python throwing an error.

The `statement` may be constructed using Python's string manipulation methods. The sequence reflected in the `arguments` must be either of a sequence or mapping type. Thus, the following data types are allowed as arguments:

- strings
- lists
- tuples
- dictionaries

If a comma-delimited list is inadvertently passed as a string, it will be evaluated as a string and will not be separated. Consequently, if one is passing values for multiple columns, one needs to use one of the other three types listed. As seen in the following project, one can construct a string of one's values and then convert them into a tuple for processing.

executemany(): Multiple INSERT statements

In *Chapter 2*, *Simple Querying* we inserted records individually using `execute()`.
Using that same method with iteration would look like this:

```python
#!/usr/bin/env python

import MySQLdb, string, sys

mydb = MySQLdb.connect(host = 'localhost',
                       user = 'skipper',
                       passwd = 'secret',
                       db = 'fish')
cursor = mydb.cursor()

data = [
        ("bass", 6.75),
        ("catfish", 5),
      ("haddock", 6.50),
      ("salmon", 9.50)
        ]

for item in data:
    cursor.execute(
        """INSERT INTO menu(name, price) VALUES("%s", %s)"""
        %(item[0], item[1]))

print "Finished!"
```

This would take care of inserting four records with a single run of the program.
But it needs to pass the statements individually through Python to do so. Using
`executemany()`, we could easily have inserted the same data with a single call:

```python
#!/usr/bin/env python

import MySQLdb, string, sys

mydb = MySQLdb.connect(host = 'localhost',
                       user = 'skipper',
                       passwd = 'secret',
                       db = 'fish')
cursor = mydb.cursor()
```

```
cursor.executemany(
        """INSERT INTO menu(name, price) VALUES (%s, %s)""",
        [
        ("bass", 6.75),
        ("catfish", 5),
        ("haddock", 6.50),
        ("salmon", 9.50)
        ] )


    print "Finished!"
```

You may notice previously that we used strings and integers in the first iterative example, but immediately a list of tuples in the second one. The executemany() function is more tolerant of mixed data types than the execute() method. As a consequence, we can get away with less precise type handling in the second where we had to explicitly handle the separate parts of item in the first. The executemany() method can handle multiple data types in one call where execute() does not.

 Just as with Cursor.execute(), executemany() supports MySQL's UPDATE statements, as well.

In either event, the results are the same:

```
mysql> select * from menu;
+----+---------+-------+
| ID | NAME    | PRICE |
+----+---------+-------+
|  1 | bass    |  6.75 |
|  2 | catfish |  5.00 |
|  3 | haddock |  6.50 |
|  4 | salmon  |  9.50 |
+----+---------+-------+
```

But the more efficient way is to use executemany().

executemany(): multiple SELECT statements

The executemany() method may be used not only to insert or update data, but may also be used to run multiple queries. As with the INSERT statement, the value here is in having an optimized iteration that affects the same basic query. If the statements that need to be processed are disparate in structure, then one needs to default to Cursor.execute().

To process several SELECT queries in succession, simply format the argument to executemany() accordingly. Consider the following code snippet that uses the Sakila database that we used in the last chapter:

```
mydb = MySQLdb.connect('localhost', 'skipper', 'secret', 'sakila')
cur = mydb.cursor()
results = cur.executemany("SELECT title FROM film WHERE rating = %s",
('R', 'NC-17'))
```

If we then print the value of results, we get an output of **405**. Like execute(), Cursor.executemany() does not return the actual results of the query in a Python program. It returns the number of affected records as a value that can be assigned to a variable. Even though the search is executed and the results returned from MySQL, MySQL for Python does not assume you want the affected records automatically. The results are returned in aggregate. That is, the output of **405** is the sum of all affected records. The value in this knows the total number of records to be returned before one processes them. Given the restricted context, executemany() tends to be used more frequently for INSERT statements than for SELECT.

It is worth noting that this example is a bit artificial. You wouldn't normally rely on the number of affected rows returned through MySQLdb. Rather, we would use MySQL's built-in COUNT() function. For more on this, see *Chapter 10, Aggregate Clauses and Functions*.

executemany(): Behind the scenes

As seen previously, it is not necessary to have an intimate knowledge of the entire process behind executemany() in order to use it. But to truly know what you are doing with it, you must follow the Python motto for learning:

Use the source, Luke!

In that vein, let's take a look at the underlying code of `executemany()`. The definition line indicates that `executemany()` requires the SQL query to be processed as well as the arguments for that statement.

```
def executemany(self, query, args):
```

As noted under *executemany(): Basic syntax* section, previously, both the statement and the arguments are mandatory. `executemany()` expects you to feed it a template for query and the values to be inserted for `args`.

```
del self.messages[:]
db = self._get_db()
if not args: return
```

We will skip the **docstring** as you can access it through `help(cursor.executemany)` in a Python shell. The method starts by deleting the contents of the messages attribute.

More on the `del` statement can be found at:
`http://docs.python.org/reference/simple_stmts.html#the-del-statement`

It then checks whether the `cursor` is still open by assigning to db the connection of the object. As mentioned previously, `args` must be declared. Here, if there are no arguments passed to the method, the method returns effectively empty-handed.

```
charset = db.character_set_name()
if isinstance(query, unicode): query = query.encode(charset)
```

Note that all queries must be strings and must be encoded for the character set used by the connection.

`MySQLdb` here checks for the character set of the database and encodes the query accordingly. `isinstance` is a built-in type checker and is here used to verify that query **is** `unicode`.

```
m = insert_values.search(query)
if not m:
    r = 0
    for a in args:
        r = r + self.execute(query, a)
    return r
```

The value of `insert_values` is defined on line 9 of the module as a regular expression:

```
insert_values = re.compile(r"\svalues\s*(\(((?<!\\)'.*?)\).*(?<!\\)?'|.)+?\))", re.IGNORECASE)
```

So, `MySQLdb` checks whether any values are available in `query`. If there are none, it calls `execute()` for every argument that is passed to it, adding the number of affected lines to the number of would-be hits and returns the total. Otherwise, it goes on.

```
p = m.start(1)
e = m.end(1)
qv = m.group(1)
```

`m` is a pattern object and therefore provides for regular expression methods. Here `p` is the index for the start of the elements matched. `e` is the end index and typically represents the length of the match. `qv` is the entire group of results, if such exist.

Next, MySQL for Python appends to the value of `qv`, the values passed by MySQL.

```
try:
    q = [ qv % db.literal(a) for a in args ]
```

`qv` is a string, so the percentage sign here serves as a string format operator to insert into the value of `qv` whatever is returned by the `db.literal()` method.

The `literal()` method of the `Connections` class simply nuances the arguments accordingly. If only one argument is passed to `executemany()`, `Connections.literal()` returns it as a single object. If more than one argument is passed, then they are converted into a sequence.

```
except TypeError, msg:
    if msg.args[0] in ("not enough arguments for format
string",
                        "not all arguments converted"):
        self.messages.append((ProgrammingError, msg.args[0]))
        self.errorhandler(self, ProgrammingError, msg.args[0])
    else:
        self.messages.append((TypeError, msg))
        self.errorhandler(self, TypeError, msg)
except:
    from sys import exc_info
    exc, value, tb = exc_info()
    del tb
    self.errorhandler(self, exc, value)
```

Then several types of errors are handled accordingly. Finally, `executemany()` prepares the number of affected records.

```
    r = self._query('\n'.join([query[:p], ',\n'.join(q),
query[e:]]))
    if not self._defer_warnings: self._warning_check()
    return r
```

After checking for any warnings, it then returns a long integer of the number of rows affected.

MySQL server has gone away

Using `executemany()` can give a speed boost to your program. However, it has its limits. If you are inserting a large amount of data, you will need to throttle back how much you process in each call or be faced with an error message similar to this one:

MySQL server has gone away.

You will get this if you are lucky. Before this, you are likely to get another message:

Lost Connection to MySQL server during query.

Both of these messages indicate that the MySQL server is overwhelmed with your data. This is because MySQL's maximum default packet size is 1 MB and the maximum data that the server will receive per packet is 1 MB.

If you encounter these error messages, you have two choices: Decrease the amount of data you are passing to MySQL in each packet or increase MySQL's tolerance for data. If you have system administrator access, the latter option can be affected by changing the `max_allowed_packet` parameter either in the command-line arguments with which the server is started or in a MySQL configuration file.

Command-line option configuration

To change the value of `max_allowed_packet` on the command-line, adapt the following example:

```
$> mysqld --max_allowed_packet=16M
```

This will change the value to 16 megabytes until the MySQL server is halted and restarted without the flagged value.

> It is important to note that the 16 megabytes are not held in reserve. MySQL does not use more memory than is necessary for any transaction. The present value only serves to cap how much memory MySQL may try to use.

If you want to make it permanent and do not want to change the configuration file for some reason, you will need to change the initialization script of your system. On Unix variants (Unix, Linux, and Mac OS X), this will be in the directory `/etc/init.d`. On Windows systems, this file could be located in different places depending on the configuration of the system, but the Windows System directory is common.

Using a configuration file

Adapting MySQL's configuration file is the simplest way to affect a permanent change in the value of max_allowed_packet. The location of the configuration file depends on your platform:

Unix/Linux: /etc/my.cnf

Windows: C:\WINDOWS\my.cnf or C:\my.cnf or C:\my.ini

Also, Windows installations may use the my.cnf or my.ini files in the installation directory of MySQL.

After locating the configuration file for your system, copy it to an archive. For example, on a Linux system, one would use the following:

```
#\etc> cp my.cnf my.cnf.original
```

The exact naming conventions available for the new filename will depend on your platform. Once that is done, you are ready to open the configuration file in your favorite text editor.

With the file opened and having system permission to write to it, locate the mysqld section in the file:

```
[mysqld]
```

One of the first values, if not the first value, in this section should be max_allowed_packet. If it is there, change the value appropriately and if it's not, amend the beginning of the mysqld section to look like this:

```
[mysqld]
max_allowed_packet=16M
```

After saving the file with the affected changes, restart the MySQL server.

More than 16 MB is often unnecessary

It is worth noting that in the preceding examples for the command-line configuration and configuration file options, we changed the value to 16 megabytes. More than this is typically unnecessary without making further configuration changes to the MySQL client.

The default packet size limit of the MySQL client is 16 megabytes. That is therefore the largest packet that the MySQL client will send by default. If you try to pass a larger packet through the client, an error message of **Packet too large** will be passed. Therefore, if you want to handle particularly large files (for example, binary files), you need to change the value of max_packet_size for both the server and the client.

Project: Converting a CSV file to a MySQL table

The CSV file is a very common way to share tabular information across several platforms and programs. Every mature spreadsheet application supports the format. Therefore, various sectors of enterprise rely on it daily.

As the name implies, CSV files contain comma-separated values. These values are often enclosed in quotation marks. This tends to make CSV a predictable format for data and makes for easy development.

But for all its uses, the CSV format is very slow for searching and for collating data. Relational databases (RDBMS) are much more efficient. Therefore, it is useful to be able to import data from a CSV file into MySQL. Unfortunately, MySQL does not do this natively and not without considerable trouble.

 For examples of what some MySQL users do to import CSV file content into MySQL, see the comments on the **mysqlimport** client: `http://dev.mysql.com/doc/refman/5.4/en/mysqlimport.html`

Further, if one tries to use **mysqlimport** for files larger than 1 MB in size, one encounters errors.

Consequently, we need a program to import CSV files with the following functionality:

- The file is comma-separated (that is, not tab, space, or semi-colon)
- The file is written using the Excel dialect of CSV
- The user will indicate at runtime the filename as well as the database, table and column headings for the INSERT command
- The program will evaluate the file's size on disk and adapt its insertion strategy to fit within MySQL's defaults

The preamble

Aside from the obvious requirement of MySQLdb, we will need two other modules to be imported into the program immediately. To parse user options, we will again use optparse. Then, to evaluate the file's size, we will use the os module.

The preamble therefore looks like this:

```
#!/usr/bin/env python

import MySQLdb
import optparse
import os
```

The options

The user options are then processed with the following code:

```
# Get options
opt = optparse.OptionParser()
opt.add_option("-d", "--database", action="store", type="string",
help="name of the local database", dest="database")
opt.add_option("-t", "--table", action="store", type="string",
help="table in the indicated database", dest="table")
opt.add_option("-f", "--file", action="store", type="string",
help="file to be processed", dest="file")
opt.add_option("-F", "--Fields", action="store", type="string",
help="Fields of file to be processed", dest="Fields")
opt, args = opt.parse_args()
```

As in previous chapters, we will pass the attributes of opt to simpler variable names.

```
database = opt.database
table = opt.table
file = opt.file
```

We should not assume that the user will know to pass the field headings without extra spaces nor can we rely on the user to avoid that mistake. Therefore, we need to strip the extraneous spaces out of the field headings as they are passed to the list fields. As MySQL will not allow spaces in columnar headings without the use of backticks, we should surround the field names with backticks by default.

```
fields = opt.Fields.split(',')
for i in xrange(0, len(fields)):
    fields[i] = "`" + fields[i].strip() + "`"
```

We now have stored all of the user input.

Defining the connection

To create the connection object and the cursor necessary for data insertion, we again use a function. As mentioned in previous projects concerning this function, one needs to be careful about the user being used in the connection.

```
def connection(database):
    """Creates a database connection and returns the cursor.  Host is
hardwired to 'localhost'."""
    try:
        mydb = MySQLdb.connect(host = 'localhost',
                               user = 'skipper',
                               passwd = 'secret',
                               db = database)
        cur = mydb.cursor()
        return cur
    except MySQLdb.Error:
        print "There was a problem in connecting to the database.
Please ensure that the database exists on the local host system."
        raise MySQLdb.Error
    except MySQLdb.Warning:
        pass
```

Of course, if the previous project programs are on the same system as this one, you can simply import the other program and call this function from there.

Creating convert

The second function that we need for this program will take care of the actual file conversion.

```
def convert(file):
    """Processes contents of file and returns a reader object, an
iterative object that returns a dictionary for each record."""

    import csv
    filehandle = open(file)
    sheet = csv.DictReader(filehandle, fields)
    return sheet
```

We will pass the function a filename `file`. It returns to us an iterative object `sheet`. The object is an iterator that returns a dictionary for each record in turn.

There is an alternative way of processing this file for conversion. Here we use `csv.DictReader()`, which returns a dictionary when its `next()` method is called. But we could use `csv.reader()`, which returns a string instead. The latter requires only the filename where the former requires both the file handle and the fields to be declared.

The basic syntax for each call is as follows:

```
csv.DictReader():
<variable> = csv.DictReader(<filehandle>, <field names>)
csv.reader():
<variable> = csv.reader(<filehandle>)
```

The main() function

Having defined functions for the database `connection` and for the file conversion, we next need to call them and then process the data they return. In addition to the two functions already mentioned, we need to get the file's size on disk using `os.path.getsize()`.

```
def main():
    """The main function creates the MySQL statement in accordance
    with the user's input and using the connection(), convert(), and
    os.path.getsize()."""

    cursor = connection(database)
    data = convert(file)
    filesize = os.path.getsize(file)
```

Next, we create two variables. The first, `values`, is to hold the data to be inserted into the MySQL statement. The second, `r`, is a counter that is incremented every time we process a line.

```
    values = []
    r = 0
```

We then need to walk through the data by record using a `for` loop.

```
    for a in data:
        if r == 0:
            columns = ','.join(fields)
```

Within the `for` loop, we use the value of `r` to gauge our location in the file. If `r` is 0, we are at the first record, the column headers. Here we have opted to use the user's field names. However, you could easily adapt this to use the table's field names.

If r is not 0, we have a record with actual data and need to process it.

```
else:
    value = ""
    for column_no in xrange(0, len(fields)):
        if column_no == 0:
            value = "'" + a[fields[column_no]]
        else:
            value = value + "', '" + a[fields[column_no]]
    value = value + "'"
```

Here we use the length of fields to determine how long the nested for loop will run. For each iteration, we use the ordinal value of the column to walk through the names of the fields as submitted by the user. We then use those values as the key by which the dictionary values of a are accessed. These are then appended to the value of value. If the field is the first one, column_no is 0 and the field contents are added without a comma being included. At the end, value needs a quote to be added.

If r is greater than 0, we are processing actual data, not column headings. The way we process the data depends on the size of the file. If the file is over 1 Mb in size, we do not want to use executemany() and risk getting an error. Instead, for this project we will process each line with a single INSERT statement.

```
if r > 0:
    if filesize <= 1000000:
        value = eval(value)
        values.append(value)
    else:
        query = """INSERT INTO %s (%s) VALUES""" %(table,
columns)
        statement = query + "(" + value +")"
        cursor.execute(statement)
```

While a few different definitions of 1 Mb abound, we here use the definition for 1 Mb on disk, which also happens to be the most conservative definition.

The actual size of 1 megabyte depends on context. Here we use the International System of Units definition which is also used by most manufacturers of hard drives and flash drives. For computer RAM, 1 Mb is 1048576 bytes (2^{20} or 1024^2). More on the size of a megabyte may be found at http://en.wikipedia.org/wiki/Megabyte#Definition

If filesize is under 1 Mb, we process `value` as a string and convert it into a tuple using Python's built-in `eval()` function. We then append the tuple as a single item of the list `values`.

It is worth noting that `eval()` comes with several security drawbacks in the real world. Frequently, it is best not to use it because Python evaluates the value in the context in about the same terms as if you entered it into the Python shell. Therefore, if you used it, you would need to protect against someone passing commands to the operating system through your Python program.

The following is an example of bad data that could be passed to `eval` that would destroy a Linux system: `"""import_('os').system('rm -rf /')"""`. This would result in a recursive deletion of the entire file tree. For the purposes of this program, we need to convert the strings to tuples. The `eval()` function is used here for the sake of simplicity.

If `filesize` is greater than 1 Mb, we form a simple INSERT statement from the data. We then use a common `Cursor.execute()` statement to process it.

```
r += 1
```

Finally, the last part of the `for` loop is to increment the counter `r` by 1. Without this, the evaluations in the rest of the loop will not give us the results we want.

Next, if the file size is less than 1 Mb, we need to form the INSERT statement template for `executemany()` and, with the data values, pass it to `executemany()` for execution. When we are done, we should give the user feedback about how many records have been affected.

```
if filesize <= 1000000:
    query = "INSERT INTO " + table + "(" + columns + ") VALUES(%s"
    for i in xrange(0, len(fields)-1):
        query = query + ", %s"
    query = query + ")"
    query = str(query)
    affected = cursor.executemany(query, values)
    print affected, "rows affected."

else:
    print r, "rows affected."
```

eResEdoE

Within the `if` loop, we create a string query that contains the basic template of the `INSERT` statement. We append to this value a string formatting `%s` for every field beyond the first one that the data includes. Finally, we finish the formation of `query` with a closing parenthesis.

At this point, `values` is a list of tuples and `query` is a string. We then pass the two to `cursor.executemany()` and capture the returned value in `affected`.

Regardless of file size, the user should always get a statement of the number of rows affected. So, we close the `if` loop with a statement to that affect. As `r` is the number of times that the simple `INSERT` statement would have been executed in the last `if` loop of the preceding `for` loop, we can use it to indicate the rows affected as part of the `else` clause.

This last statement is more reflective of the number of iterations we have had of the `for` loop than of the number of times that `cursor.execute()` has been successfully called. If one wanted to be more precise, one could instead introduce a counter to which the value returned by `cursor.execute()` is added on each successful iteration.

Calling main()

Finally, we need to call `main()`. Once again, we use the usual `if` loop:

```
if __name__ == '__main__':
    main()
```

Room to grow

The project is now finished and can take a basic CSV file and insert it into MySQL. As you use it, you will, without any doubt, see ways in which it could be better tailored to your needs. Some of these that are left as an exercise are:

- Handling tab-delimited files and files that don't speak the Excel dialect of CSV (for example, files that don't put cell contents in quotation marks)
- Dynamically evaluating the data format of the file and adjusting its processing accordingly
- Processing Excel (`*.xls`) binary files (for this use the `xlrd` module from `http://pypi.python.org/pypi/xlrd`)
- Creating a table in the given database with columns that fit the data in the CSV file (for help with this, see *Chapter 7, Creating and Dropping*)

Summary

In this chapter, we have covered how to retrieve different sets of data using MySQL for Python. We have seen:

- How to use iteration to execute several individual INSERT statements rapidly
- Cursor.executemany() is optimized for such iteration
- When one should avoid using executemany()
- Why certain errors will arise when using executemany()
- How to throttle the amount of data we INSERT and why

In the next chapter, we will look at creating and dropping tables from within Python.

7
Creating and Dropping

The secret to all effective programming lies in abstracting problems so we can leverage the power of the computer to our benefit. The more we can abstract a problem and still get the same results, the more we leverage the power of the computer, and the less work the end user has to do. Abstraction provides opportunity for automation.

In addition to allowing dynamic insertion and retrieval of information, MySQL for Python allows us to automate database and table creation and removal. In this chapter, we will see:

- How to create and delete both databases and tables in MySQL
- How to manage database instances with MySQL for Python
- Ways to automate database and table creation

At the end of the chapter, we will put these dynamics together into a web application that will allow us to perform this kind of administration on MySQL remotely.

Creating databases

Creating a database in MySQL is as simple as declaring the name of the database that you want to create. The syntax reads:

```
CREATE DATABASE <database name>;
```

An example of this is:

```
CREATE DATABASE csv;
```

As with all SQL statements, blank space is the token by which the command is divided. We first need to tell MySQL that we want to create something by using that keyword. Then we need to tell it what we want to create, a database. Finally, we give it the name of the database followed by the requisite semi-colon (when in MySQL itself).

> Note that, in order to create databases in MySQL, the account you use must have the CREATE privilege on the database.
>
> CREATE statements are also sensitive to user privileges. If a user is only granted CREATE privileges on a single database (for example, csv.*), then that user cannot create databases, but can create tables on that specific database.

Unlike some commands in MySQL, database creation is case-sensitive. So the following CREATE statements each create a different database:

```
CREATE DATABASE csv;
CREATE DATABASE Csv;
CREATE DATABASE CSV;
CREATE DATABASE C_S_V;;
```

> Whether the CREATE DATABASE statement is case-sensitive ultimately depends on the filesystem and configuration of your server. Unix-based systems are usually case-sensitive by default. However, Windows and Mac servers may not be.
>
> While Mac OS X is derived from Unix, it uses the HFS+ filesystem. So database names are not case-sensitive by default. To add the case sensitivity feature for Mac OS X, one would need to use the UFS filesystem.
>
> To configure MySQL for case-sensitivity when it is not the default, you need to set the variable lower_case_table_names. More information on that variable can be found at:
>
> http://dev.mysql.com/doc/refman/5.5/en/server-system-variables.html#sysvar_lower_case_table_names

Test first, create second

If a database already exists and you try to create one by the same name, an error will be thrown.

```
mysql> CREATE DATABASE csv;
ERROR 1007 (HY000): Can't create database 'csv'; database exists
```

To avoid this error and any ensuing fallout, we can use the IF NOT EXISTS condition in our CREATE statement. This clause immediately precedes the name of the database to be created.

```
mysql> CREATE DATABASE IF NOT EXISTS csv;
Query OK, 0 rows affected, 1 warning (0.00 sec))
```

Note that the output you get may differ slightly from version to version. MySQL 5.1.42, for example, gives this output:

```
mysql> CREATE DATABASE IF NOT EXISTS csv;
Query OK, 1 row affected, 1 warning (0.00 sec)
```

It depends on the version and configuration of your database server.

CREATE specifications

While the preceding example illustrates the most basic database creation statement, one can also add further specifications for the database immediately after declaring the name of the database. MySQL supports two ways to further define the database:

- By character set
- By collation used

Specifying the default character set

A character set is a set of symbols and encodings used to represent and store the information held in a database. If we wanted to declare the csv database to use 8-bit Unicode by default, we would define it as follows:

```
CREATE DATABASE csv CHARSET=utf8;
```

Or better:

```
CREATE DATABASE csv CHARACTER SET = utf8;
```

If we then use that database and ask for its status, we will see how that setting takes hold:

```
mysql> use csv;
Database changed
mysql> status;;
--------------
mysql  Ver 14.12 Distrib 5.0.51a, for debian-linux-gnu (i486) using
readline 5.2
```

```
Connection id:          10
Current database:       tgv
Current user:           skipper@localhost
SSL:                    Not in use
Current pager:          stdout
Using outfile:          ' '
Using delimiter:        ;
Server version:         5.0.51a-3ubuntu5.4 (Ubuntu)
Protocol version:       10
Connection:             Localhost via UNIX socket
Server characterset:    latin1
Db      characterset:   utf8
Client characterset:    latin1
Conn.   characterset:   latin1
UNIX socket:            /var/run/mysqld/mysqld.sock
Uptime:                 4 hours 36 min 47 sec

Threads: 2  Questions: 112  Slow queries: 0  Opens: 49  Flush tables: 1
Open tables: 43  Queries per second avg: 0.007
--------------
```

Specifying the collation for a database

The second specification that can be made in a database creation statement is **collation**. Where a character set is a set of symbols and encodings. A collation is a system of rules that MySQL uses to work with the database for purposes of comparison and matching.

Declaring collation

To express the collation rules for the csv database defined previously as Unicode, we would use the following definition statement:

```
CREATE DATABASE csv CHARSET=utf8 COLLATE=utf8_general_ci;
```

Or you can use:

```
CREATE DATABASE csv CHARACTER SET = utf8 COLLATE = utf8_general_ci;
```

Note that the latter CREATE statement is technically more correct. Either one works, however, and both may be seen in real-life.

In this statement, however, the collation definition is not necessary as every character set has its own set of collations available to it. For the Unicode character set, the default collation is Unicode. What this statement does do, however, is overtly define the Unicode collation to be used.

Finding available character sets and collations

To see the character sets and default collations available on your system, use the following from a MySQL shell:

```
mysql> show character set;
```

Charset	Description	Default collation	Maxlen
big5	Big5 Traditional Chinese	big5_chinese_ci	2
dec8	DEC West European	dec8_swedish_ci	1
cp850	DOS West European	cp850_general_ci	1
hp8	HP West European	hp8_english_ci	1
koi8r	KOI8-R Relcom Russian	koi8r_general_ci	1
latin1	cp1252 West European	latin1_swedish_ci	1

Not all collations can be used with every character set. Rather every character set has a group of collations with which it works. If one tries to use a collation that is not available for a given character set, MySQL will raise an error like this one:

```
mysql> CREATE DATABASE csv CHARSET=utf8 COLLATE=latin2_bin;
ERROR 1253 (42000): COLLATION 'latin2_bin' is not valid
for CHARACTER SET 'utf8'
```

Removing or deleting databases

To remove or delete a database in MySQL, we use a DROP statement. This statement is functionally the opposite of the basic CREATE statement used previously:

```
DROP DATABASE <database name>;
```

So, for csv, a DROP statement would look like this:

```
DROP DATABASE csv;
```

Note that the DROP statement not only deletes the structure of the database setup by CREATE but also irrevocably drops all of the database data, as well.

Avoiding errors

As with the CREATE statement, MySQL's DROP statement also supports a test for existence. If the database you wish to drop does not exist, MySQL will throw an error. Therefore, it is good practice to use the IF EXISTS conditional as follows:

```
DROP DATABASE IF EXISTS <database name>;
```

For a database called foo, this statement would read:

```
DROP DATABASE IF EXISTS foo;
```

Preventing (illegal) access after a DROP

By dropping a database, one simply removes it from the list of available databases that MySQL knows about.

 Using DROP does not remove user privileges to that database.

Therefore, if one drops the database csv to scrub all of its data and then creates another database of the same name, the same users who had access to the original database will have the same access to the new one. This will occur regardless of whether the table definitions are different between the two databases.

 For a detailed discussion of the REVOKE statement, see:
http://dev.mysql.com/doc/refman/5.5/en/revoke.html

To avoid this, you must revoke user privileges on the database in question. The basic syntax for REVOKE is:

```
REVOKE <privileges> ON <database.table> FROM <user>;
```

To revoke privileges, the user account that you use must have GRANT privileges as well as any access that you are trying to revoke. With those privileges, one must then state both the user and table from which you want privileges revoked.

So to revoke all access for user skipper to table filenames from the database csv, we would use this statement:

```
REVOKE ALL ON csv.filenames FROM 'skipper' @' localhost';
```

Note that this does not remove the user and does not impact on the user's access to other tables within the same database.

The easiest way to drop one database and create another is obviously to give the second a slightly different name than the first and configure network calls appropriately. However, this is not a commendable practice as it can lead to confusion in myriad ways. As we will see later in this chapter, however, Python and MySQLdb can be used to keep database connections in order.

Creating tables

In its basic structure, the MySQL statement for creating tables is very similar to that for databases. Recall that database creation is involved in simply naming the database:

```
CREATE DATABASE foo;;
```

Creating a table requires the definition of at least one column. The basic syntax looks like this (note that the backticks are optional):

```
CREATE TABLE <table name> (`<column name>` <column specifications>);
```

In practice, definition of a table bar in database foo would be as follows:

```
CREATE TABLE bar (snafu varchar(30));
```

While this is basically the statement, it is also a very flawed way of defining the table when using the MySQLdb module. Before we go into what is wrong, however, let's cover what is right.

> A comprehensive discussion of the options available when creating a table can be found in the MySQL manual: http://dev.mysql.com/doc/refman/5.4/en/create-table.html

Obviously, we declare a table named bar. MySQL requires at least one column to be defined. A column definition at its most basic is the name of the column, the type of data it will hold, and how long it will be. Here, snafu is defined as varchar (that is, variable length of characters) and of 30 characters in length. If we go over that limit on an INSERT statement, the data will almost always be truncated to 30 characters. Consider the following:

```
mysql> INSERT INTO bar(snafu) VALUES('pi');
Query OK, 1 row affected (0.08 sec)


mysql> INSERT INTO bar(snafu) VALUES('supercalifragilisticexpialidocious
');
Query OK, 1 row affected, 1 warning (0.00 sec)
```

```
mysql> SELECT * FROM bar;
+-------------------------------+
| snafu                         |
+-------------------------------+
| pi                            |
| supercalifragilisticexpialidoc |
+-------------------------------+
2 rows in set (0.00 sec)
```

Covering our bases

Among the significant issues in this statement, however, is the fact that no default is mentioned. We could therefore add blank values. Further, as there is no primary key, we can add redundant values *ad nauseam*.

```
mysql> INSERT INTO bar(snafu) VALUES('pi');
Query OK, 1 row affected (0.00 sec)

mysql> INSERT INTO bar(snafu) VALUES('');
Query OK, 1 row affected (0.00 sec)

mysql> SELECT * FROM bar;
+-------------------------------+
| snafu                         |
+-------------------------------+
| pi                            |
| supercalifragilisticexpialidoc |
| pi                            |
|                               |
+-------------------------------+
4 rows in set (0.00 sec)
```

To mitigate against these problems, we should refine our table definition. To define a column value as mandatory, we use NOT NULL in the table definition:

```
CREATE TABLE bar (snafu varchar(30) NOT NULL);
```

This only ensures that the column has a value and, by default, forces the user to input that value. If we want to ensure that the column has a value even if the user does not define it, we need to set a default:

```
CREATE TABLE bar (snafu varchar(30) NOT NULL DEFAULT '');
```

Avoiding errors

Note, however, that we have no conditionality built into this statement. If the table already exists, we will get an error. To be sure that we do not have this problem, we can use the IF NOT EXISTS clause again:

```
CREATE TABLE IF NOT EXISTS bar (snafu varchar(30) NOT NULL DEFAULT
'');
```

Creating temporary tables

Finally, if we only need the table for some temporary work and want to scrap it after we are done, we can use the TEMPORARY keyword in our definition. This creates the database for as long as the current connection is maintained.

```
mysql> CREATE TEMPORARY TABLE IF NOT EXISTS bar (`snafu` varchar(30) NOT
NULL default '');
```

Note that temporary tables are only visible to the user session that created it. So there can be no confusion on the part of other sessions on the same server. This is helpful for creating temporary datasets for debugging.

 It is worth noting that the dropping of temporary tables is logged differently when the session ends rather than when they are overtly dropped. Therefore, the best practice is to drop every temporary table you create when you are done using it, even at the end of a session.

When the database is created, MySQL will report that nothing has been affected. Since it is a temporary table, it does not show up in the list of tables. However, a query against it will return results:

```
mysql> CREATE TEMPORARY TABLE foo (`snafu` varchar(30) NOT NULL default
'');
Query OK, 0 rows affected (0.00 sec)

mysql> INSERT INTO foo(snafu) VALUES('cucumber');
Query OK, 1 row affected (0.00 sec)
```

```
mysql> show tables;
+---------------+
| Tables_in_csv |
+---------------+
| foo           |
+---------------+
1 row in set (0.00 sec)

mysql> select * from foo;
+----------+
| snafu    |
+----------+
| cucumber |
+----------+
1 row in set (0.00 sec)
```

Dropping tables

Dropping tables in MySQL follows the same pattern as dropping databases.

```
DROP TABLE <table name>;
```

We use the keyword DROP so MySQL knows what we want to do. We then indicate that we want to drop a table and follow that with the name of the table to be deleted.

 When the DROP command is executed, the table and its definition are deleted unrecoverably from the database. You should therefore exercise caution when using it.

It is worth noting that the user who passes the DROP statement to MySQL must have the DROP privilege. Otherwise, MySQL will not execute the statement.

Playing it safe

If you create a temporary table and want to ensure that only that table is dropped, use the TEMPORARY keyword:

```
DROP TEMPORARY TABLE <table name>;
```

So to drop the `araba` table defined previously, we would issue this command:

```
DROP TEMPORARY TABLE araba;
```

Of course, if we issue that command twice, MySQL will get confused. More on this is mentioned in the following section *Avoiding errors*.

Avoiding errors

As with deleting databases, we should ask MySQL to ensure that the table exists before trying to remove it. Otherwise, we can receive an error. To avoid this we use the `IF EXISTS` conditional again:

```
DROP TABLE IF EXISTS <table name>;
```

So for the table `bar` created with this `CREATE` statement (from previous command):

```
CREATE TABLE IF NOT EXISTS bar (snafu varchar(30) NOT NULL DEFAULT
'');
```

The corresponding `DROP` command would be:

```
DROP TABLE IF EXISTS bar;
```

For the temporary table, we would change the `DROP` command accordingly:

```
DROP TEMPORARY TABLE IF EXISTS foo;
```

Removing user privileges

As with dropping databases (from previous secion), dropping a table does not remove access to that table from a user's profile. Therefore, dropping it and subsequently creating another table of the same name will automatically allow the users of the first table to access the second. This will be done with the same privileges, as well. To avoid this, use the `REVOKE` command as outlined under *Preventing (illegal) access after a DROP*.

Doing it in Python

As you might expect, affecting the creation and deletion of databases and tables in Python is very similar to MySQL when using MySQL for Python. There are some differences as we shall see in this section.

For the following examples, we will work with the following code being assumed:

```
import MySQLdb
mydb = MySQLdb.connect('localhost', 'skipper', 'secret', 'csv')
cur = mydb.cursor()
```

Creating databases with MySQLdb

Where `Cursor.execute()` shows the number of affected rows in previous commands, whether `INSERT` or `SELECT`, it always returns a `0` value for the `CREATE` command of a database:

```
>>> cur.execute("""CREATE DATABASE foo""")

0L
```

Testing the output

Consequently, passing the output of the method to a variable will result in that variable equating to 0:

```
>>> res = cur.execute("CREATE DATABASE foo")
>>> print res
0
```

The only time that this does not occur is if an error is thrown (that is, if you do not include the conditional `IF NOT EXISTS`).

This is helpful when working with code that you did not write. By testing the returned value, you can have greater control over what happens in your program. This testing can be negative as follows:

```
>>> if res != 0: <do something>
```

Or can be positive:

```
>>> if res == 0: <do something>>
```

Naturally, if the statement does not execute as expected, you will want to catch the exception as shown in *Chapter 4, Exception Handling.*

Dynamically configuring the CREATE statement

The CREATE statement can be dynamically constructed in Python. To do this, we use a string formatting convention:

```
cur.execute("CREATE DATABASE IF NOT EXISTS %s" %('foo'))
```

Dropping databases with MySQLdb

Similarly to creating a database, dropping a database returns a 0 value.

```
>>> res = cur.execute("DROP DATABASE IF EXISTS foo")")
>>> print res

0
```

By leaving off the IF EXISTS clause, we can create a feedback mechanism:

```
try:
    res = cur.execute("DROP DATABASE foo")
except:
    print "Drop operation failed."
```

If the DROP is executed, program execution continues without comment. If the table has already been dropped, we get output:

Drop operation failed.

and the program then continues to execute.

Creating tables in Python

As discussed earlier in this chapter, the MySQL syntax for creating a table is similar to creating a database. The example of table bar from above reads:

```
CREATE TABLE IF NOT EXISTS bar (snafu varchar(30) NOT NULL DEFAULT
'');
```

To put this into Python, we pass the statement as an argument to Cursor.execute():

```
cursor.execute("""CREATE TABLE IF NOT EXISTS bar (snafu varchar(30)
NOT NULL DEFAULT '')""")
```

Once again, however, we are able to use Python's string formatting facilities to create dynamic statements:

```
cursor.execute("""CREATE TABLE IF NOT EXISTS %s (%s varchar(30) NOT
NULL DEFAULT '')""" %('bar', 'snafu'))
```

As before this statement creates a table bar with a column snafu.

Verifying the creation of a table

Depending on the nature of your program, it is frequently good practice to validate the creation of a table. To do so, we need to retrieve a listing of the tables in the database.

```
cursor.execute("""SHOW TABLES""")
tables = cursor.fetchall()
```

The result here is to always get the tables. Of course, there is no need for the second line if the table creation statement has failed and no tables are available. Therefore, the better way to affect this is:

```
table_no = cursor.execute("""SHOW TABLES""")
if table_no != 0:
    tables = cursor.fetchall()
```

Cursor.fetchall() returns a tuple of the tables available. To confirm the existence of the table in the database, we need to search through the list of tables.

```
created_table = 'bar'
for item in tables:
    if item[0].count(created_table) != 0:
        print item[0]
```

This will print the table name if it matches the value of created_table, bar.

All of this presumes a knowledge of the total number of tables in the database prior to your creating the last one. To ascertain whether a table has been created without counting tables, you can ask MySQL for the creation statement of the table:

```
try:
    cursor.execute("""SHOW CREATE TABLE %s""" %('bar'))
except:
    print "The table has not yet been created."
    raise
else:
    print "The table has been created."
```

The SHOW CREATE statement is addressed in more detail in *Chapter 13, Showing MySQL metadata*.

Another way to verify table creation

As with creating a database, creating a table returns a 0 value if successful. Therefore, we can again test for that. If we use the IF NOT EXISTS conditional, the statement will always return 0. Therefore, we need to leave this off in order to use this method.

 Note that many MySQL installations will issue a warning if you use IF NOT EXISTS when attempting to create a table that already exists. However, it is not good practice to rely on these warnings.

Consider the following:

```
>>> cursor.execute("""CREATE TABLE %s (%s varchar(30) NOT NULL DEFAULT
'')""" %('barge', 'snafu'))
0L
>>> cursor.execute("""CREATE TABLE IF NOT EXISTS %s (%s varchar(30) NOT
NULL DEFAULT '')""" %('barge', 'snafu'))
0L
>>> cursor.execute("""CREATE TABLE %s (%s varchar(30) NOT NULL DEFAULT
'')""" %('barge', 'snafu'))
Traceback (most recent call last):
  File "<stdin>", line 1, in <module>
  File "/var/lib/python-support/python2.5/MySQLdb/cursors.py", line 166,
in execute
    self.errorhandler(self, exc, value)
  File "/var/lib/python-support/python2.5/MySQLdb/connections.py", line
35, in defaulterrorhandler
    raise errorclass, errorvalue
_mysql_exceptions.OperationalError: (1050, "Table 'barge' already
exists")")
```

So we want to try to create the table and test the results:

```
>>> try: attempt = cursor.execute("""CREATE TABLE %s (%s varchar(30) NOT
NULL DEFAULT '')""" %('barge', 'snafu'))
... except: print "Houston, we have a problem"
...
Houston, we have a problem
```

Dropping tables with MySQLdb

Dropping a table through `MySQLdb` is very straightforward.

```
cursor.execute("DROP TABLE %s" %('barge'))
```

Of course, for the sake of feedback, it is worth sandwiching this in a `try...except` structure. As with the `DROP TABLE` statement in MySQL, you can usually just pass this statement with an `IF EXISTS` conditional and be done with it:

```
execution = cursor.execute("DROP TABLE IF EXISTS %s" %('barge'))
```

Note that, as before, the conditional element causes MySQL to always return a 0 value for successful execution. So a test for the value of execution will always test true for 0. If you want an exception if the table does not exist, use the other `DROP` statement in a `try...except` statement.

Project: Web-based administration of MySQL

The project for this chapter will set the groundwork for the next several projects. We will write a program for administering MySQL remotely through a web interface. To be sure, more sophisticated applications like PHPMyAdmin exist. The value of creating one of your own is that you can extend it and change it in the future depending on your needs. Just creating the application is a good exercise as it leaves you with code that you can import into other applications at will and gives you a better understanding of the processes involved.

By the end of this project, we want a web application that will have the following aspects:

- Ability to create MySQL statements for the following commands: CREATE, DROP, INSERT, UPDATE, and SELECT
- Execute the created statement
- Output the results of any queries and confirm the successful execution of other commands
- Be written in a modular structure that allows different functions or methods to be used independently of the others
- Use CGI to call the Python program

It is worth noting that this implementation is fairly rudimentary due to the exigencies of book media. Nevertheless, when we are done, you will have the basis for a full web application that you can develop into administrative facilities for your web-oriented MySQL database.

CGI vs PHP: What is the difference?

CGI stands for **Common Gateway Interface**. As such, it is not a language like PHP but a protocol. This means that it can be implemented in just about any programming language, and implementations of it exist in C and C++. CGI scripts are often written in Perl but may be written in other languages.

PHP stands for **Pre-Hypertext Processor** and is a language developed specifically to output HTML with speed. As such, it is optimized for web scripting and is known as one of the lightest technologies on the Web. Where heavier technologies become sluggish and can lose connectivity in the face of latency, PHP tends to be more robust.

The following sections address some of the strengths and weaknesses of each option. For this project, we will be using CGI to pass arguments to our Python program. However, with the proper coding, one could also use PHP.

> Depending on a variety of factors from language of implementation to the configuration of the web server on which it runs, CGI is reported to be either considerably slower or even faster than PHP. The performance benefits of each implementation strategy are heavily dependent on other environmental variables. Given the ubiquity of shared hosting and the fact that web developers typically do not have control over system variables in such circumstances, it is helpful to be conversant with both.
>
> CGI and PHP usually come as standard with a shared hosting solution. You can nevertheless find information on each consecutively at:
>
> `http://docs.python.org/library/cgi.html`
>
> `http://www.php.net/manual/en/install.php`

Note that this discussion does not address the matter of *persistence*. No matter which way we implement our web application, the only way that we can preserve an object between web pages is to pickle it. Pickling means converting the Python object to a byte stream for writing to a space on the server's hard disk. It also introduces a layer of complexity that we are leaving out of this project. However, if you would like to look into it further, you can find information on Python's `pickle` module at `http://docs.python.org/library/pickle.html`.

Not every Python object can be pickled. For help on determining whether something can be pickled, see *What can be pickled and unpickled?* in the following Python documentation module:

`http://docs.python.org/library/pickle.html#what-can-be-pickled-and-unpickled`.

Pickling preserves an object as a byte stream. Alternatively, we could save the session data into a database.

Basic CGI

The form dialogue of HTML requires us to include the program to which the data should be passed. For a Python program `myprogram.py`, a form line would look like this:

```
<form action="myprogram.py" method="POST">
```

Whether you use POST or GET depends on your development needs.

> More information on HTML's `form` tag and its attributes can be found at:
> `http://www.w3schools.com/TAGS/tag_form.asp`
> The difference between GET and POST is detailed in RFC 2616:
> `http://www.w3.org/Protocols/rfc2616/rfc2616-sec9.html`

Passing values to a Python program through CGI is affected by importing two modules and instantiating an object. The modules used are `cgi` and `cgitb`. The role of the `cgi` module is self-evident; importing `cgitb` gives us helpful error messages if we need to debug the program.

```
import cgi
import cgitb
```

The `cgi` module provides a class `FieldStorage` that provides a method `getvalue()` for accessing CGI input.

```
import cgi, cgitb
form = cgi.FieldStorage()
name = form.getvalue('firstname')
address = form.getvalue('surname')
phone = form.getvalue('phoneno')
```

After receiving and processing the input from CGI, the output of one's program is sent to the web client through the server. If the output is in plain text, no formatting is included. Therefore, one must be certain to include HTML formatting with it.

More detailed discussions on using CGI in Python can be found at:

`http://docs.python.org/library/cgi.html`

`http://python.about.com/od/cgiformswithpython/ss/pycgitut1.htm`

HTML tutorials abound on the Internet, but one of the best venues for learning HTML and other web-related technologies is **W3Schools**.

`http://www.w3schools.com`

Simple HTML output would look like this:

```
print """
<!DOCTYPE HTML PUBLIC "-//W3C//DTD HTML 4.01 Transitional//EN">
<html>
  <head>
    <title>Successful Input</title>
  </head>
  <body>
    <center>Information received successfully.</center>
  </body>
</html> """
```

One of the main downsides of using CGI is the problem of data persistence. Without using magic URLs, passing data from one page to another becomes a challenge.

A magic URL is a **Uniform Resource Locator (URL)** that includes unique identifying information, so the server-side program can associate it with saved data. One of the most common magic URLs is the session ID used by many news sites to track reader habits. Magic URLs are one of the most frequent security issues for web applications as web servers are not designed to tell two users apart if they use the same identifier. When one user purposely appears as another user, she/he is said to spoof that user.

The alternative would be to pass information through flags. But CGI does not support a secure way to do this. Any values that one would want to persist from one page to another would have to be embedded in the code, which is viewable and can therefore be spoofed by any user who knows that information.

Using PHP as a substitute for CGI

Depending on the configuration of the server and system variables, PHP may be a faster way to pass input to a Python program. To do this, we use the PHP command: `shell_exec()`:

```php
<?php
$somevar = $_POST["somevar"];
$escapees = array("&", ";", "\")
$replacements = array("<ampersand>", "<semicolon>", "<backslash>")
$safevar = str replace($escapees, $replacements, $somevar)
$results = shell_exec ("./myprogram.py " . $somevar) ;
print $results;
?>
```

This calls a Python program `myprogram.py` with the arguments contained in `somevar` and assigns the output to `$results`. Before handing the value of `somevar` to `myprogram.py`, we process out any known characters that could be used to break out of the execution environment. Ampersands are used to background processes on Unix-based machines. Semi-colons are used to pass multiple commands on the same line. Backslashes are used to escape out of a formatted environment. You can (and should) add to them according to the execution environment you use before using this code for any projects beyond the scope of this book. Having replaced some of the unsavory characters, we can then print `$results` or print the HTML formatting with the output intermingled appropriately.

If the previous PHP script were called `myprogram.php`, the calling form line would be:

```
<form action="myprogram.php" method="POST">
```

Aside from the aforementioned benefits of processing speed, using PHP has the benefit of introducing heterogeneity into the system. Many security issues arise because computing systems use the same technologies in the same way throughout an organization. This makes the system easy to manage, but it also makes it predictable. Using CGI, the program to be called is always shown in the HTML source code. One therefore tips one's hand and shows that the system processing the data is in Python. By using PHP to hand the data off to Python, one introduces a hidden layer of complexity that makes cracking the system more difficult.

Finally, as shown in the previous example, PHP allows us to pass command-line arguments discretely to our program. The `form` data, which the user already has, is passed overtly. But any special settings can be reserved in the PHP script and passed as an argument to the Python program at runtime.

It should be noted that the use of PHP over CGI does not impact on the HTML FORM syntax at all except to change the name of the file. PHP serves as an intermediate layer between the web page and the processing of data.

CGI versus PHP: When to use which?

CGI has been used for many years and therefore is well proven. PHP offers a cleaner and more flexible implementation than CGI for passing data between a web page and a Python program. However, depending on the implementation, it can easily result in security issues. Setting aside personal familiarity as a criterion, which you use (CGI or PHP) will largely be determined by the environment in which you are deploying.

As already mentioned, the cgitb module provides for web-based error messages. These are very helpful in the case of shared hosting, when one frequently does not have shell access. Unless one is relying on system variables, however, using PHP is still cleaner in this regard as it does not require a web server to work.

Where CGI requires a web server for testing, PHP can be run from the command-line. Therefore, one can create a local copy of one's remote directory structure and not have to run a local server. It is best practice to have such a copy for administering a website, anyway. One can then test the PHP-Python system in that context before posting it. For help on using PHP from the command line, see http://php.net/manual/en/features.commandline.php.

 A simple tutorial on using PHP in lieu of CGI can be found at: http://python.about.com/od/cgiformswithpython/ss/phpjscgi.htm

Some general considerations for this program

As already noted in this chapter, we are not going to persist data or objects on the server between pages. Therefore, we do not need a class like the MySQLStatement class that we used in *Chapter 4*. Instead, we will use functions for all MySQL operations. The only class will be for our HTML output.

Program flow

For our purposes, the program starts as soon as a user accesses the first page and enters their login information. We attempt to create a connection with the user's login credentials. If they fail, program execution breaks.

If successful, we process the user's choice of actions. If the user does not give us all the data we need for a chosen action, they receive an error message and program execution terminates.

The following six template variants correspond to the types of statements that we will program:

- CREATE DATABASE <database name>
- DROP DATABASE <database name>
- CREATE TABLE<table name>
- DROP TABLE <table name>
- SELECT * FROM table WHERE <column> = <value>
- INSERT INTO table (columns) VALUES (values)

These have all been covered in previous chapters. If anything looks unfamiliar, be sure to revisit the relevant chapter before going on.

The basic menu

For this program, we will use two web pages at first. The second page will be automatically generated by the program, but the first will be static.

The first page is a basic dialogue that asks the user to select the action that they want. We want to give the user the choice of creating, dropping, querying, or inserting data into a database.

```html
<!DOCTYPE html PUBLIC "-//W3C//DTD XHTML 1.0 Frameset//EN" "http://
www.w3.org/TR/xhtml1/DTD/xhtml1-frameset.dtd">
<html xmlns="http://www.w3.org/1999/xhtml"
      xml:lang="en"
      lang="en"
      dir="ltr">
  <head>
    <title>PyMyAdmin 0.001</title>
    <meta http-equiv="Content-Type" content="text/html;
                                      charset=utf-8">
  </head>
  <body>
    <h1>PyMyAdmin Menu</h1>
    <form name="input" action="./pymyadmin.py" method="post">
      <div>AUTHENTICATION</div>
Login: <input type="text" name="user" value=""><br>
Password: <input type="password" name="password" value="">
<br><br>
      <div>DATABASES</div>
<input type="radio" name="dbact" value="create"> CREATE<br>
```

```
<input type="radio" name="dbact" value="drop"> DROP<br>
Database name: <input type="text" name="dbname" value="">
<br><br>

        <div>TABLES</div>
<input type="radio" name="tbact" value="create"> CREATE<br>
<input type="radio" name="tbact" value="drop"> DROP<br>
Database name: <input type="text" name="tbdbname" value=""><br>
Table name: <input type="text" name="tbname" value="">
<br><br>
        <div>QUERIES</div>
<input type="radio" name="qact" value="select"> SELECT<br>
<input type="radio" name="qact" value="insert"> INSERT<br>
Database name: <input type="text" name="qdbname" value=""><br>
Table name: <input type="text" name="qtbname" value=""><br>
Columns (comma-separated): <input type="text" name="columns"
value=""><br>
Values (comma-separated): <input type="text" name="values"
value=""><br>

<input type="submit" value="Submit">
    </form>
  </body>
</html>
```

When put into a browser, the page should look like this:

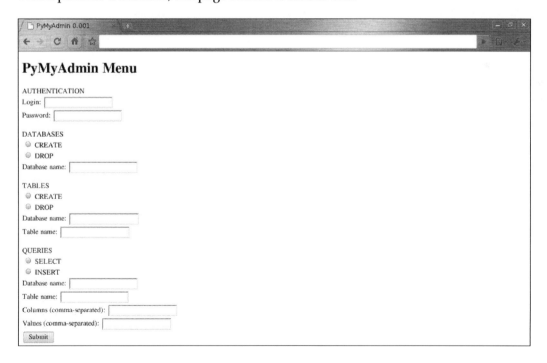

Obviously, the web design aspect of the page has been left as an exercise.

Authorization details

As you can see from this dialogue, we first ask for the authorization details. Note that the `password` dialogue is of input type password, to ensure it is hidden on entry. In the program, this data will be first used to verify the authenticity of the user's credentials before any MySQL statement is formed.

Three operational sections of the dialogue

In the subsequent three sections of the dialogue, we offer the user facilities to affect databases, tables, and insertion or retrieval. Depending on which radio button the user chooses, we will expect different parts of the form to be completed.

The variables

The web page will send us several variables, only some of which we will need for any given operation. In the order that they appear on the previous page, these are:

1. user
2. password
3. dbact
4. dbname
5. tbact
6. tbdbname
7. tbname
8. qact
9. qdbname
10. qtbname
11. columns
12. values

The first two are of obvious import. The next two, dbact and dbname, are used to create or drop a database. dbact is designed to indicate either CREATE or DROP as no other values are allowed. The value of dbname can be anything.

For table creation and dropping, we use the next three variables along with columns and values. To affect anything related to tables, we need tbact, whether to CREATE or DROP, and tbdbname, the database to be used, and tbname, the name of the table itself. Additionally, for creating a table, we need the columns and types, here indicated by columns and values.

Finally, for INSERT and SELECT statements, we use qact, qdbname, qtbname, and the last two variables. As you can guess from their names, qact is to indicate either INSERT or SELECT. qdbname is the name of the database to be used, and qtbname is the name of the table, into or out of which to process data.

Planning the functions

Some of the functions we will use will be used for multiple purposes. So we will not have createdb() and dropdb(). Rather, we will use the variable prefixes as a key to the function names. We will call dbaction() and pass the type of action as an argument. Similarly, we will use tbaction() for table administration and qaction() for queries.

We will naturally need to connect to the database. However, we will sometimes need to connect without declaring a database. So we will have connection functions that handle both.

Finally, we will need to execute the statement and return the appropriate values. This role will be performed by execute().

Code of each function

The following subsections show the code for each function. Having planned them out gives us a bird's eye view of the entire process.

Connecting without a database

The database argument on MySQLdb.connect() is optional. Therefore, we can create a connection with it in order to validate user credentials and to administer databases without knowing anything about which ones are available.

```
def connectNoDB(user, password):
    """Creates a database connection and returns the cursor.  Host is
hardwired to 'localhost'."""
    try:
        host = 'localhost'
        mydb = MySQLdb.connect(host, user, password)
        cur = mydb.cursor()
        return cur
```

```
    except MySQLdb.Error:
        print "There was a problem in connecting to the database.
Please ensure that the database exists on the local host system."
        raise MySQLdb.Error
    except MySQLdb.Warning:
        pass
```

Note that this function is hard-wired to work with the `localhost`. Without much work at all, one could make all the values of this function to be dynamic.

Connecting with a database

Obviously, we need to declare a database to do anything with a table. We could technically get by without declaring a database at first, but that would require a locution of code to declare the database eventually. It is best to do it upfront. For this, we will pull in the `connection()` function from previous projects.

```
def connection(user, password, database):
    """Creates a database connection and returns the cursor.  Host is
hardwired to 'localhost'."""
    try:
        host = 'localhost'
        mydb = MySQLdb.connect(host, user, password, database)
        cur = mydb.cursor()
        return cur
    except MySQLdb.Error:
        print "There was a problem in connecting to the database.
Please ensure that the database exists on the local host system."
        raise MySQLdb.Error
    except MySQLdb.Warning:
        pass
```

Database action

Forming the database-related statements is done by `dbaction()`.

```
def dbaction(act, name, cursor):
    if act == "create":
        statement = "CREATE DATABASE IF NOT EXISTS %s" %(name)
        output = execute(statement, cursor, 'create-db')
    elif act == "drop":
        statement = "DROP DATABASE IF EXISTS %s" %(name)
        output = execute(statement, cursor, 'drop-db')
    else:
        output = "Bad information."
    return output
```

No matter what happens, dbaction() gives us output. Using the conditional clause in both the CREATE and DROP statements, we should never have a problem with execution. Nevertheless, we include an else clause to ensure that we are covered.

Table action

The function affecting tables is more complicated than the preceding database function. This is because we need to handle column names and values as well as the basic information used for databases. The function looks like this:

```
def tbaction(act, db, name, columns, types, user, password):
    cursor = connection(user, password, db)

    if act == "create":
        tname = name + "("
        columns = columns.split(',')
        types = types.split(',')
        for i in xrange(0, len(columns)):
            col = columns[i].strip()
            val = types[i].strip()
            tname = tname + col + " " + val
            if i == len(columns)-1:
                tname = tname + ")"
            else:
                tname = tname + ", "
        statement = "CREATE TABLE IF NOT EXISTS %s" % (tname)
        results = execute(statement, cursor, 'create-tb')
    elif act == "drop":
        statement = "DROP TABLE IF EXISTS %s" % (name)
        results = execute(statement, cursor, 'drop-tb')
    return results
```

As requested in the initial web page, we expect columns and types to come in a comma-delimited format. Consequently, we need to split each and join them up so they make sense to MySQL. This is done by the for loop in the middle of the function.

Query action

For queries, we assume that the user will provide us with the following information:

- Type of action
- Database name
- Table name
- Columns involved
- Values used
- Username
- Password

The function then looks like this:

```
def qaction(qact, db, tb, columns, values, user, password):
    cursor = connection(user, password, db)

    tname = tb + "("
    columns = columns.split(',')
    values = values.split(',')
    cols = ""
    vals = ""
    for i in xrange(0, len(columns)):
        col = columns[i].strip()
        val = values[i].strip()
        cols = cols + col
        vals = vals + "'" + val + "'"
        if i != len(columns)-1:
            cols = cols + ", "
            vals = vals + ", "
    if qact == "select":
        statement = "SELECT * FROM %s WHERE %s = %s" %(tb, cols, vals)
        results = execute(statement, cursor, 'select')
    elif qact == "insert":
        statement = "INSERT INTO %s (%s) VALUES (%s)" %(tb, cols,
vals)
        results = execute(statement, cursor, 'insert')
    return results
```

Once again, we need to break apart columns and values in order to use them appropriately for MySQL.

execute()

Finally, we need a function to execute the MySQL statements that are formed by either `dbaction`, `tbaction`, or `qaction`. The `execute()` function, as you may note in the preceding code listings, takes the statement to be executed, the cursor to be used, and the type of statement to be processed. The last is essential in allowing `execute()` to handle the data returned by MySQL appropriately.

The function is as follows:

```
def execute(statement, cursor, type):
    """Attempts execution of the statement resulting from
MySQLStatement.form()."""
    while True:
        try:
            cursor.execute(statement)
            if type == "select":
                # Run query
                output = cursor.fetchall()
                results = ""
                data = ""
                for record in output:
                    for entry in record:
                        data = data + '\t' + str(entry)
                    data = data + "\n"
                    results = results + data + "\n"
            elif type == "insert":
                results = "Your information was inserted with the
following SQL statement: %s;" %(statement)
            elif type == "create-db":
                results = "The following statement has been processed
to ensure the database exists: %s;" %(statement)
            elif type == "create-tb":
                results = "The following statement has been processed
to ensure the table exists: %s;" %(statement)
            elif type == "drop-db":
                results = "The following statement has been processed
to ensure the removal of the database: %s;" %(statement)
            elif type == "drop-tb":
                results = "The following statement has been processed
to ensure the removal of the table: %s;" %(statement)
            return results

        except MySQLdb.Error, e:
            print "Some of the information you have passed is not
valid.  Please check it before trying to use this program again."
            print "The exact error information reads as follows: %s"
%(e)
```

```
        raise

    except MySQLdb.Warning:
        pass

    except Warning:
        pass
```

For purposes of feedback, the `execute()` function always returns the statement processed. If the statement is a query, it returns the results in a basic form.

As noted in previous chapters, the error-handling used here is generic for reasons of space. In real-life deployment, it should be more robust.

The HTML output

In addition to processing data, we need to return some feedback to the user. In order to prettify the page, we should enclose the output in some HTML formatting.

For this purpose, we will use a class `HTMLPage`. This will ensure that we can standardize the HTML output of the program, only changing what is necessary and not having to include the header and footer code more than once.

`HTMLPage` has a single attribute, `message`, which holds the output passed from `execute()`. Otherwise, it has four methods beyond `__init__()`:

- `header()`: Returns a standard HTML header with a generic page title
- `body()`: Compiles a HTML body that includes the value of `HTMLPage` message
- `footer()`: Returns a standard HTML closing code
- `page()`: Coordinates the three methods to form and return the HTML output

Basic definition

The definition of `HTMLPage` begins as follows:

```
class HTMLPage:
    def __init__(self):
        """Creates an instance of a web page object."""
        self.Statement = []
```

Naturally, the class needs a way to reference itself. For our purposes, `HTMLPage` is a regular Python object, so we do not need to declare any inheritance.

The message attribute

`HTMLPage.message` simply receives the value and assigns it to itself.

```
def message(self, message):
    self.message = message
```

Essentially, `message` is a means of holding the output from `execute()` as an attribute of the class object.

Defining header()

The `header()` method, as discussed, simply returns a HTML header. By defining it distinctly, we can readily reuse this code and modify it as needed.

```
def header(self):
    """Prints generic HTML header with title of application."""
    output = """
<!DOCTYPE html PUBLIC "-//W3C//DTD XHTML 1.0 Frameset//EN" "http://
www.w3.org/TR/xhtml1/DTD/xhtml1-frameset.dtd">
<html xmlns="http://www.w3.org/1999/xhtml" xml:lang="en" lang="en"
dir="ltr">
  <head>
    <title>PyMyAdmin 0.001</title>
    <meta http-equiv="Content-Type" content="text/html;
        charset=utf-8" />
  </head>
<body>
"""
    return output
```

As this is straightforward HTML code, we could have made it an attribute. However, by using a method, we are ready to render the code dynamically if needed. For example, we could not change the page title dynamically if `header()` were an attribute. As it is, we can render it dynamically with ease using this function.

Defining footer()

To match `header()`, we use `footer()`:

```
def footer(self):
    """Print generic HTML footer to ensure every page closes
neatly."""
    output = """
</body>
</html>
"""
    return output
```

Normally, this would be an attribute. However, there are circumstances when this should be rendered as a function. Some web-tracking scripts rely on JavaScript with unique identifiers to be issued at the end of a page. To form such pages dynamically, one would need to use a method instead of an attribute.

Defining body()

The `body()` method combines a title with the output of `execute()`.

```
def body(self):
    output = ""
    title = "<h1>PyMyAdmin Results</h1>"
    output = output + title + "<br>" + self.message
    return output
```

Defining page()

Finally, we define a method to coordinate the methods of `HTMLPage` to form a web page for output.

```
def page(self):
    """Creates webpage from output."""
    header = self.header()
    body = self.body()
    footer = self.footer()
    output = header + body + footer
    return output
```

Getting the data

Obviously, none of this data processing counts for anything if we cannot get the data that the user sends to us. Depending on whether you use CGI or PHP to call the Python program will determine how you accept the information.

Using CGI

To receive the information through CGI, we import `cgi` and `cgitb`, as discussed previously. We then assign the variables from the `cgi.FieldStorage()` object we create.

```
#!/usr/bin/python

import MySQLdb
import cgi, cgitb
```

```
form = cgi.FieldStorage()

user = form.getvalue('user')
password = form.getvalue('password')
dbact = form.getvalue('dbact')
dbname = form.getvalue('dbname')

tbact = form.getvalue('tbact')
tbdbname = form.getvalue('tbdbname')
tbname = form.getvalue('tbname')

qact = form.getvalue('qact')
qdbname = form.getvalue('qdbname')
qtbname = form.getvalue('qtbname')
columns = form.getvalue('columns')
values = form.getvalue('values')
```

Note that CGI always requires absolute paths. We cannot therefore use a shebang line of #!/usr/bin/env python.

Using PHP

For PHP, we do not use any of the CGI modules. Instead, because PHP calls the program as from a command-line, we can use the optparse module to weed through the options.

```
#!/usr/bin/env python

import MySQLdb
import optparse

opt = optparse.OptionParser()
opt.add_option("-U", "--user",
               action="store",
               type="string",
               help="user account to use for login",
               dest="user")
opt.add_option("-P", "--password",
               action="store",
               type="string",
               help="password to use for login",
               dest="password")
opt.add_option("-d", "--dbact",
               action="store",
```

```
                       type="string",
                       help="kind of db action to be affected",
                       dest="dbact")
    opt.add_option("-D", "--dbname",
                       action="store",
                       type="string",
                       help="name of db to be affected",
                       dest="dbname")
    opt.add_option("-t", "--tbact",
                       action="store",
                       type="string",
                       help="kind of table action to be affected",
                       dest="tbact")
    opt.add_option("-Q", "--tbdbact",
                       action="store",
                       type="string",
                       help="name of database containing table to be
affected",
                       dest="tbdbname")
    opt.add_option("-N", "--tbname",
                       action="store",
                       type="string",
                       help="name of table to be affected",
                       dest="tbname")
    opt.add_option("-q", "--qact",
                       action-"store",
                       type="string",
                       help="kind of query to affect",
                       dest="qact")
    opt.add_option("-Z", "--qdbname",
                       action="store",
                       type="string",
                       help="database to be used for query",
                       dest="qdbname")
    opt.add_option("-Y", "--qtbname",
                       action="store",
                       type="string",
                       help="table to be used for query",
                       dest="qtbname")
    opt.add_option("-c", "--columns",
                       action="store",
                       type="string",
                       help="columns to be used in query",
                       dest="columns")
```

```
opt.add_option("-v", "--values",
                action="store",
                type="string",
                help="values to be used in query",
                dest="values")
opt, args = opt.parse_args()
```

Defining main()

With the variables input into the program and the functions and class defined, we can then code the `main()` function to orchestrate the program's execution.

```
def main():
    """The main function creates and controls the MySQLStatement
instance in accordance with the user's input."""
    output = ""

    while 1:
        try:
            cursor = connectNoDB(opt.user, opt.password)
            authenticate = 1
        except:
            output = "Bad login information.  Please verify the
username and password that you are using before trying to login
again."
            authenticate = 0

        if authenticate == 1:
            errmsg = "You have not specified the information necessary
for the action you chose.  Please check your information and specify
it correctly in the dialogue."

            if opt.dbact is not None:
                output = dbaction(opt.dbact, opt.dbname, cursor)
            elif opt.tbact is not None:
                output = tbaction(opt.tbact, opt.tbdbname, opt.tbname,
opt.columns, opt.values, opt.user, opt.password)
            elif opt.qact is not None:
                output = qaction(opt.qact, opt.qdbname, opt.qtbname,
opt.columns, opt.values, opt.user, opt.password)
            else:
                output = errmsg

            printout = HTMLPage()
```

```
printout.message(output)
output = printout.page()

print output
break
```

First, we check whether the user's credentials are acceptable to MySQL. If they are not, we simply issue a statement that their login information is bad. Otherwise, we continue. Based upon what kind of action is specified, we call different functions. If no radio button is ticked, the user receives the error message `errmsg`.

After all processing has been done, we form the page. The `HTMLPage` object is `printout`. We set the value of `HTMLPage.message` to whatever output we generated in the `if...elif...else` clause. After the page is formed by `HTMLPage.page()`, we output it and break the `while` loop.

Room to grow

This project forms the basis for further development, some of which will be done in the upcoming chapters. In writing this program and later extending its functionality, be wary of trying to formulate too complicated of statements before you have good processes in place for less complex commands.

Some places where this project could (and should) be developed further before deploying it in real-life scenarios are:

- Implementing UPDATE and DELETE statements in addition to SELECT and INSERT
- Using DESCRIBE to offer the user information about tables
- Implementing fuller exception-handling

Summary

In this chapter, we have covered how to create and remove databases and tables with MySQL for Python. We have seen:

- How to use MySQLdb to create and delete both databases and tables
- How we can manage database instances with MySQL for Python
- Ways to automate database and table creation

In the next chapter, we will look at regulating MySQL user access within Python.

8
Creating Users and Granting Access

There is arguably no part of database programming that requires greater care in implementation than creating users and granting access. While the careless or malicious deletion of data is catastrophic, it can only occur at the hands of a trusted insider (whether a programmer or a database administrator) after a sufficient access control system is properly put into place.

MySQL for Python allows us to automate user creation and to administer access controls. In this chapter, we will see:

- How to create and remove users in MySQL
- Why removing a user is not as easy as DROPping (using DROP) them
- The limits of MySQLdb's ability to GRANT access
- Ways to automate user creation and access control

The project for this chapter will build on the web application that we began in the last chapter.

A word on security

On October 2, 2007, a colocation data centre run by C I Host in Chicago, Illinois (U.S.A) was robbed for the fourth time in two years. Robbers took $15,000 worth of servers.

On December 6, 2007, thieves stole $4 million worth of servers from a Verizon data centre in London, England.

On May 5, 2008, Peter Gabriel's official website went offline. Users of his Real World-Peter Gabriel and WOMAD services lost all access. The reason is that thieves had stolen the servers from a data centre run by a Carphone Warehouse subsidiary named Rednet Ltd.

As mentioned previously, if an adequate access control system is in place, rogue users are **trusted insiders** by definition. However, it is worth noting that such a control system is not merely software. Every avenue of attack—from brute force password cracking to using social engineering on a receptionist, is a vector of attack against a database. By virtue of its involving human users, an adequate access control system must provide adequate security policies and practices for that human component. All the software access controls in the world will not prevent a snookered staffer from disclosing their login information.

An adequate access control system involves security on every level of access—the local host, the LAN/WAN, the wider Internet, and any physical access to any machine located in those areas. If a user from an untrusted area gains physical access to a machine within an area of greater trust, the chance of damage to the database rises. Therefore, software security must always be buttressed by physical security.

At the time of writing this book, we live in a world where bootable CDs are easily obtained, passwords can be read out of RAM, and quantum encryption is available on an IC chip. Therefore, even full-disk encryption serves to slow and not stop thieves from accessing data. At the present point of technology, when physical security is breached, all IT security is increasingly worthless.

Creating users in MySQL

To create a user in MySQL, our user account must have the *universal* CREATE USER privilege. In general, no user beyond the database administrator should have this as it allows the user to create, remove, rename, and revoke the privileges of users on the database. We will look at the granting of privileges later in this chapter.

Alternatively, if a user has universal INSERT privileges, that user can insert a new user and relevant data into the user table of the mysql database. This method is prone to error and can endanger the stability of the entire MySQL installation if something goes wrong. Therefore, we do not deal with it here.

When creating a user, we need to specify both the user's name or ID and the user's password. The basic syntax for user creation is as follows:

```
CREATE USER <userid>;
```

Breaking the statement up by its token, we first tell MySQL that we want to CREATE something. Then we clarify the object being created as a USER account. That account should be named with the given userid. An example of this statement is:

```
CREATE USER exemplar;
```

 Note that if NO_AUTO_CREATE_USER is enabled in your MySQL configuration, this type of user creation will fail. This is particularly true in SQL_MODE.

While this statement will create a user, it is perhaps the least secure way to do so. MySQL offers two ways of securing user accounts at the time of account creation—passwords and host restrictions.

Forcing the use of a password

To force the use of a password, we need to declare one at the time of creating the user. To do this, we append an IDENTIFIED BY clause to the previous user creation syntax.

```
CREATE USER <userid> IDENTIFIED BY '<password>';
```

To use this for our exemplary user, the statement would read as follows:

```
CREATE USER 'exemplar' IDENTIFIED BY 'MoreSecurity';
```

This forces the use of a password to log in. In the first user creation statement, if the user did not offer a password, they would still be allowed access simply by using an existing user ID.

To reset a password for an account that is already created, use a SET PASSWORD statement:

```
SET PASSWORD FOR 'exemplar'@'localhost' = PASSWORD('dogcatcher')
```

Which hostname you use depends on how the account was created. See the next section for more.

Restricting the client's host

In addition to requiring a password, MySQL also provides the ability to restrict the host from which the login may come. This clarification comes immediately after userid.

```
CREATE USER <userid>@'<host name>' IDENTIFIED BY '<password>';
```

If we want the user `exemplar` to login only from the localhost, the machine on which MySQL is running—we would use the following command:

```
CREATE USER 'exemplar'@'localhost' IDENTIFIED BY 'MoreSecurity';
```

If we want the user to log in from `http://www.sample.com/` only, we would change the preceding statement to this:

```
CREATE USER 'exemplar'@'sample.com' IDENTIFIED BY 'MoreSecurity';
```

In doing so, however, we make it impossible for them to log in from `localhost`. To ensure that the user can log in from any host, we need to issue two CREATE statements that can effectively create one user for the local host and one for the remote client.

To quantify the host for all hosts, we use MySQL's pattern matching in lieu of a hostname. In order to allow the user to truly login from any host then, we need to issue the following two commands:

```
CREATE USER 'exemplar'@'localhost' IDENTIFIED BY 'MoreSecurity';
CREATE USER 'exemplar'@'%' IDENTIFIED BY 'MoreSecurity';
```

You will recall that the first user creation statement did not specify the host to be used by the user. If the hostname is not specified in the CREATE statement, MySQL uses `%` by default.

The user's identity on a MySQL database is determined by their user ID and the hostname from which they log in. It is possible for these two items to match more than one row in the MySQL `user` tables. When that happens, MySQL uses the first match it finds.

As MySQL uses its own user tables to validate logins, it is worth asking why we don't simply modify MySQL's own tables instead of issuing CREATE statements. One can do this, and there are instructions for doing so in the MySQL documentation. However, doing so leaves one open to errors and possible data corruption.

If one corrupts the data in the user tables, it is possible to lose the ability to contact the database altogether. This would then require manually restarting MySQL using `mysqld_safe`:

```
mysqld_safe --skip-grant-tables &
```

This method works on Unix-based systems. Windows systems are more complex. For more information, see the MySQL manual: `http://dev.mysql.com/doc/refman/5.5/en/resetting-permissions.html`

Creating users from Python

The ability to create users is obviously an administrative task. By default, this means that one must log in as `root`, or any other user who has administrative rights, to use them. If your Python program does not login as `root`, it will not be able to affect user creation. Therefore, one's connection credentials must read accordingly:

```
import MySQLdb
mydb = MySQLdb.connect(host = 'localhost',
                            user = 'root',
                            passwd = 'rootsecret')
cursor = mydb.cursor()
```

From here, one can similarly form the statement to the other CREATE statements that we have used.

```
statement = """CREATE USER 'exemplar'@'localhost' IDENTIFIED BY
'MoreSecurity'"""
cursor.execute(statement)
```

In a Python shell, passing the statement through `cursor.execute()` will return `0L`. If you execute this code in a Python program file, you will not get such feedback (unless you overtly tell Python to print it). But for debugging purposes, you have two choices: check the MySQL users table or try to use the login.

The latter is simply a matter of creating a second connection. This is best placed in a `try...except` structure:

```
try:
    mydb2 = MySQLdb.connect(host = 'localhost',
                                user = 'exemplar',
                                passwd = 'MoreSecurity')
    cursor2 = mydb2.cursor()
except:
    raise
```

We can check the MySQL users table manually or within a program. To affect a check manually, log into MySQL and select the `mysql` database for use.

```
use mysql;
```

Within `mysql`, read out from the `user` table.

```
SELECT * FROM users;
```

Depending on how many users are registered in the database, this table will probably run off the screen. However, the last entry should be the account just created. Alternatively, use a WHERE clause to quantify what you want.

```
SELECT * FROM users WHERE User = '<userid>';
```

So for the user `exemplar`, we would enter the following statement:

```
SELECT * FROM user WHERE User='exemplar';
```

Within Python, we can issue the last statement as follows:

```
mycheck = MySQLdb.connect(host = 'localhost',
                          user = 'root',
                          passwd = 'rootsecret',
                          db = 'mysql')
checker = mycheck.cursor()
statement = """SELECT * FROM user WHERE User='exemplar'"""
results = checker.execute(statement)
if results == 1:
    print "Success!"
else:
    print "Failure."
```

Using the user ID in the statement saves us from having to match each record against that value.

Removing users in MySQL

As with creating databases and tables, the opposite of creating a user is to DROP. As we shall see, removing a user does not revert any changes that they have made to the database(s) to which they had access. If a user had the ability to create users, removing them will not remove the users they created.

Unlike databases and tables, dropping a user requires that you also specify the hostname of the user's record. Therefore, one cannot always enter:

```
DROP USER exemplar;
```

This will only work if the user was created without specifying the hostname.

If it exists, one must include the hostname. For best practice, the basic syntax is:

```
DROP USER <userid>@<hostname>;
```

Therefore to drop user `exemplar`, we would pass the following statement:

```
DROP USER 'exemplar'@@'localhost';
```

Note that this will not impact that user's ability to log in from another host if that user had permission to connect from the other host.

`DROP`, by design, only removes the user's account and its privileges. It does not in any way affect any database objects that the user created. Therefore, if a user has created false database structures such as databases, tables, and records, then all of that will persist after the user is removed from the system.

One very important aspect of `DROP` that is critical to remember is that `DROP` does not impact on existing user sessions. If a user is logged into the server when the `DROP` statement is issued, the `DROP` statement will not take effect until the user has logged out. The user's subsequent attempts at logging in will then fail.

DROPping users in Python

Dropping a user in Python is as easy as passing the MySQL statement through `Cursor.execute()`. So the syntax is:

```
DROP USER exemplar@localhost;
```

This previous syntax can be changed to:

```
mydb = MySQLdb.connect(host = 'localhost',
                       user = 'root',
                       passwd = 'rootsecret')
cursor = mydb.cursor()
statement = """DROP USER exemplar@localhost"""
cursor.execute(statement)
```

However, any part of the statement can be dynamically created through the use of string formatting conventions.

GRANT access in MySQL

After creating a user account, one still needs to tell MySQL what kind of privileges to assign to it. MySQL supports a wide range of privileges (see the table of privileges on page 9). A user can only grant any privilege that they have themselves.

As with creating a user, granting access can be done by modifying the `mysql` tables directly. However, this method is error-prone and dangerous to the stability of the system and is, therefore, not recommended.

Important dynamics of GRANTing access

Where CREATE USER causes MySQL to add a user account, it does not specify that user's privileges. In order to grant a user privileges, the account of the user granting the privileges must meet two conditions:

- Be able to exercise those privileges in their account
- Have the GRANT OPTION privilege on their account

Therefore, it is not just users who have a particular privilege or only users with the GRANT OPTION privilege who can authorize a particular privilege for a user, but only users who meet both requirements.

Further, privileges that are granted do not take effect until the user's first login after the command is issued. Therefore, if the user is logged into the server at the time you grant access, the changes will not take effect immediately.

The GRANT statement in MySQL

The syntax of a GRANT statement is as follows:

```
GRANT <privileges> ON <database>.<table>
    TO '<userid>'@'<hostname>';
```

Proceeding from the end of the statement, the userid and hostname follow the same pattern as with the CREATE USER statement. Therefore, if a user is created with a hostname specified as localhost and you grant access to that user with a hostname of '%', they will encounter a 1044 error stating access is denied.

The database and table values must be specified individually or collectively. This allows us to customize access to individual tables as necessary. For example, to specify access to the city table of the world database, we would use world.city.

In many instances, however, you are likely to grant the same access to a user for all tables of a database. To do this, we use the universal quantifier ('*'). So to specify all tables in the world database, we would use world.*.

We can apply the asterisk to the database field as well. To specify all databases and all tables, we can use *.*. MySQL also recognizes the shorthand * for this.

Finally, the privileges can be singular or a series of comma-separated values. If, for example, you want a user to only be able to read from a database, you would grant them only the SELECT privilege. For many users and applications, reading and writing is necessary but no ability to modify the database structure is warranted. In such cases, we can grant the user account both SELECT and INSERT privileges with SELECT, INSERT.

To learn which privileges have been granted to the user account you are using, use the statement SHOW GRANTS FOR <user>@hostname>;.

With this in mind, if we wanted to grant a user `tempo` all access to all tables in the `music` database but only when accessing the server locally, we would use this statement:

```
GRANT ALL PRIVILEGES ON music.* TO 'tempo'@'localhost';
```

Similarly, if we wanted to restrict access to reading and writing when logging in remotely, we would change the above statement to read:

```
GRANT SELECT,INSERT ON music.* TO 'tempo'@'%';
```

If we wanted user `conductor` to have complete access to everything when logged in locally, we would use:

```
GRANT ALL PRIVILEGES ON * TO 'conductor'@'localhost';
```

Building on the second example statement, we can further specify the exact privileges we want on the columns of a table by including the column numbers in parentheses after each privilege. Hence, if we want `tempo` to be able to read from columns 3 and 4 but only write to column 4 of the `sheets` table in the `music` database, we would use this command:

```
GRANT SELECT (col3,col4),INSERT (col4) ON music.sheets TO 'tempo'@'%';
```

Note that specifying columnar privileges is only available when specifying a single database table—use of the asterisk as a universal quantifier is not allowed. Further, this syntax is allowed only for three types of privileges: SELECT, INSERT, and UPDATE.

A list of privileges that are available through MySQL is reflected in the following table:

Privilege	Function	Context
ALL	Grants all privileges to user	Databases, tables, or indexes
CREATE	Creates database objects	Databases, tables, or indexes
DROP	Drops database objects	Databases or tables
GRANT OPTION	Grants privileges to other users	Databases, tables, or stored routines
REFERENCES	Supported internally but otherwise unused	Databases or tables

Privilege	Function	Context
ALTER	Allows use of ALTER TABLE	Tables
DELETE	Allows use of DELETE	Tables
INDEX	Enables creation and dropping of indexes	Tables
INSERT	Allows data insertion	Tables
SELECT	Allows reading from a database	Tables
UPDATE	Allows use of UPDATE	Tables
CREATE TEMPORARY TABLES	Allows user to create temporary tables	Tables
LOCK TABLES	Enables the use of LOCK TABLES for tables on which SELECT has been granted	Tables
TRIGGER	Allows the automation of certain events in a table under conditions set by the user	Tables
CREATE VIEW	Enables the creation and deletion of views	Views
SHOW VIEW	Allows the showing of views	Views
ALTER ROUTINE	Allows user to alter and delete stored routines	Stored routines
CREATE ROUTINE	Enables the creation of stored routines	Stored routines
EXECUTE	Allows the execution of stored routines	Stored routines
FILE	Enables file access on localhost	File access
CREATE USER	Enables the creation of users	Server administration
PROCESS	Enables the user to view all processes with SHOW PROCESSLIST	Server administration
RELOAD	Enables use of FLUSH	Server administration
REPLICATION CLIENT	Allows user to query about master and slave servers	Server administration
REPLICATION SLAVE	Allows slave servers to read binary logs from the master server	Server administration
SHOW DATABASES	Allows user to view available databases	Server administration
SHUTDOWN	Enables the use of mysqladmin shutdown	Server administration

Privilege	Function	Context
SUPER	Enables the use of several superuser privileges	Server administration
ALL [PRIVILEGES]	Grants all privileges to the user that are available to the grantor	Server administration
USAGE	Allows access to the user	Server administration

MySQL does not support the standard SQL UNDER **privilege and does not support the use of TRIGGER until MySQL 5.1.6.**

More information on MySQL privileges can be found at
`http://dev.mysql.com/doc/refman/5.5/en/privileges-provided.html`

Using REQUIREments of access

Using GRANT with a REQUIRE clause causes MySQL to use SSL encryption.
The standard used by MySQL for **SSL** is the **X.509** standard of the **International Telecommunication Union's (ITU) Standardization Sector (ITU-T)**. It is a commonly used public-key encryption standard for single sign-on systems. Parts of the standard are no longer in force. You can read about the parts which still apply on the ITU website at `http://www.itu.int/rec/T-REC-X.509/en`

The REQUIRE clause takes the following arguments with their respective meanings and follows the format of their respective examples:

- **NONE**: The user account has no requirement for an SSL connection. This is the default.

  ```
  GRANT SELECT (col3,col4),INSERT (col4) ON music.sheets TO
  'tempo'@'%';
  ```

- **SSL**: The client must use an SSL-encrypted connection to log in. In most MySQL clients, this is satisfied by using the --ssl-ca option at the time of login. Specifying the key or certificate is optional.

  ```
  GRANT SELECT (col3,col4),INSERT (col4) ON music.sheets TO
  'tempo'@'%' REQUIRE SSL;
  ```

- **X509**: The client must use SSL to login. Further, the certificate must be verifiable with one of the CA vendors. This option further requires the client to use the `--ssl-ca` option as well as specifying the key and certificate using `--ssl-key` and `--ssl-cert`, respectively.

```
GRANT SELECT (col3,col4),INSERT (col4) ON music.sheets TO
'tempo'@'%' REQUIRE X509;
```

- **CIPHER**: Specifies the type and order of ciphers to be used.

```
GRANT SELECT (col3,col4),INSERT (col4) ON music.sheets TO
'tempo'@'%' REQUIRE CIPHER 'RSA-EDH-CBC3-DES-SHA';
```

- **ISSUER**: Specifies the issuer from whom the certificate used by the client is to come. The user will not be able to login without a certificate from that issuer.

```
GRANT SELECT (col3,col4),INSERT (col4) ON music.sheets TO
'tempo'@'%' REQUIRE ISSUER 'C=ZA, ST=Western Cape, L=Cape
Town, O=Thawte Consulting cc, OU=Certification Services
Division,CN=Thawte Server CA/emailAddress=server-certs@thawte.
com';
```

- **SUBJECT**: Specifies the subject contained in the certificate that is valid for that user. The use of a certificate containing any other subject is disallowed.

```
GRANT SELECT (col3,col4),INSERT (col4) ON music.sheets
TO 'tempo'@'%' REQUIRE SUBJECT 'C=US, ST=California,
L=Pasadena, O=Indiana Grones, OU=Raiders, CN=www.lostarks.com/
emailAddress=indy@lostarks.com';
```

Using a WITH clause

MySQL's `WITH` clause is helpful in limiting the resources assigned to a user. `WITH` takes the following options:

- `GRANT OPTION`: Allows the user to provide other users of any privilege that they have been granted
- `MAX_QUERIES_PER_HOUR`: Caps the number of queries that the account is allowed to request in one hour
- `MAX_UPDATES_PER_HOUR`: Limits how frequently the user is allowed to issue `UPDATE` statements to the database
- `MAX_CONNECTIONS_PER_HOUR`: Limits the number of logins that a user is allowed to make in one hour
- `MAX_USER_CONNECTIONS`: Caps the number of simultaneous connections that the user can make at one time

It is important to note that the GRANT OPTION argument to WITH has a timeless aspect. It does not statically apply to the privileges that the user has just at the time of issuance, but if left in effect, applies to any options the user has at any point in time. So, if the user is granted the GRANT OPTION for a temporary period, but the option is never removed, then the user grows in responsibilities and privileges, that user can grant those privileges to any other user. Therefore, one must remove the GRANT OPTION when it is not longer appropriate.

 Note also that if a user with access to a particular MySQL database has the ALTER privilege and is then granted the GRANT OPTION privilege, that user can then grant ALTER privileges to a user who has access to the mysql database, thus circumventing the administrative privileges otherwise needed.

The WITH clause follows all other options given in a GRANT statement. So, to grant user tempo the GRANT OPTION, we would use the following statement:

```
GRANT SELECT (col3,col4),INSERT (col4) ON music.sheets TO 'tempo'@'%'
WITH GRANT OPTION;
```

If we want to limit the number of queries that the user can have in one hour to five, as well, we simply add to the argument of the single WITH statement. We do not need to use WITH a second time.

```
GRANT SELECT,INSERT ON music.sheets TO 'tempo'@'%' WITH GRANT OPTION
MAX_QUERIES_PER_HOUR 5;
```

More information on the many uses of WITH can be found at
http://dev.mysql.com/doc/refman/5.1/en/grant.html

Granting access in Python

Using MySQLdb to enable user privileges is not more difficult than doing so in MySQL itself. As with creating and dropping users, we simply need to form the statement and pass it to MySQL through the appropriate cursor.

As with the native interface to MySQL, we only have as much authority in Python as our login allows. Therefore, if the credentials with which a cursor is created has not been given the GRANT option, an error will be thrown by MySQL and MySQLdb, subsequently.

Assuming that user `skipper` has the GRANT option as well as the other necessary privileges, we can use the following code to create a new user, set that user's password, and grant that user privileges:

```python
#!/usr/bin/env python

import MySQLdb

host = 'localhost'
user = 'skipper'
passwd = 'secret'

mydb = MySQLdb.connect(host, user, passwd)
cursor = mydb.cursor()

try:
    mkuser = 'symphony'
    creation = "CREATE USER %s@'%s'" % (mkuser, host)
    results = cursor.execute(creation)
    print "User creation returned", results

    mkpass = 'n0n3wp4ss'
    setpass = "SET PASSWORD FOR '%s'@'%s' = PASSWORD('%s')" % (mkuser,
host, mkpass)
    results = cursor.execute(setpass)
    print "Setting of password returned", results

    granting = "GRANT ALL ON *.* TO '%s'@'%s'" % (mkuser, host)
    results = cursor.execute(granting)
    print "Granting of privileges returned", results

except MySQLdb.Error, e:
    print e
```

If there is an error anywhere along the way, it is printed to screen. Otherwise, the several `print` statements are executed. As long as they all return 0, each step was successful.

Removing privileges in MySQL

To remove privileges that have been granted, one uses the REVOKE statement. One uses the same information to revoke privileges as to grant them:

- The kinds of privileges to be revoked
- The database and table involved
- The user ID
- The hostname used in granting the privilege

As with dropping and creating a user, a pattern matching hostname of % does not include localhost. That host must be revoked explicitly.

Basic syntax

The REVOKE command has the following basic syntax:

```
REVOKE <privileges> ON <database>.<table> FROM
'<userid>'@'<hostname>';
```

So to revoke all access for user tempo to the City table of the world database when logged in locally, we would use the following statement:

```
REVOKE ALL PRIVILEGES ON world.City FROM 'tempo'@'localhost';
```

If we want to revoke only INSERT privileges for remote access, we would adapt the preceding statement accordingly:

```
REVOKE INSERT ON world.City FROM 'tempo'@'%';
```

Again, it is important to remember that the following two lines affect different records in the MySQL user table:

```
REVOKE ALL PRIVILEGES ON world.City FROM 'tempo'@'localhost';
REVOKE ALL PRIVILEGES ON world.City FROM 'tempo'@'%';
```

After using REVOKE, the user still has access!?

All administrative changes in MySQL are applied to MySQL's internal databases. Therefore, any change that is effected, only takes effect the next time MySQL needs to read those administrative tables. Consequently, users can still have access to databases or tables after the revocation statement has been issued.

Often, administrative changes can wait until the user logs out. However, even then, it can take a while for the changes to take effect. Depending on how frequently MySQL reads the administrative tables, the change may not take effect even if you manually remove the permissions from the administrative tables that govern privileges (`columns_priv`, `procs_priv`, and `tables_priv`). Within MySQL, one can pass the following command:

```
FLUSH PRIVILEGES;
```

If one's login has `RELOAD` privileges.

If time is of the essence, however, and you want to force MySQL to re-read all of the administrative tables, you may want to restart it. In Linux and other Unix variants, execute the following with root privileges:

```
/etc/init.d/mysql restart
```

From Windows:

1. Click **Start** | **Control Panel** | **Administrative Controls** | **Services**.
2. Select **mysql**.
3. Right click then select **Restart** under **Options**.

Currently, there is no interface available to restart MySQL from Python without issuing OS-specific commands (that is, using the `os` module). This is not a tenable development strategy as the Python program would need to run with administrator privileges (an obvious security problem). However, Mats Kindahl, lead developer at MySQL, has started MySQL Replicant, a project designed for replicating MySQL servers, but that incidentally should include administrative tasks such as starting, restarting, and stopping. For more, including a download link, see this blog post from Kindahl's blog: `http://mysqlmusings.blogspot.com/2009/12/mysql-replicant-library-for-controlling.html`

Using REVOKE in Python

As with GRANT, revoking privileges in Python just depends on forming the statement. As seen in this code, a revision of the earlier example, the REVOKE statement uses similar context to and all the same information as the GRANT statement:

```python
#!/usr/bin/env python

import MySQLdb

host = 'localhost'
user = 'skipper'
passwd = 'secret'

mydb = MySQLdb.connect(host, user, passwd)
cursor = mydb.cursor()

try:
    mkuser = 'symphony'
    creation = "CREATE USER '%s'@'%s'" %(mkuser, host)
    results = cursor.execute(creation)
    print "User creation returned", results


    mkpass = 'n0n3wp4ss'
    setpass = "SET PASSWORD FOR '%s'@'%s' = PASSWORD('%s')" %(mkuser,
host, mkpass)
    results = cursor.execute(setpass)
    print "Setting of password returned", results

    granting = "GRANT ALL ON *.* TO '%s'@'%s'" %(mkuser, host)
    results = cursor.execute(granting)
    print "Granting of privileges returned", results

    granting = "REVOKE ALL PRIVILEGES ON *.* FROM '%s'@'%s'" %(mkuser,
host)
    results = cursor.execute(granting)
    print "Revoking of privileges returned", results


except MySQLdb.Error, e:
    print e
```

Project: Web-based user administration

In this chapter's project, we will add some user administration facilities to the web administration program that we created in the last chapter. We will therefore discuss the changes to the program and will not address those functions we have already discussed in the previous chapter.

As mentioned in the previous chapter, we should get the same results from this program regardless of whether we call it through CGI or with PHP. The output is always a HTML file. Using PHP has the advantage of allowing us to test the program from the command-line where CGI requires hard-wiring of values in the code. It is only after the program is proven locally that one should move it to a test server.

For reasons of illustration and portability, we will proceed in this project as if we called the program through PHP. This allows us to list the new options in a way that should be easier to follow.

New options in the code

The purpose of this project is to add certain user administration facilities to the program from last chapter, PyMyAdmin.py. The functionality to be added includes creating and dropping users as well as granting and revoking access to proscribed accounts.

In addition to login credentials, the CREATE USER and DROP USER statements require the declaration of a user's name. Therefore, we need to add the following to the options supported:

```
opt.add_option("-n", "--username",
               action="store",
               type="string",
               help="username to be affected",
               dest="username")
```

The account to be affected is therefore identified by opt.username.

Best practice suggests that one should set a user's password at the same time as creating the account. Therefore, we need support for this:

```
opt.add_option("-w", "--passwd",
               action="store",
               type="string",
               help="password to be used in user creation",
               dest="passwd")
```

Therefore, the affected account's password will then be contained in `opt.passwd`.

In granting and revoking privileges, we need three additional pieces of information: the relevant privileges, the database, and tables to be used.

```
opt.add_option("-r", "--privileges",
                action="store",
                type="string",
                help="privileges to be assigned to user",
                dest="privileges")
opt.add_option("-a", "--acldb",
                action="store",
                type="string",
                help="database to be affected with access rules",
                dest="acldb")
opt.add_option("-b", "--acltb",
                action="store",
                type="string",
                help="table to be affected with access rules",
                dest="acltb")
```

This data will thus reconcile to the following variables in the code:

- Privileges: `opt.privileges`
- Relevant database: `opt.acldb`
- Relevant tables: `opt.acltb`

Finally, we need a switch to indicate which of these the user wants to perform. For this we use `uact`:

```
opt.add_option("-u", "--uact",
                action="store",
                type="string",
                help="act of user administration",
                dest="uact")
```

This will naturally reconcile to `opt.uact`.

At this point, the options listed for the program when the help menu is called looks like this:

```
Usage: pymyadmin.py [options]

Options:
  -h, --help              show this help message and exit
  -U USER, --user=USER    user account to use for login
  -P PASSWORD, --password=PASSWORD
                          password to use for login
  -d DBACT, --dbact=DBACT
                          kind of db action to be affected
  -D DBNAME, --dbname=DBNAME
                          name of db to be affected
  -t TBACT, --tbact=TBACT
                          kind of table action to be affected
  -Q TBDBNAME, --tbdbact=TBDBNAME
                          name of database containing table to be
affected
  -T TBNAME, --tbname=TBNAME
                          name of table to be affected
  -q QACT, --qact=QACT    kind of query to affect
  -Z QDBNAME, --qdbname=QDBNAME
                          database to be used for query
  -Y QTBNAME, --qtbname=QTBNAME
                          table to be used for query
  -c COLUMNS, --columns=COLUMNS
                          columns to be used in query
  -v VALUES, --values=VALUES
                          values to be used in query
  -u UACT, --uact=UACT    act of user administration
  -n USERNAME, --username=USERNAME
                          username to be affected
  -w PASSWD, --passwd=PASSWD
                          password to be used in user creation
  -r PRIVILEGES, --privileges=PRIVILEGES
                          privileges to be assigned to user
  -a ACLDB, --acldb=ACLDB
                          database to be affected with access rules
  -b ACLTB, --acltb=ACLTB
                          table to be affected with access rules
```

Adding the functions: CREATE and DROP

As CREATE and DROP use the same basic data, it behooves us to use one function to
handle both.

```
def uaction(user, password, uact, username, *passwd):
    cursor = connectNoDB(user, password)
    if uact == "create-user":
        passwd = passwd[0]
        create = "CREATE USER '%s'@'localhost'" %(username)
        rescreate = execute(create, cursor, 'create-user')
        setpass = "SET PASSWORD FOR '%s'@'localhost' = PASSWORD('%s')"
%(username, passwd)
        respass = execute(setpass, cursor, 'set-pass')
        results = rescreate + respass
    else:
        drop = "DROP USER '%s'@'localhost'" %(username)
        resdrop = execute(drop, cursor, 'drop-user')
        results = resdrop
    return results
```

The main difference in the flow of the program is that we will expect to set a
password whenever the CREATE option is called. Therefore, we will fork the program
flow within the function according to whether we are creating or dropping a user.

When the CREATE option is used, this function expects a fifth value in *passwd.
Otherwise, it is never used. The program will thus execute fine without it.

If you get errors in relation to the execution of this function, it is best to insert a
print statement to show what Python is passing to MySQL and, if necessary,
the variable types being used. An example of how to do this is as follows:

```
def uaction(user, password, uact, username, *passwd):
    cursor = connectNoDB(user, password)
    if uact == "create-user":
        create = "CREATE USER '%s'@'localhost'" %(username)

        print "passwd is of type", type(passwd)
        rescreate = execute(create, cursor, 'create-user')
        setpass = "SET PASSWORD FOR '%s'@'localhost' = PASSWORD('%s')"
%(username, passwd)
        respass = execute(setpass, cursor, 'set-pass')
        results = rescreate + respass
    else:
        drop = "DROP USER '%s'@'localhost'" %(username)
        resdrop = execute(drop, cursor, 'drop-user')
        results = resdrop
    return results
```

If MySQL complains of problems in your statement, simply print it out before you pass it to `execute()`. This will ensure that it is printed before the next program call, where the statement is passed to MySQL and the problem arises. Alternatively, one could edit the `execute()` function to print the statement it receives.

Here, we are also not handling the value of `passwd` correctly. While `passwd` is a string in the main program, it is not passed as a whole. To find out how it is passed and how to handle it correctly, we need to insert such statements as the second `print` statement.

Adding CREATE and DROP to main()

Having created the functionality in `uaction()`, we can now handle the CREATE and DROP options in `main()`. To do this, we simply add another `elif` clause to the series that follows if `authenticate` equates to 1. The new `if...elif` series looks like this:

```
if authenticate == 1:
        errmsg = "You have not specified the information necessary
for the action you chose.  Please check your information and specify
it correctly in the dialogue."

        if opt.dbact is not None:
            output = dbaction(opt.dbact, opt.dbname, cursor)
        elif opt.tbact is not None:
            output = tbaction(opt.tbact, opt.tbdbname, opt.tbname,
opt.columns, opt.values, opt.user, opt.password)
        elif opt.qact is not None:
            output = qaction(opt.qact, opt.qdbname, opt.qtbname,
opt.columns, opt.values, opt.user, opt.password)
        elif opt.uact is not None:
            if opt.uact == "create":
                act = "create-user"
                output = uaction(opt.user, opt.password, act, opt.
username, opt.passwd)
            elif opt.uact == "drop":
                act = "drop-user"
                output = uaction(opt.user, opt.password, act, opt.
username)
        else:
            output = errmsg
```

Note that we create a new variable `act` to reflect the import of `opt.uact` holding a value and what that value is. This saves us from unnecessarily complicated code elsewhere.

Adding the functions: GRANT and REVOKE

Next, we need to add the functionality for GRANT and REVOKE. For each of these statements, the values involved are precisely the same. Therefore, we do not need to use optional arguments. The function looks like this:

```
def uadmin(user, password, uact, username, privileges, acldb, acltb):
    cursor = connectNoDB(user, password)
    if uact == "grant":
        grant = "GRANT %s ON %s.%s TO '%s'@'localhost'" %(privileges,
acldb, acltb, username)
        results = execute(grant, cursor, 'grant')
    else:
        revoke = "REVOKE %s ON %s.%s FROM '%s'@'localhost'"
%(privileges, acldb, acltb, username)
        results = execute(revoke, cursor, 'revoke')
    return results
```

The syntax of each statement is straightforward. As we will remind the user on the HTML page, the list of privileges should be comma delimited. If it is not, we will get an error from MySQL. For real-world deployment, one would do well to check for this or put the operational parts of the function into a `try...else` clause.

Adding GRANT and REVOKE to main()

Having added facilities to handle GRANT and REVOKE, we need to tell `main()` how to handle those options. Once again, we are simply inserting another `elif` clause into the previously mentioned series. The new `main()` function then looks like this:

```
def main():
    """The main function creates and controls the MySQLStatement
instance in accordance with the user's input."""
    output = ""

    while 1:
        try:
            cursor = connectNoDB(opt.user, opt.password)
            authenticate = 1
        except:
            output = "Bad login information.  Please verify the
username and password that you are using before trying to login
again."
            authenticate = 0
```

```
        if authenticate == 1:
            errmsg = "You have not specified the information necessary
for the action you chose.  Please check your information and specify
it correctly in the dialogue."

            if opt.dbact is not None:
                output = dbaction(opt.dbact, opt.dbname, cursor)
            elif opt.tbact is not None:
                output = tbaction(opt.tbact, opt.tbdbname, opt.tbname,
opt.columns, opt.values, opt.user, opt.password)
            elif opt.qact is not None:
                output = qaction(opt.qact, opt.qdbname, opt.qtbname,
opt.columns, opt.values, opt.user, opt.password)
            elif opt.uact is not None:
                if opt.uact == "create":
                    act = "create-user"
                    output = uaction(opt.user, opt.password, act, opt.
username, opt.passwd)
                elif opt.uact == "drop":
                    act = "drop-user"
                    output = uaction(opt.user, opt.password, act, opt.
username)
                elif opt.uact == "grant" or opt.uact == "revoke":
                    output = uadmin(opt.user, opt.password, opt.uact,
opt.username, opt.privileges, opt.acldb, opt.acltb)
                else:
                    output = errmsg

        printout = HTMLPage()
        printout.message(output)
        output = printout.page()

        print output
break
```

Note that, instead of using two `elif` options for each of GRANT and REVOKE, we combine the two with a disjunctive or. All that is left is to add support for each of the four options on the HTML page.

Test the program

Before adding support on the HTML page, however, it is good practice to test what you have written. If you used the CGI method, you will need to hardwire values into the code for testing. Using PHP is the same as calling the program from the command line. Testing the program means trying all four new options and validating them in MySQL and from a MySQL login. If the output is expected, a valid HTML file, then the program executes as expected.

> To test the program from the command-line, you will necessarily need to access the terminal of your operating system and call the program with flags. If you do not know how to do this, consult your operating system's documentation.

To test user creation and dropping, open a MySQL shell as the `root` user. Using the `mysql` database, you can verify CREATE and DROP statements against the user database. The easiest way to do this is to select all from it by using:

```
SELECT * FROM user;
```

Alternatively, nuance the query with a WHERE clause.

To test the granting and revocation of access in real terms, open a MySQL shell in the name of the user to be affected. You as administrator, can then test the access granted to that user.

```
SHOW GRANTS FOR <username>@<hostname>;
```

This will show you all available permissions for the relevant account.

If you are debugging your code and start receiving errors, remember to **blackbox** the process. Don't simply try to edit the Python code and re-run it if you are getting a MySQL error. First, use `print` commands to show what statement Python is handing off to MySQL. Then ensure that those commands actually work in MySQL. Once you are confident that you have the right MySQL command and syntax, you can look at how your code passes information to `MySQLdb`. Finally, you can revisit your Python code to ensure that it is working as planned.

Remember that optional arguments (for example, `*passwd`) are passed as tuples. So, even if it is a **string** in the `main` function, it becomes a **tuple** when passed. You, therefore, have to handle it appropriately. Once you are satisfied that the program will behave as intended, it is time to implement the options in the HTML form.

New options on the page

To avail these new options to the user, we obviously need to adapt the HTML form. Insert the following just before the closing `</form>` tag:

```
<div>USER ADMINISTRATION</div>
<input type="radio" name="uact" value="create"> CREATE <br>
<input type="radio" name="uact" value="drop"> DROP <br>
<input type="radio" name="uact" value="grant"> GRANT <br>
<input type="radio" name="uact" value="revoke"> REVOKE <br>
  User name: <input type="text" name="username" value=""> <br>
  Password: <input type="password" name="passwd" value=""> <br>
  Privileges (comma-separated): <input type="text"
          name="privileges"value=""> <br>
  Database and Table:
  <input type="text" name="acldb" value="">.
  <input type="text" name="acltb" value=""> <br>
```

Note that, as a matter of good practice, one should not implement options in the form that are not yet implemented and tested in the code. To do so is a security risk.

The relevant part of the HTML page thus looks like this when rendered in a browser:

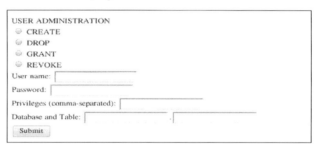

Room to grow

Where the above implementation works, several limitations exist in it. One of the primary ways that an error can arise is if the user does not enter the privileges separated by commas but by, say, semi-colons. Additional functionality that can be added includes:

- Allowing user administration for non-local hostnames
- Validating the database and table names before passing them to `execute()`
- Supporting SHOW GRANTS in order to provide a meaningful error message if a GRANT or REVOKE statement fails

We will look at other ways to augment the user-friendliness of the HTML menu in later chapters. But can you think of ways to make it easier to use?

Summary

In this chapter, we have covered how to create and remove users and privileges with MySQL for Python. We have seen:

- How to use MySQL and MySQLdb to CREATE and DROP users
- How to set user passwords
- How we can manage database privileges with MySQL for Python
- Ways to automate user creation and removal
- How to GRANT and REVOKE privileges and the conditions under which that can be done

In the next chapter, we will look at working with dates and time in MySQL for Python.

Date and Time Values

9

When beginning to program database-oriented applications, it is not uncommon to focus on processing data and to forget about matters of time and timing. If a program is simply storing addresses or otherwise dealing with data that is not naturally time-sensitive, it is easy to overlook matters of date and time. However, storing date and time for data and activity on the server allows for several desiderata, some of which are:

- Rolling back documents to an earlier draft version without affecting the current draft
- Figuring out why a process or subprocess jammed up or failed
- Forensic analysis of a compromised server

In this chapter, we will see:

- What data types MySQL supports for date and time
- When to use which data type and in what format and range
- What functions MySQL supports for managing temporal values
- The most frequently used functions for managing date and time

As mentioned in the previous chapter, the project for this chapter will build on the web application we began earlier. After looking at MySQL's date and time support and how to use it in Python, we will add similar functionality to our web-based administration program.

Date and time data types in MySQL

MySQL supports five data types for temporal matters: DATETIME, DATE, TIMESTAMP, TIME, and YEAR. These serve as types to be used when architecting a table like INT and VARCHAR that were employed in earlier chapters.

DATETIME

The DATETIME data type is used to specify a value that includes both the date and the time. It is important to realize that DATETIME accepts its values from the user like any other data type. It does not automatically generate values. For that purpose, one should use the TIMESTAMP type (seen later in this chapter).

Output format

The DATETIME type receives data in several formats, but returns it in only one.

```
YYYY-MM-DD HH:MM:SS
```

For example, the BBC's evening report of the Berlin Wall being torn down began at nine o'clock in the evening on November 10, 1989 and ran for 37 minutes and 9 seconds. A DATETIME value depicting the moment of its conclusion would read:

```
1989-10-10 21:37:09
```

Input formats

Where MySQL always returns DATETIME values in the same format, it will accept values in several formats:

- Four- or two-digit years

Either YYYY-MM-DD HH:MM:SS or YY-MM-DD HH:MM:SS is acceptable

- Any delimiter, as long as it is consistently applied

The above sample date could be input as 1989.10.10 21@37@09 or 89/10/10 21*37*09.

- No delimiters

So we could just input 19891010213709, and MySQL would understand it appropriately.

- No delimiters with a two-digit year

So 891010213709 is fair game.

DATETIME values may also be passed from DATE and TIME functions like NOW(). See the section on DATE and TIME functions, below.

Input range

MySQL insists that all dates be after the turn of the first millennium CE— 1000-01-01. The turn of the millennium here is literal. The exact beginning of acceptable dates and times is 1000-01-01 00:00:00.

On the far terminus of the range, MySQL cannot handle dates that are seen post the end of New Year's Eve 9999, or 9999-12-31 23:59:59.

Where MySQL can handle the sundry formats mentioned above, these must always reconcile to a date-time combination within this range. If a value does not, MySQL will record a zero value. So a value of either 0999-13-45 25:73:62 or 10000-14-35 25:61:61 would become 0000-00-00 00:00:00.

This is something to watch out for. When MySQL renders your data with this series of zeroes, it offers no signifier of the correction. Therefore, you will not be able to tell a bad value from a good one as both will look like 0000-00-00 00:00:00.

Using DATETIME in a CREATE statement

As mentioned previously, DATETIME is a data type. It is therefore used in table creation to specify the data type of a column. If, for example, we were keeping a record of dates and times of birth, a table creation statement might read as follows:

```
CREATE TABLE birthtimes(birthid INT NOT NULL AUTO_INCREMENT PRIMARY
KEY, babyname VARCHAR(30) DEFAULT '', birthtime DATETIME);
```

We would then populate that table with INSERT statements like:

```
INSERT INTO birthtimes(babyname, birthtime) VALUES('Johnny', '2005-12-
02 03:15:46');
```

DATE

The DATE type is a shorthand means of using only the first half of the DATETIME value format.

Output and Input formats

The format of output for such types follows that of DATETIME:

- YYYY-MM-DD

For input, DATE accepts any of the following formats:

- Four- or two-digit years

Either `YYYY-MM-DD` or `YY-MM-DD`

- Any delimiter, as long as it is consistently applied

So `YYYY/MM/DD` or `YY/MM/DD` or `YYYY*MM*DD`. Again, consistency is the key.

- No delimiters

So `YYYYMMDD` is allowed, and MySQL massages it to suit its needs.

- No delimiters with a two-digit year

So we can use `YYMMDD`.

Input range

`DATE` also has a similar range to `DATETIME`—from `1000-01-01` through `9999-12-31`. As with the first data type that we discussed in this chapter, values outside this range will be zeroed out to `0000-00-00` with no warning being given.

TIMESTAMP

The `TIMESTAMP` data type differs from the previous two in several important ways. `TIMESTAMP` values follow the same format as `DATETIME`'s long form:

```
YYYY-MM-DD HH:MM:SS
```

This is a fixed width and cannot be changed, even by setting a default (see the following section for more on this).

Input of values

`TIMESTAMP` is an auto-generated data type. Therefore, it's value is not specified in an `INSERT` statement but is culled from the server's local time. For the local time, MySQL uses the clock of the hardware on which it is running by accessing the operating system's clock.

Internally, MySQL always deals in **UTC** (**Universal Time, Coordinated**—a so-called backronym for **Coordinated Universal Time**). In common use, UTC is the same as **Greenwich Mean Time (GMT)**, though the two may differ by up to 0.9 seconds.

If the server is not on UTC, the server's time is converted to UTC for purposes of data storage and then converted back when that value is requested. Therefore, if a record was saved under one time zone and retrieved after the time zone value was changed (for example, Daylight Saving Time, British Summer Time, or similar), the value that is returned will be different than the value that was given by the user.

Range

The TIMESTAMP type differs from DATETIME, wherein its range is much more restricted. MySQL uses the Unix epoch as the beginning of its range: 1970-01-01 00:00:01. The terminus for valid timestamps is 2038-01-19 03:14:07. All times are in UTC.

Why January 19, 2038 at 3:14:07? Initially, MySQL was developed for Unix-like systems. All Unix systems currently share a bug called variously the year 2038 bug, the Y2K28 bug, or just the Unix Millenium Bug. The issue results from the problem of 32-bit signed integers being used to save dates and how those values are processed internally, in binary. The timestamp for the MySQL terminus is as follows:

2038-01-19 03:14:07 in binary is 11111111 11111111 11111111 11111111

As all addition inside a computer occurs in binary, the computer will simply add one to this value which will then bring the binary value of the timestamp to the following:

00000000 00000000 00000000 00000000 or 1901-12-13 20:45:52

The one at the far left of the number drops off the display and disappears from the system. It is not clear how many systems will be impacted by this bug. It is known that Unix-like systems are not alone in being impacted. For more on the year 2038 bug, including AOL's database crash of May 2006, see http://en.wikipedia.org/wiki/Year_2038_problem

Invalid TIMESTAMP values are converted to 0. Therefore, if a date of 1963-11-22 12:30:00 is used, it cannot be a TIMESTAMP type, but must be a DATETIME.

Defaults, initialization, and updating

MySQL allows timestamps to be set manually or automatically. If set manually, you need to give a default value. If set automatically, MySQL will use the system time to initialize the table. Updating can occur under either circumstance.

To affect a default TIMESTAMP value that is not coordinated with the system time, one would use the following in a table creation statement:

```
TIMESTAMP DEFAULT 0
```

If one wanted to coordinate the timestamp to the system time only at startup, set it to default to the current time:

```
TIMESTAMP DEFAULT CURRENT_TIMESTAMP
```

This sets the timestamp at initialization.

If the table is created with the argument for TIMESTAMP as ON UPDATE CURRENT_ TIMESTAMP, the TIMESTAMP value will automatically be updated to the current timestamp. One can set the default to 0 and still allow updates as appropriate with the following clause:

```
TIMESTAMP DEFAULT 0 ON UPDATE CURRENT_TIMESTAMP
```

This sets an initial timestamp of 0, but requests updating to the current timestamp.

To set the timestamp to the system time at initialization and then update it, we combine the two statements:

```
TIMESTAMP DEFAULT CURRENT_TIMESTAMP ON UPDATE CURRENT_TIMESTAMP
```

YEAR

As the name implies, the YEAR data type stores only year values. Whether the year is treated as a two-digit or four-digit value depends on how the type is set.

Two-digit YEAR values

The two-digit YEAR value is set with the following syntax:

```
YEAR(2)
```

A two-digit YEAR type is obviously only valid for up to 99 years. So YEAR(2) is used to specify years from 1970, the start of the aforementioned epoch, through 2069.

Four-digit YEAR values

Four-digit YEAR values are specified with the following:

```
YEAR(4)
```

These values naturally have a wider range than the two-digit form. Four-digit years may range from 1901 through 2155.

Valid input

Obviously, two-digit YEAR values require two-digit input. Four-digit YEAR values will accept two-digit input, as well. However, the consequent value may not be what is intended. For example, let's assume we create a dummy table called yeareg using the following statement:

```
CREATE TABLE yeareg(ID INT NOT NULL AUTO_INCREMENT PRIMARY KEY, year
YEAR(4));
```

We can populate that table with four-digit values without a problem:

```
INSERT INTO yeareg(year) VALUES('1923');

Query OK, 1 row affected (0.00 sec)
```

But if we use only two digits, the result is quite different:

```
mysql> INSERT INTO yeareg(year) VALUES('23');

Query OK, 1 row affected (0.00 sec)


mysql> SELECT * FROM yeareg;

+----+------+
| ID | year |
+----+------+
|  1 | 1923 |
|  2 | 2023 |
+----+------+

2 rows in set (0.00 sec)
```

Two-digit values are assumed to belong in the 21st century. The only exceptions are values from 70 through 99 and the value 00. These are rendered automatically as the years between 1970 and 1999 and, in the case of the last, the year 2000.

As with the other data types discussed in this chapter, MySQL does not guess if it is given invalid data. Data outside the above ranges will be zeroed out as 00 or 0000, depending on which size of YEAR value is expected.

TIME

The TIME data type is used for one of three purposes. It can represent:

- A time of day
- An elapsed time
- An interval of time

Because of its multiple applications, TIME has a slightly different format and set of constraints that might appear intuitive.

Format

The TIME type accepts input in multiple formats, but outputs data in only one. The output format for TIME is:

```
HH:MM:SS
```

For input, however, one can input hours, minutes, and seconds in several formats:

- As a string in the form HHMMSS: So '234545' is valid.
- As an integer in the same form HHMMSS: So a numeric value 123456 is also valid.
- As a string using colons for delimiters: This follows the output format HH:MM:SS

TIME also accepts shorthand for extremely large or small quantities in terms of days as well as fractions of a second. To specify a day, simply place the day value in front of the regular time.

```
D HH:MM:SS
```

For large values, it converts the number of days into the respective number of hours and adds it to the hour value. So:

```
1 23:59:59
```

is the same as:

```
47:49:49
```

and that is how MySQL records it in the database. Note, however, that using the day value requires the use of the colon as a delimiter. Therefore, the following is **INVALID**:

```
1235959
```

Fractions of a second, on the other hand, are dropped. The value is always, in effect, rounded down. Therefore, the following are both equal in the eyes of MySQL:

```
1 12:01:01.1
1 12:01.01.9
```

Either way, the value that is stored is:

```
36:01:01
```

Invalid values

Invalid TIME values are zeroed out to `00:00:00`. While it shows that a transaction has occurred, zero values cannot be distinguished from midnight.

Valid values for each of the columns are as follows:

- **Days**: A whole number from 1 to 34
- **Hours**: A whole number between -838 and 838
- **Minutes**: A whole number less than or equal to 59
- **Seconds**: A number less than or equal to 59
- **Fractions**: Positive decimal value less than 1

For reasons of storage, the limits of MySQL's TIME type range from `-838:59:59` to `838:59:59`. Any value that does not make sense as a time within these constraints will result in an erroneous value being stored. Precisely which value is stored will depend on the error. Exceeding the limits of minutes and seconds results in a zeroed value. Examples include:

```
5 23:01:61
20:61:23
18:75:75
```

However, if the hours and minutes are valid, but the number of hours represented by the day and hour values exceeds 838, either negatively or positively, MySQL will reduce that number to the respective terminus of either `-838:59:59` or `838:59:59`.

If you want to ensure that MySQL handles your TIME values securely and outputs any errors, use MySQL's STRICT_ALL_TABLES mode. STRICT_ALL_TABLES returns an error and aborts any operation in which a problem with the data arises. Note, however, that this can result in the partial completion of multi-line operations and so can cause trouble. Using STRICT_ALL_TABLES in development is a good way of checking your codebase. Just remember to switch it off in production.

An alternative to STRICT_ALL_TABLES is STRICT_TRANS_TABLES. This continues to process the data, but outputs a warning when it has massaged the data to fit the column.

To use either mode, start MySQL using the executable, which is appropriate for your platform and equate one of the above modes to the flag --sql-mode. For example, one would use mysqld as follows:

```
mysqld --sql-mode="STRICT_TRANS_TABLES"
```

One can also specify the mode in the MySQL configuration file by setting the value sql-mode (my.cnf for Unix-like systems and my.ini for Windows). For more on MySQL modes, see the MySQL manual at: http://dev.mysql.com/doc/refman/5.5/en/server-sql-mode.html

If TIME is used to reference a time of day, possibly to receive the value of a function like CURRENT_TIME, the value must be within the 24 hour period.

Date and time types in Python

The date and time interfaces to MySQL for Python are very robust. As a consequence, as long as the values you pass make sense within the above parameters for formatting, neither MySQL nor Python will throw an error about aspects such as the Python data type. For example, if we go back to the yeareg table, we can pass integers and strings to it through Python without issue:

```
import MySQLdb
mydb = MySQLdb.connect('localhost', 'skipper', 'secret', 'datetime')
cursor = mydb.cursor()
x = 2012
statement = "INSERT INTO yeareg(year) VALUES('%s')" %(x)
results = cursor.execute(statement)
x = str(x)
statement = "INSERT INTO yeareg(year) VALUES('%s')" %(x)
results = cursor.execute(statement)
```

In the first statement, we pass a string. In the second, an integer. Yet both statements will be executed by MySQL without issue.

```
mysql> SELECT * FROM yeareg;
+----+------+
| ID | year |
+----+------+
|  1 | 1923 |
|  2 | 2023 |
|  3 | 2013 |
|  3 | 2013 |
+----+------+
4 rows in set (0.00 sec)
```

However, passing invalid values will result in an OperationalError being thrown. Further, while this is possible, it is not advisable. Best practice holds that your program should submit data in a format suited to its target type, so strings should be formatted as strings and integers as integers.

Date and time functions

MySQL's time-related functions are used to manipulate date and time data types. As such, they are very helpful tools for accessing data with optimum speed and minimal overhead.

The MySQL list of date and time-related functions are legion. The full list is contained in the table below (Source: *MySQL 5.5 Reference Manual*):

Name	Description
ADDDATE()	Add time values (intervals) to a date value
ADDTIME()	Add time
CONVERT_TZ()	Convert from one time zone to another
CURDATE()	Return the current date
CURRENT_DATE(), CURRENT_DATE	Synonyms for CURDATE()
CURRENT_TIME(), CURRENT_TIME	Synonyms for CURTIME()
CURRENT_TIMESTAMP(), CURRENT_TIMESTAMP	Synonyms for NOW()
CURTIME()	Return the current time

Name	Description
DATE_ADD()	Add time values (intervals) to a date value
DATE_FORMAT()	Format date as specified
DATE_SUB()	Subtract two dates
DATE()	Extract the date part of a date or datetime expression
DATEDIFF()	Subtract two dates
DAY()	Synonym for DAYOFMONTH()
DAYNAME()	Return the name of the weekday
DAYOFMONTH()	Return the day of the month (0-31)
DAYOFWEEK()	Return the weekday index of the argument
DAYOFYEAR()	Return the day of the year (1-366)
EXTRACT	Extract part of a date
FROM_DAYS()	Convert a day number to a date
FROM_UNIXTIME()	Format Unix timestamp as a date
GET_FORMAT()	Return a date format string
HOUR()	Extract the hour
LAST_DAY	Return the last day of the month for the argument
LOCALTIME(), LOCALTIME	Synonym for NOW()
LOCALTIMESTAMP, LOCALTIMESTAMP()	Synonym for NOW()
MAKEDATE()	Create a date from the year and day of year
MAKETIME	MAKETIME()
MICROSECOND()	Return the microseconds from argument
MINUTE()	Return the minute from the argument
MONTH()	Return the month from the date passed
MONTHNAME()	Return the name of the month
NOW()	Return the current date and time
PERIOD_ADD()	Add a period to a year-month
PERIOD_DIFF()	Return the number of months between periods
QUARTER()	Return the quarter from a date argument
SEC_TO_TIME()	Converts seconds to HH:MM:SS format
SECOND()	Return the second (0-59)

Name	Description
STR_TO_DATE()	Convert a string to a date
SUBDATE()	A synonym for DATE_SUB() when invoked with three arguments
SUBTIME()	Subtract times
SYSDATE()	Return the time at which the function executes
TIME_FORMAT()	Format as time
TIME_TO_SEC()	Return the argument converted to seconds
TIME()	Extract the time portion of the expression passed
TIMEDIFF()	Subtract time
TIMESTAMP()	With a single argument, this function returns the date or datetime expression; with two arguments, the sum of the arguments
TIMESTAMPADD()	Add an interval to a datetime expression
TIMESTAMPDIFF()	Subtract an interval from a datetime expression
TO_DAYS()	Return the date argument converted to days
TO_SECONDS()	Return the date or datetime argument converted to seconds since Year 0
UNIX_TIMESTAMP()	Return a Unix timestamp
UTC_DATE()	Return the current UTC date
UTC_TIME()	Return the current UTC time
UTC_TIMESTAMP()	Return the current UTC date and time
WEEK()	Return the week number
WEEKDAY()	Return the weekday index
WEEKOFYEAR()	Return the calendar week of the date (0-53)
YEAR()	Return the year
YEARWEEK()	Return the year and week

Obviously, it is not feasible to keep all of these in mind without constant use. This table helps to give a primer on each, but all are discussed in great detail in the MySQL manual. For this chapter, we will look at the most frequently used date and time-related functions.

For more on any of of the date and time functions, see the MySQL manual: `http://dev.mysql.com/doc/refman/5.5/en/date-and-time-functions.html`

NOW()

The `NOW()` function returns the current date and time from the system. Which parts of the timestamp are used is determined by the data type of the column. For example, assume three tables as follows:

`dteg` with a column `dati` of type `DATETIME`

`dateeg` with a column `date` of type `DATE`

`yeareg` with a column `year` of type `YEAR(4)`

`timeeg` with a column `time` of type `TIME`

We can use `NOW()` as a value in our `INSERT` statements. For each of the following examples, the data like the respective values would be stored:

```
INSERT INTO dteg(dati) VALUES(NOW());     →  2010-01-14 11:33:51
INSERT INTO dateeg(date) VALUES(NOW());   →  2010-01-14
INSERT INTO yeareg(year) VALUES(NOW());   →  2010
INSERT INTO timeeg(time) VALUES(NOW());   →  11:33:51
```

CURDATE()

The current date is returned by `CURDATE()`. As the name implies, this function returns the current date. If we assume the tables from the `NOW()` function (seen previously), the following examples will store the relevant part of the current date in the given column:

```
INSERT INTO dateeg(date) VALUES(CURDATE());  →  2010-01-14
INSERT INTO yeareg(year) VALUES(CURDATE());  →  2010
```

Depending on your MySQL configuration, you can use this function in statements relative to `TIME` type values, but the stored value will be zeroed out to `00:00:00`.

```
INSERT INTO timeeg(time) VALUES(CURDATE());  →  00:00:00
```

CURTIME()

The function CURTIME() returns the current time in the format HH:MM:SS. Usage of it is as follows:

```
INSERT INTO timeeg(time) VALUES(CURTIME());  →  11:55:23
```

Obviously, the date is not included in the returned value, making this function unsuitable for use where DATE, DATETIME, or YEAR values are expected. If a CURTIME() returned value should be inserted where one of these three are expected, the results are predictable. The returned value is never in the appropriate format for DATE or DATETIME types, therefore MySQL stores a zeroed value.

```
INSERT INTO dteg(dati) VALUES(CURTIME());   →  0000-00-00 00:00:00
INSERT INTO dateeg(date) VALUES(CURTIME()); →  0000-00-00
However, in the case of YEAR, a more insidious error arises.
INSERT INTO yeareg(year) VALUES(CURTIME()); →  2011
```

The column is defined as YEAR(4). But MySQL will accept two digits for the value and will convert it to four digits. Therefore, when it receives for YEAR(4) a value that does not make sense, it accepts what data it can. In this case, the hour value of **11:33:51** is read simply as 11 and converted to 2011.

DATE()

The function DATE() strips the date out of a time-related string. The string is expected to be in the format of DATE or DATETIME, but need not be from columns of either of these types. One can simply feed a string to DATE() and receive the answer back as a table:

```
mysql> select date('2009-12-02 12:14');
+-----------------------+
| date('2009-12-02 12') |
+-----------------------+
| 2009-12-02            |
+-----------------------+
1 row in set (0.00 sec)
```

For DATE(), the only part that matters is the date aspect of the string. One can include just about anything after the date, including text.

```
mysql> select date('2009-12-02 Wednesday');
+------------------------------+
| date('2009-12-02 Wednesday') |
+------------------------------+
| 2009-12-02                   |
+------------------------------+
1 row in set, 1 warning (0.00 sec)
```

If there is a time or time-like datum after the date, it does not need to be properly formatted.

```
mysql> select date('2009-12-02 11am');
+-------------------------+
| date('2009-12-02 11am') |
+-------------------------+
| 2009-12-02              |
+-------------------------+
1 row in set, 1 warning (0.00 sec)
```

The date, however, must come first in the string passed to DATE(). Otherwise, MySQL returns NULL results.

DATE_SUB() and DATE_ADD()

The DATE_ADD() and DATE_SUB() functions are used to modify date values according to specific intervals of time. DATE_ADD() adds an interval of time. DATE_SUB() subtracts an interval of time. Their syntax is essentially the same:

```
DATE_ADD(date, INTERVAL amount unit)
DA  TE_SUB(date, INTERVAL amount unit)
```

In each case, date is the value to be modified. The keyword INTERVAL is required to introduce the amount and unit of time to be used.

In practice, these functions can be used as:

```
mysql> SELECT DATE_ADD(now(), INTERVAL 20 minute);
+-------------------------------------+
| DATE_ADD(now(), INTERVAL 20 minute) |
+-------------------------------------+
| 2010-01-14 13:04:48                 |
+-------------------------------------+
1 row in set (0.00 sec)
```

And it can also be used as:

```
mysql> SELECT DATE_SUB(now(), INTERVAL 20 minute);
+-------------------------------------+
| DATE_SUB(now(), INTERVAL 20 minute) |
+-------------------------------------+
| 2010-01-14 12:25:22                 |
+-------------------------------------+
1 row in set (0.00 sec)
```

The format and type of the returned value depends on the argument passed to the function. If the date is a DATETIME or TIMESTAMP value or it is a DATE and the INTERVAL value using hours, minutes, or seconds, then the returned value will be a DATETIME value. Otherwise, these functions return a string.

An alternative to DATE_SUB() is to increment the date value by a negative number. So instead of the last example, we could have simply modified the first one as follows:

```
mysql> SELECT DATE_ADD(now(), INTERVAL -20 minute);
+--------------------------------------+
| DATE_ADD(now(), INTERVAL -20 minute) |
+--------------------------------------+
| 2010-01-14 12:24:51                  |
+--------------------------------------+
1 row in set (0.00 sec)
```

Just as with DATE(), we can substitute a DATE or DATETIME formatted string for the date.

```
mysql> SELECT '2009-12-24' + INTERVAL 1 DAY;
+-------------------------------+
| '2009-12-24' + INTERVAL 1 DAY |
+-------------------------------+
| 2009-12-25                    |
+-------------------------------+
1 row in set (0.00 sec)
```

Additionally, both support shorthand ways of affecting the same end. Instead of using DATE_ADD() or DATE_SUB(), we can simply use the plus sign + or the minus sign - respectively. The syntax in these cases is:

```
date + INTERVAL amount unit
date - INTERVAL amount unit
```

For example, to add 20 days to today, we use:

```
mysql> SELECT NOW() + INTERVAL 20 DAY;
+-----------------------+
| NOW() + INTERVAL 20 DAY |
+-----------------------+
| 2010-02-03 12:50:13   |
+-----------------------+
1 row in set (0.00 sec)
```

and

```
mysql> SELECT INTERVAL 20 DAY + '2009-12-24';
+-------------------------------+
| INTERVAL 20 DAY + '2009-12-24' |
+-------------------------------+
| 2010-01-13                    |
+-------------------------------+
1 row in set (0.01 sec)
```

Similarly, to subtract is as follows:

```
mysql> SELECT NOW() - INTERVAL 20 DAY;
+------------------------+
| NOW() - INTERVAL 20 DAY |
+------------------------+
| 2009-12-25 12:48:47    |
+------------------------+
1 row in set (0.00 sec)
```

However, basic logic applies to the syntax here. When adding, we can juggle the two addends without impacting on the sum. With subtraction, however, the INTERVAL clause must come second because it makes no sense to subtract a date from an interval of time.

Both functions accept several different units of time. However, unlike with the TIME data type, mentioned previously, all amounts must relate precisely to the unit used. One cannot, for example, pass day values with an hour unit. A complete listing of the options and the expected quantity type for each is as follows:

For a unit of type	A valid Amount must be in
MICROSECOND	Microseconds
SECOND	Seconds
MINUTE	Minutes
HOUR	Hours
DAY	Days
WEEK	Weeks
MONTH	Months
QUARTER	Quarters
YEAR	Years
SECOND_MICROSECOND	Seconds and microseconds with format 'seconds.microseconds'
MINUTE_MICROSECOND	Minutes, seconds, and microseconds with format 'MINUTES:SECONDS.MICROSECONDS'
MINUTE_SECOND	Minutes and seconds with format 'MINUTES:SECONDS'
HOUR_MICROSECOND	The variables of time, including microseconds, with format 'HOURS:MINUTES:SECONDS.MICROSECONDS'
HOUR_SECOND	The variable of time with format 'HOURS:MINUTES:SECONDS'
HOUR_MINUTE	The basic time with format 'HOURS:MINUTES'

For a unit of type	A valid Amount must be in
DAY_MICROSECOND	The basic variables of time as well as number of days and microseconds with format 'DAYS HOURS:MINUTES:SECONDS.MICROSECONDS'
DAY_SECOND	The same as day_microsecond excluding microseconds with format 'DAYS HOURS:MINUTES:SECONDS'
DAY_MINUTE	Days, hours, and minutes with format 'DAYS HOURS:MINUTES'
DAY_HOUR	Days and hours with format 'DAYS HOURS'
YEAR_MONTH	Years and months with format 'YEARS-MONTHS'

DATEDIFF()

The DATEDIFF() function is used to calculate the number of days between dates. It requires two arguments, both in the DATE format:

```
DATEDIFF(first_date, second_date);
```

In practice, it can calculate just about any number of days.

```
mysql> SELECT DATEDIFF('2009-12-25', '2010-01-14');
+--------------------------------------+
| DATEDIFF('2009-12-25', '2010-01-14') |
+--------------------------------------+
|                                  -20 |
+--------------------------------------+
1 row in set (0.00 sec)
```

It also does not require explicit dates, but can accept output from other time-related functions.

```
mysql> SELECT DATEDIFF('2001-09-11', DATE(NOW()));
+-----------------------------------+
| DATEDIFF('2001-09-11', NOW())     |
+-----------------------------------+
|                             -3047 |
+-----------------------------------+
1 row in set (0.00 sec)
```

Any results passed to DATEDIFF() must be as DATE formatted values. If it is unclear whether a value will be in the appropriate format, you can pass it through DATE() first.

```
mysql> SELECT DATEDIFF('2001-09-11', DATE(NOW()));
+------------------------------------+
| DATEDIFF('2001-09-11', DATE(NOW()) |
+------------------------------------+
|                              -3047 |
+------------------------------------+
1 row in set (0.00 sec)
```

However, bad data will not be made good by DATE():

```
mysql> SELECT DATEDIFF('2001-09-11', DATE(CURTIME()));
+----------------------------------------+
| DATEDIFF('2001-09-11', DATE(CURTIME()) |
+----------------------------------------+
|                                   NULL |
+----------------------------------------+
1 row in set, 1 warning (0.00 sec)
```

DATE_FORMAT()

The DATE_FORMAT() function is very helpful for creating human-friendly date and time strings automatically. It requires two arguments—a date and the formatting structure for the output. For example, the expression %W denotes the day of the week for DATE_FORMAT(). We can therefore learn what day of the week a particular date is by using:

```
mysql> SELECT DATE_FORMAT('2001-09-11', '%W');
+--------------------------------+
| DATE_FORMAT('2001-09-11', '%W') |
+--------------------------------+
| Tuesday                        |
+--------------------------------+
1 row in set (0.07 sec)
```

The supported formats and their abbreviations are listed below. Note that they bear many similarities to the Unix command date, but there are many differences.

Specifier	Description
%a	Abbreviated weekday name (Sun, Mon,and so on)
%b	Abbreviated month name (Jan, Feb, and so on)
%c	Numeric month value without a leading 0 in single-digit values (0, 1, 2, and so on)
%D	Day of the month with English suffix (0th, 1st, 2nd, 3rd, ...)
%d	Numeric day of the month with a leading 0 for single-digit values (00-31)
%e	Numeric day of the month with no leading 0 for single-digit values (0-31)
%f	Microseconds (000000..999999)
%H	Hour based on a 24-hour day and with a leading 0 (00 through 23)
%h	Hour based on two 12-hour segments with a leading 0 (01, 02, 03, and so on.)
%I	Two-digit hour based on two 12-hour segments (01, 02, 03, and so on)
%i	Numeric value of minutes with leading 0 (00, 01, 02, and so on)
%j	Three-digit day of the year (001, 002, through to 366)
%k	Hour based on 24-hour day and with no leading 0 (0, 1, 2, and so on)
%l	Hour based on two 12-hour segments and with no leading 0 (1, 2, and so on)
%M	Full name of the m (January, February, and so on)
%m	Numeric value of the month with leading 0 (00, 01, 02, and so on)
%p	AM or PM
%r	Time based on two 12-hour segments (hh:mm:ss followed by AM or PM)
%S	Seconds with leading 0 (00, 01, 02, and so on)
%s	Seconds with leading 0 (00, 01, 02, and so on)
%T	Time based on 24-hour clock (hh:mm:ss)
%U	Week (00 to 53), where Sunday is the first day of the week
%u	Week (00 to 53), where Monday is the first day of the week
%V	Week (01 to 53), where Sunday is the first day of the week; used with %X
%v	Week (01 to 53), where Monday is the first day of the week; used with %x
%W	Full name of day (Sunday through Saturday)
%w	Numeric value of the day of the week (0 [Sunday] through 6 [Saturday])
%X	Numeric, four-digit value of year for the week where Sunday is the first day of the week; used with %V

Specifier	Description
%x	Numeric, four-digit value of year for the week where Monday is the first day of the week; used with %v
%Y	Numeric, four-digit year
%y	Numeric, two-digit year
%%	The '%' character
%x	x for any "x" not listed above

These sundry formatting specifiers can then be combined for customized date formats. For example, a more human-friendly format of the aforementioned BBC report on the day the Berlin Wall fell (November 10, 1989 at 9 o'clock in the evening) might be formatted as follows:

```
mysql> SELECT DATE_FORMAT('1989-10-11 21:37:09:04', '%W %d %M %Y at %h:%m
%p and %s seconds');
+-----------------------------------------------------------------------
----------+
| DATE_FORMAT('1989-10-11 21:37:09:04', '%W %d %M %Y at %h:%m %p and %s
seconds') |
+-----------------------------------------------------------------------
----------+
| Wednesday 11 October 1989 at 09:10 PM and 09 seconds
|
+-----------------------------------------------------------------------
----------+
1 row in set, 1 warning (0.00 sec)
```

EXTRACT()

The EXTRACT() function returns a designated part from a date string. It requires only the unit needed and the date from which to draw the data.

```
mysql> SELECT EXTRACT(SECOND FROM '1989-10-11 21:00:09');
+---------------------------------------------+
| EXTRACT(SECOND FROM '1989-10-11 21:00:09') |
+---------------------------------------------+
|                                          9 |
+---------------------------------------------+
1 row in set (0.00 sec)
```

It works with the same units of time as DATE_ADD() and DATE_SUB().

TIME()

Like DATE(), the TIME() function is used to extract the time (as opposed to date) value from a DATE or DATETIME string. Where DATE() expects the relevant information to be first in the string, TIME() looks to the next set of data in the string. It accepts one argument—the string to be evaluated.

```
mysql> SELECT TIME('1989-10-11 21:00:09');
+----------------------------+
| TIME('1989-10-11 21:00:09') |
+----------------------------+
| 21:00:09                   |
+----------------------------+
1 row in set (0.00 sec)
```

It is further worth noting that the format of the time value is expected to be HH:MM:SS. If more information follows the time, even without a space delimiter, it is ignored.

```
mysql> SELECT TIME('1989-10-11 21:00:09abcdef');
+----------------------------------+
| TIME('1989-10-11 21:00:09abcdef') |
+----------------------------------+
| 21:00:09                         |
+----------------------------------+
1 row in set, 1 warning (0.00 sec)
```

Project: Logging user activity

Between July 2005 and January 2007, a major international clothing retailer suffered a data breach that amounted to the theft of 45.6 million credit card numbers. TJX is the parent company of stores such as TJMaxx, Bob's Stores, Marshalls, HomeGoods, and AJ Wright stores in the United States, as well as Winners and HomeSense stores in Canada, and TKMaxx stores across Europe. The credit card information from most, if not all, of these stores was electronically burgled over an undetermined amount of time. After the breach was discovered, TJX spokeswoman Sherry Lang went on record as saying: "*There is a lot of information we don't know, and may never be able to know, which is why this investigation has been so laborious*" (Sources: AP, CNET).

Computer forensic examinations rely extensively on computer logs. Without sufficient logging, as seen in the case of TJX, one cannot tell where things went wrong if catastrophe strikes. While MySQL keeps its own logs, the fact that these are known makes them a target for cleansing or deletion by anyone who would break into the system. In security terms, homogeneity makes breaking into a system much easier. Therefore, it is worth it to make one's system sufficiently different from out-of-the-box solutions, in order to render it difficult to break into.

> Note that while heterogeneity goes a long way to assuring the security of a system, a balance must be struck. One must be careful not to make the layout so complex or wildly unique such that it is difficult to administer either by the system administrator or by the other support staff, including new-hires.

Aside from such extreme circumstances, logging is also very helpful for debugging and for learning about your users' needs. Studying web logs indicates the browsing habits of users from entry to exit. Therefore, database logging can ensure that you know which data is being accessed most frequently and in what way.

By default, MySQL keeps its logging feature switched off. To turn it on, edit the my.cnf file (or my.ini on Windows). Under the section entitled *Logging and Replication*, you will find a number of logs that can be switched on or off at runtime. By default, these logs record a bevy of information that can be quite useful. Particularly detailed is the general query log. However, as the comment in the MySQL 5 default configuration reads:

```
# Be aware that this log type is a performance killer.
```

Information on each log type can be found in the MySQL manual at:
`http://dev.mysql.com/doc/refman/5.5/en/server-logs.html`

Suffice it to say, however, that MySQL logs can be helpful in their detail. However, that detail can be costly in server performance. For this reason, many MySQL installations do not use the general log, but only the error log. This records debugging information for the performance of MySQL—when it was started, when it stopped, and what, if any, errors caused the server to die. It is not oriented toward security or usage patterns per se.

It is therefore helpful to maintain one's own customized log. In this project, we will revise the project from the previous chapter to introduce such logging. The emendations will follow this specification:

- Log all MySQL activity sent through MySQLdb except its own
- The log will include the username and statement submitted for processing
- If the expected database and table are not available, they will be created
- All logging will occur before any MySQL statement is submitted
- If the logging is unsuccessful, the MySQL statement will not be processed
- The log infrastructure should be created by the program, not by a MySQL script or command-line

The log framework

For reasons of simplicity, the log for this project will be another MySQL database. In real-world deployment, you would want to store your log files off the local server for security reasons. Using the flexible connect() method of MySQL for Python, one can affect such a change of host with relative ease.

The database that we use is called logdb. Obviously, you can name yours as you like, as long as you are consistent in using that name.

Within logdb, the table for logging activity will be called entry_log. Its architecture is as follows:

```
mysql> describe entry_log;
```

Field	Type	Null	Key	Default	Extra
transaction	int(11)	NO	PRI	NULL	auto_increment
username	varchar(30)	NO		NULL	
query	varchar(256)	NO		NULL	
qtime	timestamp	NO		CURRENT_TIMESTAMP	

As the table shows, every transaction has its own identifier. In addition to the username and query, every entry will also be given a timestamp of when it was performed.

To affect this table, we will use the following CREATE statement as a basis:

```
CREATE TABLE entry_log(transaction INT NOT NULL AUTO_INCREMENT PRIMARY
KEY, username VARCHAR(30) NOT NULL, query VARCHAR(256) NOT NULL, qtime
TIMESTAMP);
```

However, we will not do this from within MySQL. The specification reads that we should not have to set up tables and databases in MySQL itself. Rather we will let Python and MySQLdb do the dirty work for us.

The logger() function

To affect the new logging functionality, we will create a separate function called logger(). It will accept as an argument the statement to be passed to MySQL and will also use the username submitted with the program.

For the sake of security, we will not allow any of the login details to be changed. They will be hardcoded into the connect() dialogue. So the first lines of the function will look like this:

```
def logger(statement):
    """Logs each transaction in a MySQL database."""
    mydb = MySQLdb.connect('localhost', 'loguser', 'secretphrase')
    cursor = mydb.cursor()
```

Note that we do not indicate the database we will use. This is because the login could fail if we specify a database that does not exist. Therefore, we need to ensure that the database exists before we try to use it.

Creating the database

Having created the cursor, we now need to ensure the database is available. For this, we will rely on the IF NOT EXISTS clause:

```
createdb = "CREATE DATABASE IF NOT EXISTS logdb"
```

As discussed in earlier chapters, this ensures that the command will not fail. For reasons of debugging, we then pass the results of cursor.execute() to a variable.

```
resdb = cursor.execute(createdb)
```

This ensures that we can learn the results of this execution if we need to. If there is any question of whether the database will be created, we can test the value of `resdb` and respond accordingly.

Using the database

Before we can issue any statements pertaining to the database or table, we need to tell MySQL that we will use the `logdb` database.

```
usedb = "USE logdb"
resuse = cursor.execute(usedb)
```

Again, by storing the results of each `execute()` call, we are able to test the success of the process.

Creating the table

With the database created, we next need to ensure that the table is available. We will use the preceding statement, but again include the `IF NOT EXISTS` clause:

```
createtb = "CREATE TABLE IF NOT EXISTS entry_log(transaction INT
UNSIGNED NOT NULL AUTO_INCREMENT PRIMARY KEY, username VARCHAR(30) NOT
NULL, query VARCHAR(256) NOT NULL, qtime TIMESTAMP)"
restb = cursor.execute(createtb)
```

The result is a flexible way of ensuring that the database `logdb` and the table `entry_log` are available to us.

As this function will log all activity, we can test the values one-by-one if something is awry. For example, if no queries are being processed and no log entries made, we are not guaranteed that Python or MySQL will throw an error. However, we can test each of the `resdb`, `resuse`, and `restb` values and print out messages upon success. That will allow us to see how far the program goes before exiting, thus indicating the point of error.

Forming the INSERT statement

Having the database infrastructure in place, we can then form and execute an `INSERT` statement to log the activity. As previously indicated, `logger()` will take the statement value and submit it. We will also use the global value of the username. In a CGI implementation, this latter value may be user. In PHP, it will be referenced as `opt.user` as part of the options parsed by `optparse`.

An important issue when passing a MySQL statement as part of another MySQL statement is the issue of quotation marks—whether single or double. Therefore, we need to message the value of statement before we submit it as part of the INSERT statement for logdb.

```
statement = statement.replace("'", "\\'")
statement = statement.replace('"', '\\"')
statement = "'" + statement + "'"
user = "'" + opt.user + "'"
```

Here we use Python's ability to handle arguments in either single or double quotes to replace—first the single quotes and then the double in the value statement. In order to ensure the quotes are properly escaped in the ensuing MySQL statement, we must escape the escape character (\) by reduplicating it.

Then we sandwich each of the statement and opt.user (or user) values between quotes and assign them to statement and user, respectively. This is in preparation for the VALUES field in the INSERT statement.

Finally, we form the statement to be executed:

```
entry = "INSERT INTO entry_log(username, query) VALUES(%s, %s)"
% (user, statement)
```

And later we pass it to execute()

```
reslog = cursor.execute(entry)
```

As we will see in the next section, the results saved to reslog are important for the successful deployment of the log functionality. For now, however, we will simply return that value as the end product of the function.

```
return reslog
```

Ensure logging occurs

As mentioned in the specification for this project, the log must record all activity passed to MySQL. The natural implication of this requirement is to modify the execute() function to call logger() and not to process any statement until logger() records it successfully.

First we pass the statement received by execute() to logger() as the first thing to be done in execute():

```
def execute(statement, cursor, type):
    """Attempts execution of the statement."""
    reslog = logger(statement)
```

Next, we test the value of `reslog`. Recall that every successful `INSERT` statement returns a value of 1 if successful. So we can affect the test with a switch called success.

```
if reslog == 1:
    success = 1
else:
    success = 0
```

This `if...else` structure determines whether to turn success on or off. As usual, `True` and `False` can be used in lieu of 1 and 0, respectively.

For the effects of the switch to be implemented, we then need to change the while statement on which `execute()` operates. Currently, it reads as:

```
while True:
```

We then need to change it to read:

```
while success == 1:
```

Alternatively, we could just use one of the following conditionals:

```
while success
```

Or, we can use:

```
while reslog > 0
```

From this point, `execute()` will only process statements after `logger()` has recorded them. As we hardcoded everything in `logger()` that we could, this renders it much more secure than a dynamic log function.

Room to grow

While this program works, there are more than a few ways to improve it. Obviously, before you use it in the wild, you should change the host used by `connect()` in `logger()`. Logs should never be in the same place as the activity they record.

Other points for improvement that you might consider trying out are:

- Instead of writing to a database, write the log to a file and post it to a remote machine
- Record the user's IP address by searching the web server's logs
- Keep separate logs for each user
- Record whether a query successfully returned any hits or was erroneous

- Record unsuccessful logins, sending an email to the database administrator if too many are received in the name of the same user within a certain amount of time

A lot of information will be logged by the likes of the web server, MySQL itself, and other logging applications in the stack. However, this program allows you to customize what information you log, combining it with other information that the others may not record.

Summary

In this chapter, we have covered how to log user activity with MySQL for Python. We have seen:

- The several data types for date and time that MySQL supports
- When different data types should be used and with what format and range
- The date and time functions that can be accessed through MySQL for Python
- Frequently used functions for handling matters of date and time

In the next chapter, we will look at using aggregate functions in MySQL for Python.

10
Aggregate Functions and Clauses

It is not overstating things to say that MySQL queries can return a significant amount of data. As we have seen with the SELECT statement, using clauses such as WHERE reduces the number of hits that MySQL returns. Similarly, one can reduce the amount of data returned by specifying the columns to be returned. Such features save us from having to write our own algorithms to weed through the data. However, even after narrowing the data, we sometimes still need to perform calculations with the data for purposes such as tallying a sum, averaging out results, or finding the range of a dataset. MySQL saves us this trouble as well, by providing functions that return the answers to our questions without bothering us with the data. These summative operations are called **aggregate functions**.

In this chapter, we will see how:

- MySQL saves us time and effort by pre-processing data
- To perform several calculations using MySQL's optimized algorithms
- To group and order returned data by column

The project for this chapter will once again build on the project from the earlier chapters. After becoming more conversant with MySQL's aggregate functions and learning how to use them in Python, we will add some aggregate functionality to the web-based administration program.

Calculations in MySQL

Letting the database server take the burden of calculations can reduce latency across a network. Most web servers, for example, not only serve up web pages, but also perform the processing for any scripts used to form those pages. If the script needs to perform calculations of large amounts of data, the processing time of the server will increase accordingly. Similar bottlenecks can occur on LANs and even desktop systems that are normally optimized for user-based interactions, not heavy data processing.

Computer clusters are another matter altogether. Depending on the size of the cluster, one can lay much heavier loads on individual machines and the cluster will be able to bear the burden. While using a cluster for processing data takes the load off the database server, this can still result in latency as one part of the processing machinery (the database) may operate much slower than the rest of the parts.

MySQL provides several optimized ways of performing calculations on data. Their functionality spans from statistics to bitwise operations, but the most commonly used functions are:

- `COUNT()`
- `SUM()`
- `MAX()`
- `MIN()`
- `AVG()`

A listing of the less frequently used numeric functions can be found at `http://dev.mysql.com/doc/refman/5.5/en/group-by-functions.html`

Each of these functions is called by inserting the function's name and argument immediately after `SELECT`. The function call stands in lieu of the column names to be returned.

In the subsequent sections, we will be using the film table of the `sakila` database.

COUNT()

The COUNT() function returns the number of records affected. It does not return the data itself. Its basic syntax is:

```
SELECT COUNT(<column name>) FROM <table name>;
```

In practice, it looks like this:

```
SELECT COUNT(title) FROM film;
```

This query returns the following results:

```
+--------------+
| COUNT(title) |
+--------------+
|         1000 |
+--------------+
```

In contrast, consider a table such as follows:

```
+----+-------------------+------+
| ID | activity          | year |
+----+-------------------+------+
|  1 | NULL              | 2010 |
|  2 | learn piano       | 2009 |
|  3 | climb Kilimanjaro | 2008 |
|  4 | learn Python      | 2005 |
|  5 | tour outerspace   | NULL |
+----+-------------------+------+
```

If we run a similar query against these five records, we get different results:

```
SELECT COUNT(activity) FROM diarytb;
```

The preceding statement returns the following results:

```
+-----------------+
| COUNT(activity) |
+-----------------+
|               4 |
+-----------------+
1 row in set (0.00 sec)
```

The COUNT() function returns a count of only non-NULL values by default. Similar results would therefore be returned for the following:

```
SELECT COUNT(year) FROM diarytb;
```

To return both non-NULL and NULL values, we must use a universal quantifier:

```
SELECT COUNT(*) FROM diarytb;
```

```
+----------+
| COUNT(*) |
+----------+
|        5 |
+----------+
```

In the case of the film table from sakila, no record was NULL. Therefore, the number of returned records was the same as the total number of records in the table.

 As you may notice, COUNT() does not care if the data is alphabetic or numeric, it merely counts affected records. Of all of the functions mentioned, COUNT(), MAX(), and MIN() are the only ones that can handle string data.

SUM()

As the name suggests, SUM() returns the total of a series of numeric values. The basic syntax is as follows:

```
SELECT SUM(<column name>) FROM <table name>;
```

SUM() only works on numeric values. If one passes string values to it, MySQL will throw an error.

Using sakila again, we can ascertain the length of all films in the table with the following query:

```
SELECT SUM(length) FROM film;
```

The result is the cumulative length in whatever unit is presumed for the column, in this case, minutes:

```
+-------------+
| SUM(length) |
+-------------+
|      115272 |
+-------------+
```

MAX()

The MAX() function takes a column as its argument and returns the largest value of the query results. The basic syntax of MAX() is as follows:

```
SELECT MAX(<column name>) FROM <table name>;
```

In practice, it looks like this:

```
SELECT MAX(length) FROM film;
```

Which returns the following results from sakila:

```
+-------------+
| MAX(length) |
+-------------+
|         185 |
+-------------+
```

Obviously, MAX() returns the highest number for numeric values. For string values, however, it returns the highest index value of a set of strings.

```
mysql> SELECT MAX(title) FROM film;
+------------+
| MAX(title) |
+------------+
| ZORRO ARK  |
+------------+
1 row in set (0.00 sec)
```

 For information on how MySQL indexes strings, see the MySQL manual: http://dev.mysql.com/doc/refman/5.5/en/mysql-indexes.html

If no records are affected, MAX() returns NULL.

```
mysql> SELECT MAX(title) FROM film WHERE title='CARMAGEDDON';
+------------+
| MAX(title) |
+------------+
| NULL       |
+------------+
```

MIN()

The MIN() function is the obvious complement to MAX() and performs similarly to it. As with MAX(), MIN() follows the SELECT keyword and takes a column name as an argument:

```
SELECT MIN(<column name>) FROM <table name>;
```

In sakila, we can get the minimum running time as follows:

```
mysql> SELECT MIN(length) FROM film;
+-------------+
| MIN(length) |
+-------------+
|          46 |
+-------------+
```

As with MAX(), MIN() also accepts strings and returns the string with the lowest index value:

```
mysql> SELECT MIN(title) FROM film;
+------------------+
| MIN(title)       |
+------------------+
| ACADEMY DINOSAUR |
+------------------+
```

AVG()

The AVG() function returns the mean of a numeric range. It follows the same format as the other aggregate functions in its syntax:

```
SELECT AVG(<column name>) FROM <table name>;
```

The results of AVG() are calculated by dividing the sum of the resulting numeric series by the number of records affected.

```
mysql> SELECT AVG(length) FROM film;
+-------------+
| AVG(length) |
+-------------+
|    115.2720 |
+-------------+
```

The different kinds of average

It is important to note what kind of average is meant by MySQL's AVG() function. The English word 'average' can mean any of three things: mean, median, or mode. Only mean is implied by MySQL's AVG().

Mean

Mean is calculated by dividing the sum of a numeric series by the number of items in that series. For the film table of sakila, this is 115272 ÷ 1000, or 115.2720.

Median

Median is the middle item of a series (for example, the sixth item of a series of eleven items). If the number of items is odd, the middle item is the median. If the number of items is even, the median is the average of the two numbers in the middle of the series. A simple example of how to determine the median of an odd number of items is the following query:

```
SELECT <column> FROM <table> ORDER BY <column> DESC LIMIT <half the
total number of items>, 1;
```

To determine the median of an even number of items we limit the results by two:

```
SELECT <column> FROM <table> ORDER BY <column> DESC LIMIT <half the
total number of items>, 2;
```

and then take the mean of the two results.

In the case of the film table of `sakila`, this query will return two instances of the same value. Instead, one must broaden the range until a different number is returned. Then one takes the mean of the two unique values.

```
mysql> select length from film order by length limit 500, 5;
+--------+
| length |
+--------+
|    114 |
|    114 |
|    114 |
|    114 |
|    115 |
+--------+
```

The median is then (114 + 115) ÷ 2, or 114.5.

Mode

Mode is the item that occurs most frequently in a series, of which there may be none or more than one. If all values in the series are unique, there is no mode. If more than one value has the highest rate of occurrence, there is more than one mode. As a result, modes are tricky to ascertain through MySQL itself. However, the following will work in many circumstances:

```
SELECT COUNT(value) AS mode FROM table GROUP BY value ORDER BY mode
DESC LIMIT 1;
```

If no results are to be returned, `AVG()` returns `NULL`.

```
SELECT AVG(release_year) FROM film WHERE title='The Osterman Weekend';
```

```
+-------------------+
| AVG(release_year) |
+-------------------+
|              NULL |
+-------------------+
```

Trimming results

MySQL allows for two different ways of trimming results when using aggregate functions. One is a keyword that removes redundant data. The other is a function that pools the data into a single string value.

DISTINCT

The purpose of DISTINCT is to ensure that all results are unique. The examples above do not discriminate between duplicate values. Each value is treated as a separate record without quantitative comparison to the others, thus allowing for redundancy in the results.

This redundancy works well when comprehensiveness is required but can otherwise skew the results of a query. For example, if we want to know how many unique ratings are used in the film table of sakila, we would not want to use this query:

```
SELECT COUNT(rating) FROM film;
```

The results show every record that has a value for the rating column.

```
+---------------+
| COUNT(rating) |
+---------------+
|          1000 |
+---------------+
```

Instead of retrieving the actual values and process 1000 records in our program, we can pass the burden onto the MySQL server by using the DISTINCT keyword:

```
SELECT COUNT(DISTINCT rating) FROM film;
```

This results in a much smaller return:

```
+------------------------+
| COUNT(DISTINCT rating) |
+------------------------+
|                      5 |
+------------------------+
```

If we want to return the ratings themselves, we can use DISTINCT without the COUNT() function:

```
SELECT DISTINCT rating FROM film;
```

The results will be as follows:

```
+--------+
| rating |
+--------+
| PG     |
| G      |
| NC-17  |
| PG-13  |
| R      |
+--------+
```

By default, the results are returned in the order they appear in the table. To sort them otherwise, use the ORDER BY function that is detailed later in this chapter.

Of the functions discussed earlier in this chapter, DISTINCT can be used with the following:

- COUNT()
- MAX()
- MIN()
- AVG()

While the DISTINCT keyword can be used with MAX() and MIN(), the benefits are negligible. The MAX() function finds the highest value of a dataset and MIN() the lowest. As DISTINCT simply weeds out the duplicates, there is no significant benefit to be had in using it. The net results are the same.

When using DISTINCT with AVG(), however, the results can be dramatically affected. For example, the raw average (that is, mean) length of the records in film is returned as follows:

```
mysql> SELECT AVG(length) FROM film;
+-------------+
| AVG(length) |
+-------------+
|    115.2720 |
+-------------+
```

However, if we sort out the duplicate lengths, we get a different value.

```
mysql> SELECT AVG(DISTINCT length) FROM film;
+----------------------+
| AVG(DISTINCT length) |
+----------------------+
|             115.5000 |
+----------------------+
```

Consequently, it is important to know which value you are seeking and also to form the query accordingly.

GROUP_CONCAT()

The GROUP_CONCAT() function collates all of the results into a single string value and returns it. Its basic syntax is:

```
SELECT GROUP_CONCAT(<column name>) FROM <table name>;
```

In practice, it looks like this:

```
SELECT GROUP_CONCAT(length) FROM film;
```

The results of this query will be a lot of MySQL formatting that sandwiches a series of values:

```
|  86,48,50,117,130,169,62,54,114,63,126,136,150,94,46,180,82,57,113,
79,129,85,92,181,74,86,179,91,168,82,92,119,153,62,147,127,121,68, 99,
148,137,170,170,113,83,108,153,118,162,182,75,173,87,113,65,129,90,122
,160,89,175,106,73,151,100,53,77,122,85,142,100,93,150,162,163,103,61,
85,114,148,103,71,50,102,63,121,76,179,63,63,98,72,121,176,123,169,56,
73,136,161,73,60,133,119,125,61,63,67,89,53,52,120,75,61,167,70,135,85
,176,92,151,114,85,163,61,179,112,183,179,110,152,114,117,51,70,146,66
,71,114,87,185,122,142,61,124,107,101,132,150,101,143,90,165,81,150,16
4,143,124,58,65,70,95,139,55,70,149,109,67,76, 120,59,112,65,180,122,8
7,172,115,173,184,166,185,112,92,146,64,57,136,139,172,143,50,153,104,
112,69,112,184,56,133,176,161,84,106,58,144,121,89,99,130,165,185,104,
59,57,113,120,122,51,106,100,64,76,81, 76,56,88,143,87,107,63,147,141,
94,68,100,47,57,122,120,125,68,49, 139,177,154,47,177,176,170,133,135,
61,159,175,178,110,96,116,132, 171,119,154,101,168,141,140,96,98,85,14
8,153,107,67,85,115,126,155,152,177,143,92,85,77,51,1 |
```

When interacting with MySQL from Python, this can be very helpful for getting all of the results in one go. If you parse the results, it is important to note that MySQL does not insert spaces into the results. Rather, each comma follows or precedes each value immediately.

Specifying the delimiter

If commas are not your delimiter of choice, GROUP_CONCAT() allows you to specify the delimiter by using the SEPARATOR keyword followed by the delimiter in quotes.

```
mysql> SELECT GROUP_CONCAT(length SEPARATOR ':') FROM film;
```

This command returns the same values separated by colons instead of commas.

 It is important to note that the delimiter only goes between values, so we cannot use SEPARATOR to format the results for printing. No delimiter would go before the first value.

The GROUP_CONCAT() function further allows multi-character delimiters. For example:

```
mysql> SELECT GROUP_CONCAT(length SEPARATOR ' and ') FROM film;
```

The command returns the following:

```
| 86 and 48 and 50 and 117 and 130 and 169 and 62 and 54 and 114 and
63 and 126 and 136 and 150 and 94 and 46 and 180 and 82 and 57 and 113
and 79 and 129 and 85 and 92 and 181 and 74 and 86 and 179 and 91 and
168 and 82 and 92 and 119 and 153 and 62 and 147 and 127 and 121 and
68 and 99 and 148 and 137 and 170 and 170 and 113 and 83 and 108 and
153 and 118 and 162 and 182 and 75 and 173 and 87 and 113 and 65 and
129 and 90 and 122 and 160 and 89 and 175 and 106 and 73 and 151 and
100 and 53 and 77 and 122 and 85 and 142 and 100 and 93 and 150 and
162 and 163 and 103 and 61 and 85 and 114 and 148 and 103 and 71 and
50 and 102 and 63 and 121 and 76 and 179 and 63 and 63 and 98 and 72
and 121 and 176 and 123 and 169 and 56 and 73 and 136 and 161 and 73
and 60 and 133 and 119 and 125 and 61 and 63 and 67 and 89 and 53 and
52 and 120 and 75 and 61 and 167 and 70 and 135 and 85 and 176 and 92
and 151 and 114 and 85 and 163 and 61 and 179 and 112 and 183 and 179
and 110 and 152 and 114 and 117 and 51 and 70 and 146 a |
```

Oops! MySQL has cut off our results in midstream. By default, GROUP_CONCAT() returns a maximum length of 1024 characters. When the results hit that limit, MySQL truncates the value.

Customizing the maximum length

When dealing with large amounts of results, a limit of 1024 can be very frustrating. One way around this is to set the maximum length of GROUP_CONCAT() to a higher value for your MySQL session. We do this by passing the following code inside of a MySQL shell:

```
SET SESSION group_concat_max_len = 10240;
```

Now, we can pass the same query as before and get the results in their entirety. Any value can be passed here, but this sets the length to ten times the default. Whatever value we set, the amount of data transported is still bound by the local value for `max_allowed_packet`, which defaults to 1 GB. On MySQL versions prior to 5.084, however, we can set that variable, too, with this command:

```
SET SESSION max_allowed_packet = 10000;
```

As of MySQL 5.0.84, `max_allowed_packet` is available on a read-only basis; changes must therefore be affected via a configuration file (or via a command-line option, if available).

> For more on MySQL system variables, see: `http://dev.mysql.com/doc/refman/5.0/en/server-system-variables.html`

If you do not know which version of MySQL you are using or are unsure of the relevant configuration, the following command will show whether your change has taken effect:

```
SHOW VARIABLES LIKE 'max_allowed_packet';
```

If you are uncertain what a system variable is called, you can show all of them:

```
SHOW VARIABLES;
```

> To differentiate between what variables pertain to the current session and, which pertain to the entire database environment, use the keywords SESSION and GLOBAL, respectively:
> ```
> SHOW SESSION VARIABLES;
> SHOW GLOBAL VARIABLES;
> ```

Using GROUP_CONCAT() with DISTINCT

The GROUP_CONCAT() function only concatenates results, it does not sort them. As a result, we can wind up with a lot more data than we need. To refine the data further, we can use DISTINCT. Compare the results of these two queries:

```
mysql> SELECT GROUP_CONCAT(length) FROM film;
```

The preceding command returns:

```
| 86,48,50,117,130,169,62,54,114,63,126,136,150,94,46,180,82,57,113,
79,129,85,92,181,74,86,179,91,168,82,92,119,153,62,147,127,121,68,
99,148,137,170,170,113,83,108,153,118,162,182,75,173,87,113,65,129,90,
122,160,89,175,106,73,151,100,53,77,122,85,142,100,93,150,162,163,103,
61,85,114,148,103,71,50,102,63,121,76,179,63,63,98,72,121,176,123,169,
56,73,136,161,73,60,133,119,125,61,63,67,89,53,52,120,75,61,167,70,135
,85,176,92,151,114,85,163,61,179,112,183,179,110,152,114,117,51,70,146
,66,71,114,87,185,122,142,61,124,107,101,132,150,101,143,90,165,81,150
,164,143,124,58,65,70,95,139,55,70,149,109,67,76, 120,59,112,65,180,12
2,87,172,115,173,184,166,185,112,92,146,64,57,136,139,172,143,50,153,1
04,112,69,112,184,56,133,176,161,84,106,58,144,121,89,99,130,165,185,1
04,59,57,113,120,122,51,106,100,64,76,81,76,56,88,143,87,107,63,147,14
1,94,68,100,47,57,122,120,125,68,49,139,177,154,47,177,176,170,133,135
,61,159,175,178,110,96,116,132,171,119,154,101,168,141,140,96,98,85,14
8,153,107,67,85,115,126,155,152,177,143,92,85,77,51,1 |
```

but

```
mysql> SELECT GROUP_CONCAT(DISTINCT length) FROM film;
```

returns a concatenation of only the unique values, amounting to less than half the length:

```
| 86,48,50,117,130,169,62,54,114,63,126,136,150,94,46,180,82,57,113,
79,129,85,92,181,74,179,91,168,119,153,147,127,121,68,99,148,137,170,8
3,108,118,162,182,75,173,87,65,90,122,160,89,175,106,73,151,100,53,77,
142,93,163,103,61,71,102,76,98,72,176,123,56,161,60,133,125,67,52,120,
167,70,135,112,183,110,152,51,146,66,185,124,107,101,132, 143,165,81,1
64,58,95,139,55,149,109,59,172,115,184,166,64,104,69,84,144,88,141,47,
49,177,154,159,178,96,116,171,140,155,158,174,138,97,131,156,80,145,11
1,128,157,78,105,134 |
```

To further sort the results of GROUP_CONCAT(), we need to indicate the order by which to sort the results. For this, we turn to server-side sorting in the next section.

Server-side sorting in MySQL

When sorting results, MySQL allows for two types of ordering: by group and by item. Below, we look at each in turn in terms of their respective clauses:

- GROUP BY
- ORDER BY

Despite their syntactical similarities, each has its distinct applications and limitations.

GROUP BY

The GROUP BY clause is used to organize results according to the structure of the data returned. The clause itself is appended to the end of the SELECT statement. The basic syntax is:

```
SELECT <column name(s)> FROM <table name> GROUP BY <column name as key>;
```

As a rule, GROUP BY cannot be used in conjunction with a universal quantifier ('*') instead of the column name(s). Rather, the column used as the key for sorting must be stated among the column names indicated for the query.

Using the world database, we can ascertain what the database records as the official language of each country in the world, with the following query:

```
SELECT CountryCode, Language FROM CountryLanguage WHERE IsOfficial='T' GROUP BY CountryCode;
```

The results are indexed alphabetically according to the first column retrieved. As one might imagine, they run quite long. If we wanted to trim the results to the language of German, we can use a WHERE clause:

```
SELECT CountryCode, Language, Percentage FROM CountryLanguage WHERE Language LIKE 'German' AND IsOfficial='T' GROUP BY CountryCode;
```

The results will be:

```
+-------------+----------+------------+
| CountryCode | Language | Percentage |
+-------------+----------+------------+
| AUT         | German   |       92.0 |
| BEL         | German   |        1.0 |
| CHE         | German   |       63.6 |
| DEU         | German   |       91.3 |
| LIE         | German   |       89.0 |
| LUX         | German   |        2.3 |
+-------------+----------+------------+
```

Using the sakila database, we can use GROUP BY to ascertain how long most films are borrowed. The rental_duration for any film is between three and seven days. Therefore, we key the sorting to that column and count the number of corresponding records.

```
SELECT rental_duration, COUNT(title) FROM film GROUP BY rental_duration;
```

The result is:

```
+-----------------+--------------+
| rental_duration | COUNT(title) |
+-----------------+--------------+
|               3 |          203 |
|               4 |          203 |
|               5 |          191 |
|               6 |          212 |
|               7 |          191 |
+-----------------+--------------+
```

We can tell from these results that most films are returned within four days. If we had used the AVG() function, however, we would have received different results:

```
mysql> SELECT AVG(rental_duration) FROM film;
+----------------------+
| AVG(rental_duration) |
+----------------------+
|               4.9850 |
+----------------------+
```

Therefore, we can see (again) that the mean is not always the best average to take.

ORDER BY

Unlike GROUP BY, the ORDER BY clause causes no categorization whatsoever. Rather, it strictly sorts the records returned according to an indicated pattern. Where the 1000 titles of film will result in a single row if grouped by release_year, the ORDER BY clause will return 1000 records.

The basic syntax for this clause is:

```
SELECT <column name> FROM <table name> ORDER BY <column name>;
```

Using a universal quantifier

The ORDER BY clause also differs from GROUP BY in that it works with universal quantification of the columns selected. So rather than specify the columns to be returned, one can simply use the asterisk; however, one must still use a valid column name as a key for the sorting. So to adopt the GROUP BY example, we can use:

```
SELECT rental_duration, title FROM film ORDER BY rental_duration;
```

We can get the rental duration and title from `film` sorted according to increased rental periods. In addition, we can return all columns with the following:

```
SELECT * FROM film ORDER BY rental_duration;
```

Sorting alphabetically or from low-to-high

MySQL treats strings according to their index equivalents. Therefore, alphabetic sorting is the same as sorting in ascending order. To do so, we use the `ASC` keyword immediately after the column to be used as a key. The following returns the results in alphabetical order by title:

```
SELECT title, rating, length FROM film WHERE title LIKE 'Y%' ORDER BY
title ASC;
```

To keep all the results on screen, this example uses a `WHERE` clause to reduce the relevant results to film titles that begin with 'Y'. The result of this query is:

```
+-----------------+--------+--------+
| title           | rating | length |
+-----------------+--------+--------+
| YENTL IDAHO     | R      |     86 |
| YOUNG LANGUAGE  | G      |    183 |
| YOUTH KICK      | NC-17  |    179 |
+-----------------+--------+--------+
```

If we trade out the `WHERE` clause for a `LIMIT` clause at the end of the statement, we can learn the top ten of a series very quickly. This query returns the ten shortest films in the `sakila` database:

```
SELECT title, rating, length FROM film ORDER BY length ASC LIMIT 10;
```

The results are as follows:

```
+---------------------+--------+--------+
| title               | rating | length |
+---------------------+--------+--------+
| ALIEN CENTER        | NC-17  |     46 |
| IRON MOON           | PG     |     46 |
| KWAI HOMEWARD       | PG-13  |     46 |
| LABYRINTH LEAGUE    | PG-13  |     46 |
| RIDGEMONT SUBMARINE | PG-13  |     46 |
| DIVORCE SHINING     | G      |     47 |
| DOWNHILL ENOUGH     | G      |     47 |
| HALLOWEEN NUTS      | PG-13  |     47 |
| HANOVER GALAXY      | NC-17  |     47 |
| HAWK CHILL          | PG-13  |     47 |
+---------------------+--------+--------+
```

Reversing the alphabet or sorting high-to-low

Where ASC overtly indicates that sorting should be in ascending order, we can reverse that sort with the DESC keyword. Adapting the last example, we can ascertain the twenty longest films in the sakila database with the following query:

```
SELECT title, rating, length FROM film ORDER BY length DESC LIMIT 20;
```

The results are as follows:

```
+--------------------+--------+--------+
| title              | rating | length |
+--------------------+--------+--------+
| CHICAGO NORTH      | PG-13  |    185 |
| CONTROL ANTHEM     | G      |    185 |
| DARN FORRESTER     | G      |    185 |
| GANGS PRIDE        | PG-13  |    185 |
| HOME PITY          | R      |    185 |
| MUSCLE BRIGHT      | G      |    185 |
| POND SEATTLE       | PG-13  |    185 |
| SOLDIERS EVOLUTION | R      |    185 |
| SWEET BROTHERHOOD  | R      |    185 |
| WORST BANGER       | PG     |    185 |
| CONSPIRACY SPIRIT  | PG-13  |    184 |
| CRYSTAL BREAKING   | NC-17  |    184 |
| KING EVOLUTION     | NC-17  |    184 |
| MOONWALKER FOOL    | G      |    184 |
| SMOOCHY CONTROL    | R      |    184 |
| SONS INTERVIEW     | NC-17  |    184 |
| SORORITY QUEEN     | NC-17  |    184 |
| THEORY MERMAID     | PG-13  |    184 |
| CATCH AMISTAD      | G      |    183 |
| FRONTIER CABIN     | PG-13  |    183 |
+--------------------+--------+--------+
```

> You will notice that all of the ten longest films have the same length. To determine the twenty longest lengths in the database, we would need to use a GROUP BY clause in conjunction with GROUP_CONCAT:
>
> SELECT GROUP_CONCAT(title), rating, GROUP_CONCAT(DISTINCT length) FROM film GROUP BY length DESC LIMIT 20;
>
> The ORDER BY clause cannot be used in conjunction with the calculating and concatenating functions.

Like sorting in ascending order, sorting in descending order uses index values for strings. The index value of certain strings, however, will be determined by how the table is created. For example, if we run this query against sakila:

```
SELECT title, rating, length FROM film WHERE title LIKE 'WO%' ORDER BY rating ASC;
```

We get all film titles that begin with WO sorted by rating, supposedly in ascending order. However, it is not in that order. The results are as follows:

```
+-----------------------+--------+--------+
| title                 | rating | length |
+-----------------------+--------+--------+
| WORST BANGER          | PG     |    185 |
| WON DARES             | PG     |    105 |
| WONDERLAND CHRISTMAS  | PG     |    111 |
| WORDS HUNTER          | PG     |    116 |
| WORLD LEATHERNECKS    | PG-13  |    171 |
| WOMEN DORADO          | R      |    126 |
| WORKING MICROCOSMOS   | R      |     74 |
| WORKER TARZAN         | R      |    139 |
| WONKA SEA             | NC-17  |     85 |
| WONDERFUL DROP        | NC-17  |    126 |
| WOLVES DESIRE         | NC-17  |     55 |
+-----------------------+--------+--------+
```

The NC-17 ratings follow after, not before the others. The reason for this is that the rating column is of type enum. This is a type of string for which the values are enumerated at the time the table is created and the column specified. The index value for such types follows the order in which the options were specified. In the case of film, we can learn the sequence from the description. Using DESCRIBE FILM, the data type for rating is revealed to be:

```
enum('G','PG','PG-13','R','NC-17')
```

Therefore, MySQL's sorting of the ratings column will always be according to this order.

Sorting with multiple keys

The ORDER BY clause can be used with multiple keys to provide a multi-tiered sorting process.

```
SELECT rating, title, length FROM film ORDER BY rating, length;
```

It returns all columns of film sorted first by rating then by title.

To use the ASC and DESC keywords, we simply place them after the relevant key. So rating can be in ascending order and length in descending with the following query:

```
SELECT rating, title, length FROM film ORDER BY rating ASC, length
DESC;
```

Putting it in Python

As with most programming languages, the more one knows about the data and data structure, the better one can program to handle it. This is at least doubly true for database programming with aggregate functions and clauses such as those which we cover in this chapter.

Putting the SELECT statement into Python is not particularly complex, but handling the results intelligently requires a knowledge of their format. Again, setting up a basic database session in Python would look like this:

```
#!/usr/bin/env python

import MySQLdb

mydb = MySQLdb.connect('localhost', 'skipper', 'secret', 'sakila')
cursor = mydb.cursor()
```

For the statement to be run against sakila, we can use the following:

```
statement = """SELECT * FROM film WHERE title LIKE 'Z%'
                    ORDER BY rating ASC"""
```

Then we execute it:

```
runit = cursor.execute(statement)
fetch = cursor.fetchall()
```

If, at this point, we just print the value of `fetch`, we get a lot of a database formatting:

```
print fetch
((999, 'ZOOLANDER FICTION', 'A Fateful Reflection of a Waitress
And a Boat who must Discover a Sumo Wrestler in Ancient China',
2006, 1, None, 5, Decimal("2.99"), 101, Decimal("28.99"), 'R',
'Trailers,Deleted Scenes', datetime.datetime(2006, 2, 15, 5, 3,
42)), (998, 'ZHIVAGO CORE', 'A Fateful Yarn of a Composer And a Man
who must Face a Boy in The Canadian Rockies', 2006, 1, None, 6,
Decimal("0.99"), 105, Decimal("10.99"), 'NC-17', 'Deleted Scenes',
datetime.datetime(2006, 2, 15, 5, 3, 42)), (1000, 'ZORRO ARK', 'A
Intrepid Panorama of a Mad Scientist And a Boy who must Redeem
a Boy in A Monastery', 2006, 1, None, 3, Decimal("4.99"), 50,
Decimal("18.99"), 'NC-17', 'Trailers,Commentaries,Behind the Scenes',
datetime.datetime(2006, 2, 15, 5, 3, 42)))
```

Obviously, this is less than ideal. If we did not know the format of the data, we would be left to abstract the data handling. This would typically result in verbose and inefficient code.

Ideally, we should modify our SELECT statement to return only the data that we want. In this case, we are only interested in the `rating`, `title`, and `length`. So we should change the SELECT statement accordingly:

```
statement = """SELECT rating, title, length FROM film
                WHERE title LIKE 'Z%'
                ORDER BY rating ASC"""
```

This gives us more managable data. Each record is now three fields long. However, the results are still obtuse; being formatted with parentheses and commas obfuscates the data. Better then to use a `for` loop to prepare the data:

```
for i in fetch:
    print i[0],"\t", i[2],"\t", i[1]
```

While we are at it, we can preface that for a loop with a `print` statement that reflects the column headers:

```
print "Rating \tLength \tTitle"
```

The result is easier on the eyes and therefore more user-friendly:

```
Rating  Length  Title
R       101     ZOOLANDER FICTION

NC-17   105     ZHIVAGO CORE

NC-17   50      ZORRO ARK
```

Project: Incorporating aggregate functions

Building support for aggregate functions into our web application requires some revision of code that we have already written. As shown in this chapter, all aggregate functions work with the SELECT keyword. We will thus need to change how we support that kind of query. By the end of this section, we will build the following functionality into the web application:

- Support for all calculating functions
- Support for use of DISTINCT in conjunction with calculating functions
- Allowance for sorting using either ORDER BY or GROUP BY
- Return results in a tabular format

The order of development when revising a project should be inside out. Revise the relevant function and develop outward, through the main() function. After we code the initial variable assignments, we can then move on to revise the web interface to support the new functionality. The virtue of this process is that we do not introduce variables without support—to do so would seed security and stability issues.

Adding to qaction()

As all of our new functionality deals with the SELECT statement, we will need to revisit the qaction() function of the application. Currently, the code looks like this:

```
def qaction(qact, db, tb, columns, values, user, password):
    """Forms SELECT and INSERT statements, passes them to execute(),
and returns the affected rows."""
    cursor = connection(user, password, db)

    tname = tb + "("
    columns = columns.split(',')
    values = values.split(',')
    cols = ""
    vals = ""
    for i in xrange(0, len(columns)):
        col = columns[i].strip()
        val = values[i].strip()
        cols = cols + col
        vals = vals + "'" + val + "'"
        if i != len(columns)-1:
            cols = cols + ", "
```

```
            vals = vals + ", "
    if qact == "select":
        statement = "SELECT * FROM %s WHERE %s = %s" %(tb, cols, vals)
        results = execute(statement, cursor, 'select')
    elif qact == "insert":
        statement = "INSERT INTO %s (%s) VALUES (%s)" %(tb, cols,
vals)
        results = execute(statement, cursor, 'insert')
    return results
```

 If you find seven arguments to be too much, you can use `** args` instead.

To introduce additional support in this function, we need to add new variables and instructions for how to handle them without losing the original SELECT functionality.

New variables

For the calculating functions, we will use a new variable `calc`. As all calculating functions require a columnar key on which to operate, we will also use a variable `colkey`. So every calculation will have this format:

```
calc(colkey)
```

The value of `calc` will be allowed to be any one of the calculating functions. In the HTML form, we can specify them to be uppercase so they are easier to read in the resulting SQL statement. We could use `str.upper()`, but it is better to exploit our control over the program input by structuring the HTML according to what we ultimately need.

The use of DISTINCT is essentially a switch. It takes no arguments per se, but is either used or not. Therefore, we can use a variable `distinct` as a boolean, in effect. In the HTML, we can support the value as either *yes* or *no*. If `distinct` is *yes*, the calculation function would read:

```
calc(DISTINCT colkey).
```

If *no*, we will pass over it (as addressed further).

Finally, support for sorting is provided by `sort`. Naturally, if we are going to sort, we need to indicate the column by which sorting should take place. That value is represented by variable `key`. So the sorting clause will read in the format.

```
sort key
```

To pass these values into the function, we could merely append them to the function definition line (again, using `**args` could be used in lieu of our arguments here):

```
def qaction(qact, db, tb, columns, values, user, password, calc,
colkey, distinct, sort, key):
```

But that gets unwieldy. Another option, and one that could easily be employed on the other arguments to this and the other functions, is to use a convention reserved for variable-length arguments. If we say that all variables related to aggregate functions can be part of a tuple called aggregates, we can use the following:

```
def qaction(qact, db, tb, columns, values, user, password,
*aggregates):
```

For purposes of illustration, we will use the variable-length convention as shown here. However, how variable you make the length of the arguments is your choice.

We can then assign those variables in the function:

```
calc = aggregates[0]
colkey = aggregates[1]
distinct = aggregates[2]
sort = aggregates[3]
key = aggregates[4]
```

By default, we will plan on all variables equating to the string NONE. This is purely for the sake of pattern matching and could alternatively be dealt with by testing the value for equating to None or for setting up a test for it being True. A further alternative is to use `try...except` structures defaulting to NONE or a similar string.

New statement formation

The new functionality needs to support new options in two different places. Currently, the SELECT statement is formed according to this template:

```
SELECT * FROM <table> WHERE <column> = '<value>'
```

However, the calculating functions need to go where the asterisk is currently located, and the sorting clause needs to follow on the end of the statement. We should therefore be able to support both of the following options:

```
SELECT <calculating function> FROM <table> WHERE <column> =
  '<value>'
SELECT * FROM <table> WHERE <column> = '<value>' <sorting     clause>
```

To add these parts, we will use a series of `if...else` clauses.

The only time that we want to change the original statement is if we have new variables to handle. Better is to test for a positive rather than a series of negatives. However, our program needs do not allow for that easily. In which case, we might set up a conditional structure as follows:

```
        if calc != "NONE" or distinct != "NONE" or sort != "NONE" or
key != "NONE":
                <form one of the new statements>
        else:
            statement = "SELECT * FROM %s WHERE %s - %s" %(tb, cols,
vals)
```

So we default to the formation of the original statement value but allow for the creation of the alternatives if any of our new variables have been set.

We then need to build in ways of handling the variables and forming the new statements within the `if` clause of the explained structure. For the specification we have set ourselves, this will fall into two inner `if...else` structures.

Each will handle the value of one option in the alternative statements discussed. At the end of the outer `if` clause, the results of the inner `if...else` structures will be combined as building blocks to form the statement.

The first `if...else` structure will quantify any calculating functions and determine whether DISTINCT should be included. For this first variable part of the SELECT statement, we will create a new string called `selection`. It will hold either an asterisk, as per the original statement, or the verbage for the calculating function. The code reads as follows:

```
            if calc != "NONE":
                if distinct == "yes":
                    selection = "%s(DISTINCT %s)" %(calc, colkey)
                else:
                    selection = "%s(%s)" %(calc, colkey)
            else:
                selection = "*"
```

Recall that, by design, `calc` can only equate to one of the calculating functions or to NONE. If it equates to NONE, we default to the universally-quantifying asterisk.

If `calc` is not NONE, it must equate to one of the calculating functions. We then test the value of `distinct`. If `distinct` is yes, we account for that in the assignment of `selection`. Otherwise, we omit it.

The second `if...else` structure determines the ordering and grouping by the value of `sort`. The resulting building block is called **sorting**.

```
if sort != "NONE":
    sorting = "%s %s" %(sort, key)
else:
    sorting = ""
```

In the HTML of the page, we will hardwire sort to equate to either ORDER BY or GROUP BY. This value is then added to the MySQL statement formed by the program.

> It is worth noting that these values should not go unchallenged in real-life deployments. We do not do it here for the sake of space. However, one should never execute code directly from a public-facing web page because of the inherent insecurity of such an implementation. For more on this, see Wikipedia's articles or similar ones on SQL injection.

Once the two building blocks, and the selection and sorting are formed, we can then combine them together with the rest of the SELECT statement template. The assignment line reads as follows:

```
statement = "SELECT %s FROM %s WHERE %s = %s %s"
%(selection, tb, cols, vals, sorting)
```

With that completed, the resulting statement is again passed to `execute()` and the affected rows assigned to results, which is subsequently returned by the function. After these changes, the code for `qaction()` reads as follows:

```
def qaction(qact, db, tb, columns, values, user, password,
*aggregates):
    """Forms SELECT and INSERT statements, passes them to execute(),
and returns the affected rows."""
    cursor = connection(user, password, db)

    calc = aggregates[0]
    colkey = aggregates[1]
    distinct = aggregates[2]
    sort = aggregates[3]
    key = aggregates[4]

    tname = tb + "("
    columns = columns.split(',')
    values = values.split(',')
    cols = ""
    vals = ""
```

```
        for i in xrange(0, len(columns)):
            col = columns[i].strip()
            val = values[i].strip()
            cols = cols + col
            vals = vals + "'" + val + "'"
            if i != len(columns) - 1:
                cols = cols + ", "
                vals = vals + ", "
    if qact == "select":
        if calc != "NONE" or distinct != "NONE" or sort != "NONE" or
key != "NONE":
            if calc != "NONE":
                if distinct == "yes":
                    selection = "%s(DISTINCT %s)" %(calc, colkey)
                else:
                    selection = "%s(%s)" %(calc, colkey)
            else:
                selection = "*"

            if sort != "NONE":
                sorting = "%s %s" %(sort, key)
            else:
                sorting = ""
            statement = "SELECT %s FROM %s WHERE %s = %s %s"
%(selection, tb, cols, vals, sorting)
        else:
            statement = "SELECT * FROM %s WHERE %s = %s" %(tb, cols,
vals)
        results = execute(statement, cursor, 'select')

    elif qact == "insert":
        statement = "INSERT INTO %s (%s) VALUES (%s)" %(tb, cols,
vals)
        results = execute(statement, cursor, 'insert')
    return results
```

Revising main()

Now that the functionality is built into `qaction()`, we can ammend `main()`
accordingly. At present, `main()` reads as follows:

```
def main():
    """The main function creates and controls the MySQLStatement
instance in accordance with the user's input."""
    output = ""
```

```
    while 1:
        try:
            cursor = connectNoDB(opt.user, opt.password)
            authenticate = 1
        except:
            output = "Bad login information.  Please verify the
username and password that you are using before trying to login
again."
            authenticate = 0

        if authenticate == 1:
            errmsg = "You have not specified the information necessary
for the action you chose.  Please check your information and specify
it correctly in the dialogue."

            if opt.dbact is not None:
                output = dbaction(opt.dbact, opt.dbname, cursor)
            elif opt.tbact is not None:
                output = tbaction(opt.tbact, opt.tbdbname, opt.tbname,
opt.columns, opt.values, opt.user, opt.password)
            elif opt.qact is not None:
                output = qaction(opt.qact, opt.qdbname, opt.qtbname,
opt.columns, opt.values, opt.user, opt.password)
            elif opt.uact is not None:
                if opt.uact == "create":
                    act = "create-user"
                    output = uaction(opt.user, opt.password, act, opt.
username, opt.passwd)
                elif opt.uact == "drop":
                    act = "drop-user"
                    output = uaction(opt.user, opt.password, act, opt.
username)
                elif opt.uact == "grant" or opt.uact == "revoke":
                    output = uadmin(opt.user, opt.password, opt.uact,
opt.username, opt.privileges, opt.acldb, opt.acltb)
            else:
                output = errmsg

        printout = HTMLPage()
        printout.message(output)
        output = printout.page()

        print output
        break
```

The part of `main()` that needs changing, and the part in which the code of this section will be placed, is the second `elif` clause:

```
elif opt.qact is not None:
        output = qaction(opt.qact, opt.qdbname, opt.qtbname,
    opt.columns, opt.values, opt.user, opt.password)
```

Into this clause, we will quantify each of the new variables. We will further assign complementary values, such as `colkey`, based on `calc` also being indicated by the user. The code reads as follows:

```
elif opt.qact is not None:

        if opt.calc is not None:
            calc = opt.calc
            colkey = opt.colkey
        else:
            calc = "NONE"
            colkey = "NONE"
        if opt.distinct is not None:
            distinct = opt.distinct
        else:
            distinct = "NONE"
        if opt.sort is not None:
            sort = opt.sort
            key = opt.key
        else:
            sort = "NONE"
            key = "NONE"
        output = qaction(opt.qact, opt.qdbname, opt.qtbname,
    opt.columns, opt.values, opt.user, opt.password, calc, colkey,
    distinct, sort, key)
```

For safer computing, we could put the main block of this clause into a `try...except` clause. Otherwise, we leave ourselves open to possible errors if the user omits important data.

Finally, we pass the data to `qaction()` and assign the results to output. You will notice that we pass the variables overtly. Because the aggregates argument of `qaction()` is a tuple, we could also pass all of the added values (from `calc` onward) as a tuple. The choice is yours, but Python can handle either.

As before, the resulting output is passed to `HTMLPage.message()` later. The resulting HTML page is then printed as output.

Setting up the options

Having set up the new functionality, we next need to provide support for it in the options of the program. If you coded this application as a CGI program, the values will be available automatically as part of `cgi.FieldStorage()`. In PHP, however, we need to add each option as a flag. The code is as follows:

```
opt.add_option("-C", "--calculate",
               action="store",
               type="string",
               help="which calculating function to employ",
               dest="calc")
opt.add_option("-K", "--colkey",
               action="store",
               type="string",
               help="column to use when calculating",
               dest="colkey")
opt.add_option("-I", "--distinct",
               action="store",
               type="string",
               help="whether to return distinct results",
               dest="distinct")
opt.add_option("-S", "--sort",
               action="store",
               type="string",
               help="how to sort results",
               dest="sort")
opt.add_option("-k", "--key",
               action="store",
               type="string",
               help="key to use when sorting",
               dest="key")
```

We can then call the program from the command line to test the HTML output. If the program is called `pymyadmin.py`, we can call it as follows (changing the syntax according to your operating system):

```
./pymyadmin.py -U 'skipper' -P 'secret' -q 'select' -Z sakila -Y film
-c length -v '114' -C 'COUNT' -K title
```

Here, HTML will output the following to the screen:

```
<!DOCTYPE html PUBLIC "-//W3C//DTD XHTML 1.0 Frameset//EN" "http://
www.w3.org/TR/xhtml1/DTD/xhtml1-frameset.dtd">
<html xmlns="http://www.w3.org/1999/xhtml" xml:lang="en" lang="en"
dir="ltr">
  <head>
    <title>PyMyAdmin 0.001</title>
<meta http-equiv="Content-Type" content="text/html; charset=utf-8" />
  </head>
```

```
    <body>
      <h1>PyMyAdmin Results</h1>
<br>   10 <br>
<br>

    </body>
</html>
```

This is the same output that will be passed to Apache. You can test it by exporting the output to an output file. However, if you used CGI for this application, you would need to hard-wire the values into the code temporarily.

Changing the HTML form

As with the Python program, the HTML page will support the aggregate functions within the section for queries. That section of the form currently reads:

```
<div>QUERIES</div>
<input type="radio" name="qact" value="select"> SELECT
<br>
<input type="radio" name="qact" value="insert"> INSERT
<br>
Database name: <input type="text" name="qdbname" value="">
<br>
Table name: <input type="text" name="qtbname" value="">
<br>
Columns (comma-separated): <input type="text" name="columns" value="">
<br>
Values (comma-separated): <input type="text" name="values" value="">
<br><br>
```

We need to change it to provide support for the functionality we have introduced into the Python program.

As mentioned previously, the values of `calc` will be hard-wired into the HTML. With the determination of that value, we will also include a text field in which the user is to specify the value of `colkey`. The code follows the field for `Values` and reads:

```
Calculations: <select name="calc">
    <option value="COUNT">COUNT</option>
    <option value="SUM">SUM</option>
    <option value="MAX">MAX</option>
    <option value="MIN">MIN</option>
    <option value="AVG">AVG</option>
</select>
(<input type="text" name="colkey" value="">)
<br>
```

You may note that the dialogue for `colkey` is sandwiched between parentheses. The visual effect of this code is that the user will see the SQL formatting in the HTML.

Following this, we offer the user the ability to indicate the value of `distinct`.

```
DISTINCT?
<input type="radio" name="distinct" value="yes">Yes
<input type="radio" name="distinct" value="no">No
<br>
```

Finally, we need to provide the facilities for sorting. With the choice of whether to order by item or by group, we also provide a text field for the key by which to sort the values.

```
Sorting: <select name="sort">
    <option value="ORDER BY">ORDER BY</option>
    <option value="GROUP BY">GROUP BY</option>
</select>
<input type="text" name="key" value="">
<br><br>
```

Summary

In this chapter, we have covered how to use aggregate functions and clauses in Python. We have seen:

- How to use MySQL's optimized functions to calculate certain aspects of data results

- The ways that MySQL provides for sorting the data before it is returned

- How to tell MySQL render unique values

- Some of the ways that discrete values return different results than non-discrete ones

- How we can instruct MySQL to return alternative averages to the mean and its default for the function `AVG`

In the next chapter, we will see how to create joins (using `JOIN`) in MySQL for Python.

11
SELECT Alternatives

We have already seen how to restrict the data that MySQL returns by using a WHERE clause. Rather than retrieve the entire table and sort through it in Python, we passed the burden onto the server. Using WHERE restricted the number of rows that match. This is just like when we specify columns instead of using an asterisk after SELECT — it saves us from receiving the entire record for every match.

WHERE causes MySQL to ignore any row that does not match our selection. Specifying the columns then indicates to MySQL, which parts of the affected rows to return. In addition to WHERE, MySQL supports other ways of narrowing one's returns. It also allows us to match and complement the data using other tables, including combining tables or results from different queries.

In this chapter, we will see:

- How we can restrict results using WHERE and HAVING, and what the differences are between them
- When it is best to use WHERE and when one might use HAVING
- How to create temporary subtables from which to SELECT data
- How to join the results of two SELECT statements with UNION
- The various ways to JOIN tables
- The difference between an INNER JOIN and and OUTER JOIN, whether LEFT or RIGHT

The project for this chapter will again be built on the web-based database administration program that we have developed in preceding chapters. After seeing new ways to restrict and complement the data that we retrieve from a table, we will add some of that functionality into our application.

HAVING clause

The HAVING clause has similar effect to the WHERE clause. The syntax is virtually the same:

```
SELECT <some column(s)> FROM <table> HAVING <met a certain condition>;
```

Indeed, in some statements, one can be tempted to replace WHERE with HAVING because the syntax is so similar, and sometimes one would not notice much, if any, difference in the returned data. However, each has its purpose and is applied differently, as discussed later in this chapter.

WHERE versus HAVING: Syntax

The HAVING clause can only be applied to columns that have been previously indicated in the statement. For example, using the sakila database, let's say we wanted every record from film that was updated since 2005. Trying to hack from our knowledge of WHERE, we might try the following:

```
SELECT title FROM film HAVING YEAR(last_update) > '2005';
```

But we would be wrong and would be greeted with an error:

ERROR 1054 (42S22): Unknown column 'last_update' in 'having clause'

One way of resolving the problem is by using a universal quantifier:

```
SELECT * FROM film HAVING YEAR(last_update) > '2005';
```

The returned data will be the entire table because all of the records in the film were updated last in 2006. This statement works because last_update is implied in the quantifying asterisk. However, it is far from ideal and leaves it to Python to sort through the data. It is better to use this statement:

```
SELECT title, last_update FROM film HAVING YEAR(last_update) > '2005';
```

This statement will still return every record by giving us the information we want and proof of the match.

WHERE versus HAVING: Aggregate functions

A common situation in which WHERE and HAVING differ in syntax, is in the use of aggregate functions. As we have seen, a WHERE clause such as the following is allowed:

```
SELECT title, MAX(film_id), AVG(length), last_update FROM film WHERE
length > '100' GROUP BY YEAR(last_update);
```

Because all records in film were last updated in the same year, this query will return exactly one row holding—the title of the first affected record (that is, of films with `length` greater than 100 minutes), the highest ID number of the affected rows, the average length of the same, and the timestamp for the last update of the first hit.

To use HAVING in a context such as this requires a different syntax. When using HAVING with aggregate functions, it must be placed in the GROUP BY structure. The precise reasons for this are addressed more fully in the next section, but the concise cause is that HAVING is applied after aggregation is performed. So for example, to get the same information for every title that begins with X, Y, or Z, we could use the following:

```
SELECT title, MAX(film_id), AVG(length), last_update FROM film GROUP
BY title HAVING title > 'X';;
```

The results of this are as follows:

```
+-------------------+------------+------------+---------------------+
| title             | MAX(film_id) | AVG(length) | last_update        |
+-------------------+------------+------------+---------------------+
| YENTL IDAHO       |        995 |    86.0000 | 2006-02-15 05:03:42 |
| YOUNG LANGUAGE    |        996 |   183.0000 | 2006-02-15 05:03:42 |
| YOUTH KICK        |        997 |   179.0000 | 2006-02-15 05:03:42 |
| ZHIVAGO CORE      |        998 |   105.0000 | 2006-02-15 05:03:42 |
| ZOOLANDER FICTION |        999 |   101.0000 | 2006-02-15 05:03:42 |
| ZORRO ARK         |       1000 |    50.0000 | 2006-02-15 05:03:42 |
+-------------------+------------+------------+---------------------+
```

However, achieving the same results as the WHERE clause can give us further required adaptations. As mentioned above, HAVING requires the column used in its condition to have been mentioned previously in the SELECT statement. But the columns passed as arguments to calculating functions do not count as having been mentioned previously. In effect, MySQL does not see them when it evaluates a HAVING clause. Rather, it just sees their results and finds no match. Therefore, to use those results with a HAVING clause, we need to give them a name using AS. The last example could be rewritten for ease of reading as follows:

```
SELECT title, MAX(film_id) AS max, AVG(length) AS avg, last_update
FROM film GROUP BY title HAVING title > 'X';
```

And the headings of the results would be changed accordingly as:

title	max	avg	last_update
YENTL IDAHO	995	86.0000	2006-02-15 05:03:42
YOUNG LANGUAGE	996	183.0000	2006-02-15 05:03:42
YOUTH KICK	997	179.0000	2006-02-15 05:03:42
ZHIVAGO CORE	998	105.0000	2006-02-15 05:03:42
ZOOLANDER FICTION	999	101.0000	2006-02-15 05:03:42
ZORRO ARK	1000	50.0000	2006-02-15 05:03:42

Using AS, we can achieve results similar to the WHERE clause that started this section. Let's say, however, that we wanted to group by title, not the year of the last update. The WHERE version would look like this:

```
SELECT title, MAX(film_id), AVG(length), last_update FROM film WHERE
length > '100' GROUP BY title;
```

But the HAVING version cannot merely switch the order of the clauses around because, in the view of MySQL, the column length is never referenced as a column in the SELECT statement. Rather, it is an argument to AVG(). Therefore, we need to name the results of AVG() as length.

```
SELECT title, MAX(film_id), AVG(length) AS length, last_update FROM
film GROUP BY title HAVING length > '100';;
```

 Note that HAVING requires the column of its condition to have been used earlier in the clause, but GROUP BY does not.

To be sure, the use of AVG here is unnecessary. As we are grouping by a unique quality, title, the average length will be the value initially passed to AVG(). The average of a single value is that value. Consequently, the WHERE clause would be the best version to use in this case. In the next section, we will look at when one should use HAVING instead of WHERE.

WHERE versus HAVING: Application

The use of HAVING differs from WHERE in more than its syntax. However, the two clauses also differ in how they are applied.

Whenever you pass a SELECT statement to MySQL, it forms a table of results which is then optimized (that is, narrowed), based on the criteria passed to it. The condition represented in WHERE is applied **before** the optimizations are carried out. But the condition in HAVING is applied **after** the optimizations are performed, being affected as a final filter for what should be reported back. The difference is subtle, but boils down to application before the results are finalized (WHERE) and application after the results table is created (HAVING). A further example may help to clarify the difference.

Suppose we wanted to search the Country table of the world database to find which forms of government had the largest populations. We then quantify the population size by those in excess of 100 million people. A basic, unquantified query might look like this:

```
SELECT AVG(Population), GovernmentForm FROM Country GROUP BY
GovernmentForm ORDER BY Population DESC;;
```

The trouble with this query is that it gives us far more data than we need:

```
+-----------------+----------------------------------------------+
| AVG(Population) | GovernmentForm                               |
+-----------------+----------------------------------------------+
| 1277558000.0000 | People'sRepublic                             |
|   48596000.0000 | Islamic Republic                             |
|  133954700.0000 | Federal Republic                             |
|   38357333.3333 | Socialistic Republic                         |
|   22720000.0000 | Islamic Emirate                              |

...
|        1000.0000 | Independent Church State                    |
|           0.0000 | Co-administrated                            |
|           0.0000 | Dependent Territory of the US              |
+-----------------+----------------------------------------------+
```

Using conditions, we are able to modify the results on the server. However, how we narrow the query, will determine the results.

Using WHERE, we can narrow the results to countries having populations over 100 million people.

```
SELECT AVG(Population) AS Population, GovernmentForm FROM Country
WHERE Population > '100000000' GROUP BY GovernmentForm ORDER BY
Population DESC;;
```

The resulting table is drastically smaller:

```
+-----------------+-------------------------+
| AVG(Population) | GovernmentForm          |
+-----------------+-------------------------+
| 1277558000.0000 | People'sRepublic        |
|  344114800.0000 | Federal Republic        |
|  165915000.0000 | Republic                |
|  126714000.0000 | Constitutional Monarchy |
+-----------------+-------------------------+
```

The problem is that we are not looking for countries with populations larger then 100 million. We are looking for forms of government. For this, we can use the following statement with a HAVING clause:

```
SELECT AVG(Population) AS Population, GovernmentForm FROM Country
GROUP BY GovernmentForm HAVING Population > '100000000' ORDER BY
Population DESC;;
```

These results are even smaller:

```
+-----------------+------------------+
| Population      | GovernmentForm   |
+-----------------+------------------+
| 1277558000.0000 | People'sRepublic |
|  133954700.0000 | Federal Republic |
+-----------------+------------------+
```

If you want to check these results against the larger table, simply take out the HAVING clause:

```
SELECT AVG(Population) AS Population, GovernmentForm FROM Country
GROUP BY GovernmentForm ORDER BY Population DESC;;
```

The query using WHERE limited the values submitted for averaging. The condition was applied to the data before the average was calculated. Using HAVING, the average for each type of government was calculated first and then the condition was applied to the result of AVG.

Subqueries

The WHERE clause reduces the amount of data through a simple filtering process and HAVING filters the results. But MySQL also provides more robust ways of narrowing the data from which results are culled. Normally, MySQL processes a query against a database that is resident on disk. Subqueries, however, are nested SELECT statements that result in a table of results against which the main query is processed. Once the main query is processed against the results of the subquery, the latter is purged from memory.

Up to this point, if we needed to take the results from one query and use it as input for another query, we might feel constrained to use two SELECT statements and manually transfer the data. Here, however, subqueries do that for us.

For example, let's say that we wanted to find the title of every movie done by actors with the surname CHASE. The sakila database does not provide this information in one table. Using a series of SELECT statements, we would first need to retrieve the actor_id of every actor with a surname of CHASE:

```
SELECT actor_id FROM actor WHERE last_name='CHASE';
```

We would need to save those results and use them in a series of SELECT statements against film_actor to get the values for film_id:

```
SELECT film_id FROM film_actor WHERE actor_id =<actor_id>;
```

We would take each of those film identifiers and query film to get the title:

```
SELECT title FROM film WHERE film_id = <film_id>;>;
```

Doing this manually in MySQL would be an enormous headache. We could do it easily enough in Python by recycling the data into each query through loops. But that requires writing code unnecessarily and increases our I/O, costing us in speed and responsiveness. It is better to put the onus on the database server with a subquery or a join (discussed later in this book).

To form a subquery, we define the condition of the WHERE clause in terms of the results of a SELECT statement. The syntax looks like this:

```
SELECT <column reference> FROM <table 1> WHERE <a column from table 1>
<relational operator> (SELECT <a similar column  from table 2> FROM
<table 2>);
```

An example that combines the last two of our earlier SELECT statements is:

```
SELECT title FROM film WHERE film_id = (SELECT film_id FROM film_actor
WHERE film_id='17' AND actor_id='3');
```

The result is as follows:

```
+------------------+
| title            |
+------------------+
| ACADEMY DINOSAUR |
+------------------+
```

MySQL requires that subqueries result in only one row by default. For this reason, we have had to place two conditions in the subquery—a `film_id` value of 17 and an `actor_id` value of 3. Had we not done so, MySQL would have thrown an error that reads:

```
ERROR 1242 (21000): Subquery returns more than 1 row
```

> A comprehensive discussion on errors pertaining to subqueries and how to resolve them can be found in the MySQL documentation: http://dev.mysql.com/doc/refman/5.5/en/subquery-errors.html

In order to have MySQL process for each row of a series in sequence, we need to preface the subquery with one of two keywords—ANY or IN. However, ANY is used on the right side of any relational operator to cause MySQL to process any True value that is returned. IN is used to process an expression list. To dispense with the hardwired value for `film_id`, we can use either one:

```
SELECT title FROM film WHERE film_id IN (SELECT film_id FROM film_
actor WHERE actor_id='3');

SELECT title FROM film WHERE film_id = ANY (SELECT film_id FROM film_
actor WHERE actor_id='3');
```

The result will be a listing for every `title` in `film` that has an identifier of the same value as those associated with `actor_id` 3 in `film_actor`. Those are 22 in number.

But that only gets us part of the way. The actor with `actor_id` 3 is only one of those with the surname CHASE. Instead of repeating the process manually, we can nest another subquery inside of the subquery. We can specify to MySQL to draw only from those records where the `last_name` value is CHASE.

```
SELECT title FROM film WHERE film_id = ANY (SELECT film_id FROM film_
actor WHERE actor_id = ANY(SELECT actor_id FROM actor WHERE last_
name='CHASE'));));
```

The results will be 49 rows containing all actors with the specified surname. We can nest subqueries like Matryoshka dolls as long as we want and as long as the data allows, and MySQL will not care. The queries simply must make sense, return one row at a time (or use the keywords ANY or IN), and feed into the WHERE clause of the next query.

Unions

Sometimes, you may not want to limit results but, rather, combine results from multiple queries. Rather than execute two different SELECT statements in Python, you can pass the task to the server with UNION. A UNION is the combination of the results from two SELECT statements into a single result set. Unlike JOINs (discussed in the next section), a UNION does do not combine the results side-by-side, but one after the other. So where the results from the first query end, the results from the second query begin.

The basic syntax of a UNION is as follows:

```
(<SELECT statement 1>) UNION (<SELECT statement 2>);
```

Each SELECT statement is discrete as they are neither related nor can they rely on each other's data. The number of columns returned by each SELECT statement must be the same. Otherwise, MySQL will throw an error.

The data type of each column should be the same with respect to the columns of the other statement. If it is not, you can get strange results. Consider this UNION of two queries against sakila:

```
(SELECT actor_id AS id, last_name AS name FROM actor WHERE last_
name='WRAY') UNION (SELECT actor_id AS actorid, film_id AS filmid FROM
film_actor) limit 5;
```

The results are as follows:

```
+----+------+
| id | name |
+----+------+
| 63 | WRAY |
|  1 | 1    |
| 10 | 1    |
| 20 | 1    |
| 30 | 1    |
+----+------+
```

We have limited the results to **five** for purposes of illustration. In the table `actor`, there is only one record with a surname of WRAY. Consequently, by mixing data types between the two SELECT statements, the surname of the actor becomes conflated with the `film_id` from `film_actor`. Note that MySQL also does not specify where one set of results leave off and the other take up. The aliases used in the second SELECT statement are not applied.

Like subqueries, UNIONs can be applied for as long as system resources and datasets allow. Simply surround each SELECT statement with parentheses and separate each with the word UNION.

We can also specify whether to sort the results of a SELECT statement without modifying the SELECT statement itself. This is done by following the use of UNION with DISTINCT. This will also cause MySQL to sort out duplicates as it did with aggregate functions. The opposite of DISTINCT is ALL. This is the default behavior of UNION, but can nevertheless be used explicitly. For the effect of each, consider the results of the following two queries:

```
(SELECT last_name AS name FROM actor WHERE last_name='WRAY') UNION
DISTINCT (SELECT film_id AS filmid FROM film_actor) LIMIT 20;
```

```
+------+
| name |
+------+
| WRAY |
| 1    |
| 2    |
| 3    |
| 4    |
+------+
```

and

```
(SELECT last_name AS name FROM actor WHERE last_name='WRAY') UNION ALL
(SELECT film_id AS filmid FROM film_actor) LIMIT 20;
```

```
+------+
| name |
+------+
| WRAY |
| 1    |
| 1    |
| 1    |
| 1    |
+------+
```

Joins

Joins are often one of the hardest topics for MySQL newcomers to grasp. The entire concept pivots on the understanding of mathematical sets, unions, intersections, and their resulting Venn diagrams. Another way of looking at joins is to use tabular information. For an example of this, see: `http://en.wikipedia.org/wiki/Sql_join`.

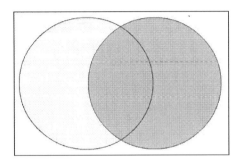

In the preceding Venn diagram, the left circle may be seen to represent one set and the right circle another. The overlapping area is called the intersection of the two sets. The set of elements that encompasses the contents of both circles is called a union, but should not be confused with the MySQL keyword UNION. With that information in mind, we can then see how MySQL allows us to access different parts of the Venn diagram through joins.

LEFT and RIGHT joins

In MySQL, each set is represented by a table. The first table referenced in the query is the set on the left. The second is represented by the circle on the right. For MySQL to know which is the primary set when forming the results, we use LEFT or RIGHT, respectively. If neither LEFT nor RIGHT is specified in the SELECT statement, LEFT is presumed. For reasons of portability, the MySQL manual further recommends against using RIGHT joins if one can use a LEFT JOIN instead. LEFT and RIGHT joins are types of OUTER joins, which are dealt with in the next section.

The basic syntax for LEFT and RIGHT JOIN is:

```
SELECT <columns to be returned> FROM <table 1> <LEFT or RIGHT> JOIN
<table 2> ON <key column from table 1> <relational operator> <key
column from table2>;
```

Whichever table is specified as primary is returned in full by default (subject to selection criteria). Where there is a disparity between the lengths of the two sets, a LEFT JOIN will result in the left set being exhausted. A RIGHT JOIN will use the right set similarly. If the non-primary set is shorter than the primary, a NULL value will be returned as a complement to the primary sets values. If the primary is shorter, the non-primary set will be truncated to fit.

Using the world database, we can perform a JOIN that returns every actor for each film by the film identifier. Alternatively, we can return every film for each actor by actor. Whether we join to the right or to the left determines which is returned. A LEFT JOIN of the datasets looks like this (we use LIMIT here to keep the example manageable):

```
SELECT actor.actor_id AS id, actor.first_name AS first, actor.last_
name AS last, film_actor.film_id AS film FROM actor LEFT JOIN film_
actor ON actor.actor_id=film_actor.actor_id LIMIT 10;;
```

The results

```
+----+----------+---------+------+
| id | first    | last    | film |
+----+----------+---------+------+
|  1 | PENELOPE | GUINESS |    1 |
|  1 | PENELOPE | GUINESS |   23 |
|  1 | PENELOPE | GUINESS |   25 |
|  1 | PENELOPE | GUINESS |  106 |
|  1 | PENELOPE | GUINESS |  140 |
|  1 | PENELOPE | GUINESS |  166 |
|  1 | PENELOPE | GUINESS |  277 |
|  1 | PENELOPE | GUINESS |  361 |
|  1 | PENELOPE | GUINESS |  438 |
|  1 | PENELOPE | GUINESS |  499 |
+----+----------+---------+------+
```

Clearly, we get every film for each actor. To get every actor for each film, we can change the query to a RIGHT JOIN:

```
SELECT actor.actor_id AS id, actor.first_name AS first, actor.last_
name AS last, film_actor.film_id AS film FROM actor RIGHT JOIN film_
actor ON actor.actor_id=film_actor.actor_id LIMIT 10;
```

and get the following results:

```
+------+-----------+---------+------+
| id   | first     | last    | film |
+------+-----------+---------+------+
|    1 | PENELOPE  | GUINESS |    1 |
|   10 | CHRISTIAN | GABLE   |    1 |
|   20 | LUCILLE   | TRACY   |    1 |
|   30 | SANDRA    | PECK    |    1 |
|   40 | JOHNNY    | CAGE    |    1 |
|   53 | MENA      | TEMPLE  |    1 |
|  108 | WARREN    | NOLTE   |    1 |
|  162 | OPRAH     | KILMER  |    1 |
|  188 | ROCK      | DUKAKIS |    1 |
|  198 | MARY      | KEITEL  |    1 |
+------+-----------+---------+------+
```

As with every other part of MySQL, whether the results you get are valid for the question you need to answer depends on how well you phrase your query.

OUTER joins

As the name implies, OUTER joins differ from INNER joins in what they encompass; the latter is discussed in the next section. The OUTER JOIN is so called because it always includes one of the tables in addition to the intersection of the two. The table to be included is indicated by the terms LEFT and RIGHT. The resulting joins are called LEFT [OUTER] JOIN and RIGHT [OUTER] JOIN, respectively.

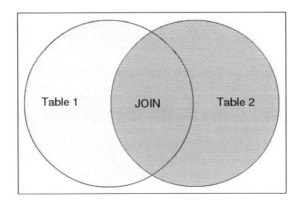

In the preceding Venn diagram, a LEFT OUTER JOIN would include the intersection labeled JOIN as well as Table 1. A RIGHT OUTER JOIN includes the intersection and the contents of Table 2. Now we can see how it makes sense to call these OUTER joins because they contain data that are outside the region where the two tables are joined.

The syntax of an OUTER JOIN is as follows:

```
SELECT <column reference> FROM <table 1> <LEFT or RIGHT> OUTER JOIN
<table 2> ON (<key column from table 1> = <key column from table
2>);>);>);>);>);
```

Against the sakila database, for example, we can run this JOIN:

```
SELECT actor.*, film_actor.* FROM film_actor LEFT OUTER JOIN actor ON
(YEAR(actor.last_update) = YEAR(film_actor.last_update)) limit 5;
```

The syntax of a RIGHT OUTER JOIN would be the same save for the obvious use of RIGHT instead of LEFT. For the effective difference of each, see the previous section on LEFT and RIGHT joins.

INNER joins

In MySQL, an INNER JOIN is simply the intersection of the two sets to the exclusion of anything that does not overlap. A diagram of it is as follows:

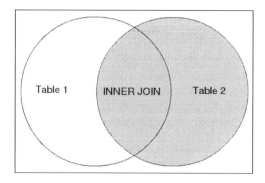

As seen here, the INNER JOIN gives us the inner part of the diagram.

To affect an inner join, MySQL naturally requires you to specify which tables are to be compared. It also requires the specific columns from each table to be specified as well as the key values to be used for forming the intersection. The basic syntax of the INNER JOIN is as follows:

```
SELECT <columns to be returned> FROM <table 1> INNER JOIN <table 2>
ON <key column from table 1> <relational operator> <key column from
table2>;
```

So for example, if we wanted to use the `world` database and find every city that lies in a country of the same name, we might try to cull out all the city names from `City` and all the country names from `Country`. Of course, the only way to relate the two with certainty is to cull out the `CountryCode` from `City` and match it to `Code` from `Country`. All of this requires a lot more processing than needed. The better option would be to use an `INNER JOIN` between the `City` and `Country` tables:

```
SELECT City.Name AS Name, Country.Name AS Country, Country.Region AS
Region FROM City INNER JOIN Country ON City.Name = Country.Name;
```

As different column names may carry different meanings in different tables, it is not a bad idea to use `AS` again to create custom headings. The results of this query are as follows:

Name	Country	Region
Djibouti	Djibouti	Eastern Africa
Mexico	Mexico	Central America
Gibraltar	Gibraltar	Southern Europe
Armenia	Armenia	Middle East
Kuwait	Kuwait	Middle East
Macao	Macao	Eastern Asia
San Marino	San Marino	Southern Europe
Singapore	Singapore	Southeast Asia

We can further apply conditions to the data of the join by appending a `WHERE` clause to the statement.

```
SELECT City.CountryCode AS Code, City.Name AS Name, Country.Name AS
Country, Country.Region AS Region FROM City INNER JOIN Country ON
City.Name = Country.Name WHERE Country.Region LIKE 'South%';
```

This returns only those results where the region begins with `South`:

Code	Name	Country	Region
GIB	Gibraltar	Gibraltar	Southern Europe
SMR	San Marino	San Marino	Southern Europe
SGP	Singapore	Singapore	Southeast Asia

However, INNER joins are quite powerful. They are unsurprisingly very common in MySQL programming.

NATURAL joins

A NATURAL JOIN combines the two tables based on their commonalities. If neither LEFT nor RIGHT is specified, then neither is given precedence, which often results in an empty set. However, the table which is given precedence is reproduced in the results. For every record of the precedent table, a record is produced in the results. Where the columns have overlapping data, only one record will be reproduced.

If the precedent table is longer or fuller than the other set, the results from the latter will be represented with NULL values. If the precedent table is shorter, the other table is truncated to match.

The basic syntax of NATURAL joins is as follows:

```
SELECT <columns> FROM <table 1> NATURAL <LEFT or RIGHT> JOIN <table 2>;
```

In practice, it would look like this query of the world database:

```
SELECT * FROM City NATURAL LEFT JOIN Country;
```

In the results, you will see that everywhere Country has no column whose name is the same as that of the value in City, a NULL value is inserted. Using NATURAL RIGHT JOIN instead gives results that defer to the second table over the first.

Another example that shows the way MySQL automatically sorts the data on a NATURAL JOIN is seen with the sakila database:

```
SELECT * FROM actor NATURAL LEFT JOIN film_actor LIMIT 5;
```

We limit the results for sake of space, but they illustrate that actor_id, being common to both tables, is only reproduced once.

```
+----------+---------------------+------------+-------------+---------+
| actor_id | last_update         | first_name | last_name   | film_id |
+----------+---------------------+------------+-------------+---------+
|        1 | 2006-02-15 04:34:33 | PENELOPE   | GUINESS     |    NULL |
|        2 | 2006-02-15 04:34:33 | NICK       | WAHLBERG    |    NULL |
|        3 | 2006-02-15 04:34:33 | ED         | CHASE       |    NULL |
|        4 | 2006-02-15 04:34:33 | JENNIFER   | DAVIS       |    NULL |
|        5 | 2006-02-15 04:34:33 | JOHNNY     | LOLLOBRIGIDA|    NULL |
+----------+---------------------+------------+-------------+---------+
```

CROSS joins

Where INNER joins give us the intersection of the two sets and OUTER joins give us the intersection with one of the sets, the CROSS JOIN gives us both sets. The basic syntax is as follows:

```
SELECT <columns from table 1>, <columns from table 2> FROM <table 1>
CROSS JOIN <table 2>;
```

An example using the world database is:

```
SELECT City.*, Country.* FROM City CROSS JOIN Country;
```

Without a conditional clause, every record of table 2 will be returned for every record of table 1. If each table has 1000 records, the table returned will be the product of those two sets, or one million records. We can limit the results with a WHERE clause as follows:

```
SELECT City.*, Country.* FROM City CROSS JOIN Country WHERE City.Name
LIKE 'C%';
```

This query restricts the number of results by quantifying the value of the Name column in the City (table 1) set of data. Even so, we still get 67,159 records returned.

Depending on which columns you specify, you can retrieve all or few of the fields for each record. In the following example, we simply retrieve the city and country name for each row, again quantifying the results with a WHERE clause.

```
SELECT City.Name, Country.Name FROM City CROSS JOIN Country WHERE
City.Name LIKE 'C%';
```

Greater precision in forming a query naturally leads to faster processing. Results vary on different servers, but the unqualified query takes over 12 minutes to return where the second query takes around 80 seconds and the third 20 seconds.

Doing it in Python

As we have seen in previous chapters, processing a SELECT query in Python is as simple as execute() and fetchall(). However, Python also allows us to build statements dynamically, and this applies to joins, unions, and subqueries as well.

Subqueries

If we want column from `table1`, but the column reference for the subquery is `colref`, from both `table1` and `table2`, we can write the following:

```python
#!/usr/bin/env python

import MySQLdb

mydb = MySQLdb.connect('localhost', 'skipper', 'secret', 'sakila')
cursor = mydb.cursor()

table1 = 'film'
table2 = 'film_actor'
column = 'film_id, title'
colref = 'film_id'

statement = "SELECT %s FROM %s WHERE %s IN (SELECT %s FROM %s)" \
%(column, table1, colref, colref, table2)

cursor.execute(statement)
results = cursor.fetchall()

for i in results: print i[0], '\t', i[1]
```

The results obviously will be the title and identifier for each title in film. We can further nuance this for reader input to allow searches by the name of the actor.

```python
#!/usr/bin/env python

import MySQLdb
import sys

mydb = MySQLdb.connect('localhost', 'skipper', 'secret', 'sakila')
cursor = mydb.cursor()

table1 = 'film'
column = 'film_id, title'
colref = 'film_id'

sub1ref = 'film_id'
table2 = 'film_actor'

sub2ref = 'actor_id'
table3 = 'actor'
```

```
firstname = sys.argv[1]
surname = sys.argv[2]

statement = "SELECT %s FROM %s WHERE %s IN (SELECT %s FROM %s WHERE %s
= ANY (SELECT %s from %s WHERE first_name='%s' AND last_name = '%s'))"
%(column, table1, colref, colref, table2, sub2ref, sub2\
ref, table3, firstname, surname)

cursor.execute(statement)
results = cursor.fetchall()

for i in results: print i[0], '\t', i[1]
```

Unions

As with subqueries, we can create the two statements of a UNION and join them dynamically. For example:

```
#!/usr/bin/env python

import MySQLdb

mydb = MySQLdb.connect('localhost', 'skipper', 'secret', 'sakila')
cursor = mydb.cursor()

statement1 = "SELECT actor_id FROM actor"
statement2 = "SELECT film_id FROM film"
union = "(%s) UNION (%s)" %(statement1, statement2)

cursor.execute(union)
results = cursor.fetchall()

for i in results: print i[0]
```

Joins

As mentioned in the earlier section on joins, which JOIN you use will depend on the results you want. Here an INNER JOIN will be illustrated, but the same process applies to the formation of the other kinds of joins.

```
#!/usr/bin/env python

import MySQLdb
```

```
mydb = MySQLdb.connect('localhost', 'skipper', 'secret', 'world')
cursor = mydb.cursor()


table1 = 'City'
table2 = 'Country'


col1 = "CountryCode"
col2 = "Region"


colref1 = table1 + "." + col1
colref2 = table2 + "." + col2
colref _ colref1 + ", " + colref2


keyref1 = 'Name'
keyref2 = 'Name'
key1 = table1 + "." + keyref1
key2 = table2 + "." + keyref2


statement = "SELECT %s FROM %s INNER JOIN %s ON %s = %s" %(colref,
table1, table2, key1, key2)


cursor.execute(statement)
results = cursor.fetchall()


for i in results: print i[0], '\t', i[1]
```

After opening a connection to the database and creating a cursor, we define the parts of the statement, concatenating strings as necessary. We then insert the sundry values into the value of statement.

Remember that the statement remains a string until it is passed to cursor. execute() as an argument. It can be then amended at any time. If you find it too difficult to manage the variables that are to be inserted into the statement, simply break the statement down into parts and combine it at the end. Should a problem with the statement persist, you can use a print statement just before the statement is executed to find out what is being passed to MySQL.

Project: Implement HAVING

For the project of this chapter, we will introduce support for HAVING under sorting in our basic database administration web application. Basically, a full-fledged web-based administration application should have support for JOIN and, to a certain extent, subqueries. However, this functionality will be left for room to grow.

The goals of this project are straightforward:

- Implement support for HAVING in the Python back-end of the application
- Code the HTML front-end to allow HAVING in conjunction with sorting

When we are done, we will also look at some ways that this application could (and should) be dressed up.

Revising the Python backend

Before implementing a user interface for any functionality, one naturally needs to code support into the program itself. In the case of HAVING, we need to do the following in pymyadmin.py:

- Revise the qaction function to insert HAVING into the MySQL statement that it passes to execute()
- Revise the qaction function call in main()
- Code support for appropriate option-handling—whether as CGI or as a command-line option passed by PHP

Revising qaction()

Currently, the qaction() function looks like this:

```
def qaction(qact, db, tb, columns, values, user, password,
*aggregates):
    """Forms SELECT and INSERT statements, passes them to execute(),
and returns the affected rows."""
    cursor = connection(user, password, db)

    calc = aggregates[0]
    colkey = aggregates[1]
    distinct = aggregates[2]
    sort = aggregates[3]
    key = aggregates[4]

    tname = tb + "("
    columns = columns.split(',')
    values = values.split(',')
    cols = ""
    vals = ""
    for i in xrange(0, len(columns)):
        col = columns[i].strip()
        val = values[i].strip()
```

```
                cols = cols + col
                vals = vals + "'" + val + "'"
                if i != len(columns) - 1:
                    cols = cols + ", "
                    vals = vals + ", ""
        if qact == "select":
            if calc != "NONE" or distinct != "NONE" or sort != "NONE" or
key != "NONE":
                if calc != "NONE":
                    if distinct == "yes":
                        selection = "%s(DISTINCT %s)" %(calc, colkey)
                    else:
                        selection = "%s(%s)" %(calc, colkey)
                else:
                    selection = "*"

                if sort != "NONE":
                    sorting = "%s %s" %(sort, key)
                else:
                    sorting = ""
                statement = "SELECT %s FROM %s WHERE %s = %s %s"
%(selection, tb, cols, vals, sorting)
            else:
                statement = "SELECT * FROM %s WHERE %s = %s" %(tb, cols,
vals)
            results = execute(statement, cursor, 'select')

        elif qact == "insert":
            statement = "INSERT INTO %s (%s) VALUES (%s)" %(tb, cols,
vals)
            results = execute(statement, cursor, 'insert')
        return results
```

In order to add facility for HAVING, we need to add some internal variables to carry the value of the column and value keys, the arguments for HAVING. We do not need to change the variable arguments of the function definition because the HAVING arguments will be passed as part of aggregates [].

After the assignment key = aggregates [4], seen previously, we should add:

```
        hcol = aggregates[5]
        hval = aggregates[6]
```

The need for HAVING will be qualified by the presence of a value for hcol. Find the test for sorting with the following if clause:

```
if sort != "NONE":":   ## or:  if sort is not None:
    sorting = "%s %s" %(sort, key)
else:
    sorting = ""
```

To assign a value for HAVING, we need to test whether sorting is desired and then whether hcol has any value. If sort and hcol both have a value other than NONE, we then prepare a value having. The if...else statement looks like this:

```
if hcol != "NONE" and sort != "NONE":
    having = "HAVING %s = '%s'" %(hcol, hval)
else:
    having = ""
```

With a value for having, we revise the SELECT statement to include having:

```
statement = "SELECT %s FROM %s WHERE %s = %s %s %s"
%(selection, tb, cols, vals, sorting, having)
```

Just as with sorting, nothing is added if no value is to be appended.

Revising main()

With support for HAVING implemented in qaction(), we can build support for it in main(). It is worth noting that we implemented HAVING in qaction in a way that does not require its use. If we wanted, we could create separate calls for each in main(), or another calling function.

To create support for HAVING in main(), we create another if...else clause in the while loop. Currently, for usage with PHP, the while loop reads as follows:

```
while 1:
    try:
        cursor = connectNoDB(opt.user, opt.password)
        authenticate = 1
    except:
        output = "Bad login information.  Please verify the
username and password that you are using before trying to login
again."
        authenticate = 0

    if authenticate == 1:
```

```
                    errmsg = "You have not specified the information necessary
for the action you chose.  Please check your information and specify
it correctly in the dialogue."

            if opt.dbact is not None:
                output = dbaction(opt.dbact, opt.dbname, cursor)
            elif opt.tbact is not None:
                output = tbaction(opt.tbact, opt.tbdbname, opt.tbname,
opt.columns, opt.values, opt.user, opt.password)
            elif opt.qact is not None:

                if opt.calc is not None:
                    calc = opt.calc
                    colkey = opt.colkey
                else:
                    calc = "NONE"
                    colkey = "NONE"
                if opt.distinct is not None:
                    distinct = opt.distinct
                else:
                    distinct = "NONE"
                if opt.sort is not None:
                    sort = opt.sort
                    key = opt.key
                else:
                    sort = "NONE"
                    key = "NONE"
                output = qaction(opt.qact, opt.qdbname, opt.qtbname,
opt.columns, opt.values, opt.user, opt.password, calc, colkey,
distinct, sort, key)

            elif opt.uact is not None:
                if opt.uact == "create":
                    act = "create-user"
                    output = uaction(opt.user, opt.password, act, opt.
username, opt.passwd)
                elif opt.uact == "drop":
                    act = "drop-user"
                    output = uaction(opt.user, opt.password, act, opt.
username)
                elif opt.uact == "grant" or opt.uact == "revoke":
                    output = uadmin(opt.user, opt.password, opt.uact,
opt.username, opt.privileges, opt.acldb, opt.acltb)
                else:
                    output = errmsg
```

```
printout = HTMLPage()
printout.message(output)
output = printout.page()

print output
break
```

The variable names used here would be different if the application is run under CGI because of the CGI modules. See *Chapter 7, Creating and Dropping* for more on the differences between using CGI and PHP and how to work with each.

It is possible to create a program that will run with both CGI and PHP by either testing how the program is called or by using a `try...except` structure for the options. However, coding such as that would only come into play if you needed to deploy the system in both environments and wanted to conserve on code.

We need to insert our `if...else` structure just after the `if...else` structure for the assignment of `sort` and `key`. When we are done, that code section should read as follows:

```
if opt.sort is not None:
    sort = opt.sort
    key = opt.key
else:
    sort = "NONE"
    key = "NONE"
if opt.hcol is not None  and opt.hval is not None:
    hcol = opt.hcol
    hval = opt.hval
else:
    hcol = "NONE"
    hval = "NONE"
```

In addition to testing the value of `opt.hcol`, we should also test for `None` in `hval`. Otherwise, we can get an error.

After the values of `hcol` and `hval` are assigned, we need to append each to the arguments for `qaction()` in appropriate order. If we conflate them, `qaction()` will assign their values in the wrong order.

```
output = qaction(opt.qact, opt.qdbname, opt.qtbname,
opt.columns, opt.values, opt.user, opt.password, calc, colkey,
distinct, sort, key, hcol, hval)
```

With that, HAVING is supported by the main() function. We still need to build support into the options of the program.

Revising the options

As with previous chapters, how you code support for the options, depends on whether you are coding for CGI or PHP. See *Chapter 7* for the difference on each. Heretofore, we have been coding for PHP due to its relative simplicity in executing, debugging and because PHP tends to execute faster than CGI when using default configurations.

Currently, the beginning of our options-handling for sorting looks like this (including the introductory code for optparse):

```
import optparse
# Get options
opt = optparse.OptionParser()
...
opt.add_option("-S", "--sort",
               action="store",
               type="string",
               help="how to sort results",
               dest="sort")
opt.add_option("-k", "--key",
               action="store",
               type="string",
               help="key to use when sorting",
               dest="key")
```

To add option support for HAVING, we need to support hcol and hval. Therefore, we need to add the following:

```
opt.add_option("-H", "--hcol",
               action="store",
               type="string",
               help="column to use for HAVING",
               dest="hcol")
opt.add_option("-V", "--hval",
               action="store",
               type="string",
               help="value to use for HAVING",
               dest="hval")
```

To be sure, Python does not care where in the list of options you put the assignment. As long as it is before the assignment of `opt` and `args`, it will be assigned with all of the other option values. However, for the sake of maintenance, it is best to add it after the sorting options are handled:

```
    opt.add_option("-H", "--hcol",
                action="store",
                type="string",
                help="column to use for HAVING",
                dest="hcol")
    opt.add_option("-V", "--hval",
                action="store",
                type="string",
                help="value to use for HAVING",
                dest="hval")
```

With that, we finish implementing support for HAVING in our administration application. However, we still need to create support for it in the HTML interface.

Revising the HTML interface

Currently, the section for queries in the HTML code reads as follows:

```
<div>QUERIES</div>
<input type="radio" name="qact" value="select"> SELECT<br>
<input type="radio" name="qact" value="insert"> INSERT<br>
  Database name: <input type="text" name="qdbname" value=""><br>
  Table name: <input type="text" name="qtbname" value=""><br>
  Columns (comma-separated: <input type="text"
                                  name="columns" value=""><br>
  Values (comma-separated: <input type="text"
                                name="values"value=""><br>Calculations:
<select name="calc">
  <option value="COUNT">COUNT</option>
  <option value="SUM">SUM</option>
  <option value="MAX">MAX</option>
  <option value="MIN">MIN</option>
  <option value="AVG">AVG</option>
</select>
(<input type="text" name="colkey" value="">)<br>
DISTINCT?
<input type="radio" name="distinct" value="yes">Yes
<input type="radio" name="distinct" value="no">No
<br>Sorting:
```

```
<select name="sort">
  <option value="ORDER BY">ORDER BY</option>
  <option value="GROUP BY">GROUP BY</option>
</select>
<input type="text" name="key" value="">
<br><br>
```

To finalize our implementation of HAVING for sorting, we need to solicit values for hcol and hval from the user. After the value of key is assigned and before the double line-breaks, we should insert the following dialogue:

```
<br>
HAVING <br>
Column: <input type="text" name="hcol" value="">
<br>
Value: <input type="text" name="hval" value="">
```

Then the dialogue is finished. As is illustrated in the following section *Room to grow*, there are several things that we can and should add to this application before we consider it complete.

Room to grow

With HAVING implemented for sorting in our administration application, we will leave this project for others in subsequent chapters. As has been alluded several times, this application could use more coding to make it more useful and usable than it is at present. In particular, some issues that you should address are:

- How would you implement the various kinds of joins and subqueries?
- As HAVING is used outside of sorting, how would you allow a user to use it in a generic SELECT statement?
- Currently, the tabular information returned by SELECT is not formatted. How would you allow for its formatting while being sensitive to the fact that not all statements will be SELECT statements?
- Aside from being monochrome, the page is now much more verbose than when we started. How could you use CSS to create a tab-based menu system instead of the sub-headers to simplify the interface and keep everything on one screen?

Summary

In this chapter, we have covered how to use HAVING clauses, subqueries, and joins in Python. We have also seen:

- How to restrict results using HAVING
- How HAVING differs from WHERE
- When it is best to use the following—WHERE or HAVING
- How to narrow data even further with subqueries
- Using UNION to concatenate two results sets before they are returned
- The various ways to join tables, including the difference between a LEFT JOIN and a RIGHT JOIN as well as the differences between INNER joins, OUTER joins, NATURAL joins, and CROSS joins

In the next chapter, we will look at several more of MySQL's powerful functions and how to use them best in Python.

12
String Functions

We have already seen how we can pass the burden of certain processes onto the database server. The MySQL aggregate functions are optimized for their tasks. This reduces the amount of I/O passed back to Python and results in less data for our programs to process. In addition to the aggregate functions, MySQL also provides other functions that help us process data before it is returned to Python.

In this chapter, we will see:

- The way MySQL allows us to combine strings and return the single, resulting value
- How to extract part of a string or the location of a part, thus saving on processing
- How to convert cases of results

All of this can be done through MySQL for Python. After we have seen the common ways to juggle strings in MySQL, we will then apply it in this chapter's project.

Preparing results before their return

MySQL offers a bevy of functions for preparing results before returning them. Here we will look at the more common ones. Before we begin, it is worth noting that all MySQL functions are limited by the size of the `max_allowed_packet` variable. If the value(s) to be returned exceed the maximum allowed packet size, MySQL will return a NULL value.

For information on fine-tuning server variables such as max_allowed_packet, see:
`http://dev.mysql.com/doc/refman/5.5/en/server-parameters.html`

CONCAT() function

The CONCAT() function allows us to concatenate, or join, two or more values. The basic syntax is as follows:

```
SELECT CONCAT(value1, value2);
```

The values can be either string or numeric values:

```
SELECT CONCAT(22, '/', 7);
+--------------------+
| CONCAT(22, '/', 7) |
+--------------------+
| 22/7               |
+--------------------+
SELECT CONCAT('pi = ', 22, '/', 7);
+-----------------------------+
| CONCAT('pi = ', 22, '/', 7) |
+-----------------------------+
| pi = 22/7                   |
+-----------------------------+
```

However, as in Python, a string value passed without quotes causes MySQL to throw an error:

```
SELECT CONCAT(pi, ' = ', 3, '.', 14156);

ERROR 1054 (42S22): Unknown column 'pi' in 'field list'
```

It may seem strange that MySQL should complain about a 'field list', but that is exactly what it sees when it looks at CONCAT(). Further, one is able to use field names in the argument of CONCAT() to affect calculations or formatting. Using the sakila database, for example, we can return the length of each title in terms of hours as follows:

```
SELECT title, CONCAT(length/60, ' hours') FROM film;
```

If we append WHERE title LIKE 'WAR%' after film, we get the following results:

```
+------------------+----------------------------+
| title            | CONCAT(length/60, ' hours') |
+------------------+----------------------------+
| WAR NOTTING      | 1.3333 hours               |
| WARDROBE PHANTOM | 2.9667 hours               |
| WARLOCK WEREWOLF | 1.3833 hours               |
| WARS PLUTO       | 2.1333 hours               |
+------------------+----------------------------+
```

As usual, we can use AS to clean up the results if we want:

```
SELECT title AS Title, CONCAT(length/60, ' hours') AS
Length FROM film WHERE title LIKE 'WAR%';
```

```
+------------------+--------------+
| Title            | Length       |
+------------------+--------------+
| WAR NOTTING      | 1.3333 hours |
...
```

SUBSTRING() or MID()

The function calls SUBSTRING() and MID() are synonymous. Which one you choose is a matter of style. Their purpose is to allow you to extract a substring, or the midsection, of a value within the bounds of certain index points. The syntax is as follows:

```
SELECT SUBSTRING(value, position, length);
SELECT MID(value, position, length);
```

The value must adhere to the usual rules—quotes for strings. The first index point is the beginning point within the value and is a required argument. The second index value is optional. Its absence causes the return of the string from the initial index point to the end of the value. For a string, "I'm afraid not", we can get everything from the fifth position onward:

```
SELECT SUBSTRING("I'm afraid not", 5);
+--------------------------------+
| SUBSTRING("I'm afraid not", 5) |
+--------------------------------+
| afraid not                     |
+--------------------------------+
```

While the second index point is optional, it has a very different meaning in MySQL from Python when it is used. Contrary to its meaning when specifying a range, say, in xrange() and similar Python functions, the second index point is *not* an absolute index in the word, but it is the number of positions forward from the first index point.

An example for extracting the middle word from the string, "I'm afraid not is":

```
select mid("I'm afraid not", 4,8);
+---------------------------------+
| mid("I'm afraid not", 4,8) |
+---------------------------------+
| afraid          |
+---------------------------------+
```

Finally, if we don't want to specify a precise range within the value, we don't have to. MySQL's SUBSTRING() and MID() functions allow for counting backward from the end of the value. Just use a negative number for the number of places from the end, from where you want MySQL to count.

```
SELECT SUBSTRING("I'm afraid not",-3);
+------------------------------+
| SUBSTRING("I'm afraid not",-3) |
+------------------------------+
| not          |
+------------------------------+
```

TRIM()

The TRIM() function performs the same job as Python's built-in strip() function: it strips leading and trailing whitespaces from results. However, TRIM() is also more flexible than strip() in that it can be customized to strip a specified value(s) from the beginning of a value, the end of a value, or both.

Basic syntax

The basic syntax is:

```
SELECT TRIM(<some value>);
```

It looks like this in real life:

```
SELECT TRIM(' Barstow                ') AS spot;
```

In order to show the stripping of the string, the `results` column is given a smaller title than the string itself.

```
+---------+
| spot    |
+---------+
| Barstow |
+---------+
```

`TRIM()` can be applied to numeric values as well:

```
    SELECT trim( 1234567890                        ) AS numbers;
```

This results in the following output:

```
+------------+
| numbers    |
+------------+
| 1234567890 |
+------------+
```

Options

In addition to this basic syntax, `TRIM()` also supports the option of specifying whether the value to be removed is at the beginning or end of the value, or both. To do this, we specify either `LEADING`, `TRAILING`, or `BOTH` in the argument. We also must specify then precisely what we want trimmed as shown in the following session:

```
mysql> SELECT TRIM(LEADING ' ' FROM '    Barstow    ') AS spot;
+----------------+
| spot           |
+----------------+
| Barstow        |
+----------------+
1 row in set (0.00 sec)


mysql> SELECT TRIM(TRAILING ' ' FROM '    Barstow    ') AS spot;
+----------------+
| spot           |
+----------------+
|     Barstow    |
```

```
+----------------+
1 row in set (0.00 sec)


mysql> SELECT TRIM(BOTH ' ' FROM '    Barstow    ') AS spot;

+---------+
| spot    |
+---------+
| Barstow |
+---------+

1 row in set (0.00 sec)
```

Obviously, the default for TRIM() is to strip whitespace from both sides. However, as you might deduce from the previous examples, we can also specify precise values to pull instead of whitespaces.

```
mysql> SELECT TRIM(LEADING 'B' FROM 'Barstow') AS spot;

+--------+
| spot   |
+--------+
| arstow |
+--------+

1 row in set (0.00 sec)
```

Note that we removed the whitespace from the argument. If we hadn't, the stripping would not have done what we wanted. For example, try the following statement on your own:

```
    SELECT TRIM(LEADING 'B' FROM '    Barstow    ') as spot;
```

Alternatives

There are also two variants to TRIM() that offer a shorthand for the LEADING and TRAILING options. Instead of passing those words with their necessary additional syntax, we can strip whitespace from the left of the value with LTRIM(), and from the right with RTRIM(), as follows:

```
mysql> SELECT LTRIM('  Barstow  ') as spot;

+--------------+
| spot         |
+--------------+
| Barstow      |
```

```
+-------------+
1 row in set (0.00 sec)


mysql> SELECT RTRIM('  Barstow  ') as spot;

+-------------+
| spot        |
+-------------+
|   Barstow |
+-------------+
1 row in set (0.00 sec)
```

REPLACE()

The REPLACE() substitutes one value for another within a given stream of text, whether string or numeric. For string values, the operation is case-sensitive. Unlike Python's substitution functions, it does not work with regular expressions (as of MySQL 5.5). The basic syntax is:

```
SELECT REPLACE(base value, value to be replaced, replacement value);
```

A string-based example is:

```
mysql> SELECT REPLACE("I'm afraid not", 'fraid ', ' frayed k') as spot;

+--------------------+
| spot               |
+--------------------+
| I'm a frayed knot |
+--------------------+
1 row in set (0.00 sec)
```

But it also works with numeric values because the result is first converted to a string:

```
mysql> SELECT REPLACE(22/7, 3, 2) as num;

+--------+
| num |
+--------+
| 2.1429 |
+--------+
1 row in set (0.00 sec)
```

In this case, quotes are optional:

```
mysql> SELECT REPLACE(10/3, '3', '2') as spot;
+--------+
| spot |
+--------+
| 2.2222 |
+--------+
1 row in set (0.00 sec)
```

Note that the replacement is indiscriminate—all instances of the first value are changed to the second. One must consequently be careful in how REPLACE() is applied. REPLACE() is multibyte safe.

INSERT()

INSERT() functions similarly to REPLACE() in that it injects a substring into a value. Whether it overwrites part or all of that value is determined by the arguments you pass to it. The basic syntax is as follows:

```
SELECT INSERT(base value, position, length, string to be inserted);
```

An example is:

```
mysql> SELECT INSERT("I'm afraid", 4, 0, ' not ') as clause;
+----------------+
| clause         |
+----------------+
| I'm not afraid |
+----------------+
1 row in set (0.00 sec)
```

This inserts the word not surrounded by two blank spaces just after the "m" in I'm. As the length of the insertion is 0 characters, no part of the original value is overwritten. However, because of that, the resulting value has two spaces between "not" and "afraid" instead of just one. We could either truncate the value to be inserted by one space or we can overwrite the space before "afraid".

To truncate "not", we would use TRIM:

```
mysql> SELECT INSERT("I'm afraid", 4, 0, RTRIM(' not ')) as clause;
+----------------+
| clause         |
+----------------+
| I'm not afraid |
+----------------+
1 row in set (0.00 sec)
```

But a less obtuse way of affecting the same results is to increase the length by one:

```
mysql> SELECT INSERT("I'm afraid", 4, 1, ' not ') as clause;
+----------------+
| clause         |
+----------------+
| I'm not afraid |
+----------------+
1 row in set (0.00 sec)
```

INSERT() works well with multi-byte characters as either the base value or the insertion string. If the position exceeds the length of the base value, the base value itself is returned:

```
mysql> SELECT INSERT("I'm afraid", 23, 1, ' not ') as clause;
+------------+
| clause     |
+------------+
| I'm afraid |
+------------+
1 row in set (0.00 sec)
```

If the length of the insertion exceeds the length of the original base value but the position of insertion is valid, the rest of the base value is overwritten:

```
mysql> SELECT INSERT("I'm afraid", 4, 23, ' not ') as clause;
+----------+
| clause |
+----------+
| I'm not |
+----------+
1 row in set (0.00 sec)
```

All four of the arguments for INSERT() are required, and an error is thrown if any of them is missing.

REGEXP

Technically speaking, REGEXP does not appear as a function. However, it is included here because it operates on strings, such as SUBSTRING() and because it is listed among the string functions in the MySQL documentation. The syntax for the REGEXP phrase is:

```
value REGEXP pattern
```

REGEXP is more a keyword token to distinguish a part of the SELECT statement as being special, as being a regular expression. MySQL evaluates regular expressions on the fly, compiling them as needed, instead of compiling them as one usually does in Python.

If the pattern match is a success, REGEXP causes MySQL to return 1; otherwise, it returns 0. Here a carat (^) is used to test the beginning of the value.

```
mysql> SELECT 'Barstow' REGEXP '^B';
+-----------------------+
| 'Barstow' REGEXP '^B' |
+-----------------------+
|                     1 |
+-----------------------+
1 row in set (0.00 sec)

mysql> SELECT 'Barstow' REGEXP '^C';
+-----------------------+
| 'Barstow' REGEXP '^C' |
```

```
+----------------------+
|            0 |
+----------------------+
1 row in set (0.00 sec)
```

The nature of the value against which the pattern is checked can be either a precise value or a representation of search results (for example, column name). Therefore, REGEXP can appear in the column specification or in other clauses like WHERE. Consider the following example using sakila:

```
mysql> SELECT title FROM film WHERE title REGEXP '^TA.{3}K';
+-----------+
| title     |
+-----------+
| TAXI KICK |
+-----------+
1 row in set (0.00 sec)
```

The carat matches the beginning of the value to be assessed similar to the way it matches the beginning of a line in Python. The dot after TA matches any single character. The {3} is a complex way of rendering . . . —that is, three characters in succession. As it turns out, there is only one title in film that begins with TA and that has three characters before K.

A complete list of MySQL's regular expression meta-characters follow:

Meta-character	Meaning
.	Match any character
?	Match zero or one
*	Match zero or more
+	Match one or more
{n}	Match n times
{m,n}	Match m through n times
{n,}	Match n or more times
^	Beginning of line
$	End of line
[[:<:]]	Match beginning of words
[[:>:]]	Match ending of words

Meta-character	Meaning
[:class:]	Match a character class
[abc]	Match one of enclosed chars
[^xyz]	Match any character not enclosed
|	Separates alternatives

Most of these will be familiar from working with Python's regular expressions. However, character classes are foreign to Python. They are part of MySQL's support for the **POSIX** standard.

> **POSIX** stands for **Portable Operating System Interface for Unix**, a standard created by the IEEE as IEEE 1003 and adopted by the International Standards Organisation as ISO/IEC 9945. It initially defined a common **Application Programming Interface** (**API**) for use across Unix-like operating systems. But, the platforms that are at least partially compliant with it have since been extended to include Microsoft Windows among others.

A character class is essentially shorthand for a large number of characters. Instead of writing every letter of the alphabet like this:

```
mysql> SELECT 'Barstow' REGEXP '[abcdefghijklmnopqrstuvwxyz]';
```

We can use [:alpha:] to represent every alphabetic character and get the same results:

```
mysql> SELECT 'Barstow' REGEXP '[:alpha:]';
+-----------------------------+
| 'Barstow' REGEXP '[:alpha:]' |
+-----------------------------+
|                           1 |
+-----------------------------+
1 row in set (0.00 sec)
```

Character classes can include every alphanumeric character, punctuation, or several others. A complete list of POSIX character classes are listed with their definition and ASCII `regex` equivalent as follows:

POSIX	Description	ASCII
`[:alnum:]`	Alphanumeric characters	`[a-zA-Z0-9]`
`[:alpha:]`	Alphabetic characters	`[a-zA-Z]`
`[:ascii:]`	ASCII characters	`[\x00-\x7F]`
`[:blank:]`	Space and tab	`[ \t]`
`[:cntrl:]`	Control characters	`[\x00-\x1F\x7F]`
`[:digit:]`	Digits	`[0-9]`
`[:graph:]`	Visible characters	`[\x21-\x7E]`
`[:lower:]`	Lowercase letters	`[a-z]`
`[:print:]`	Visible characters and spaces	`[\x20-\x7E]`
`[:punct:]`	Punctuation and symbols	`[!"#$%&'()*+,\-./:;<=>?@[\\\]^_`{|}~]`
`[:space:]`	All whitespace characters, including line breaks	`[ \t\r\n\v\f]`
`[:upper:]`	Uppercase letters	`[A-Z]`
`[:word:]`	Word characters	`[A-Za-z0-9_]`
`[:xdigit:]`	Hexadecimal digits	`[A-Fa-f0-9]`

Accessing and using index data

Here you will see how to calcualte the length of a value with LENGTH() function.

LENGTH()

Like `len()` in Python, the `LENGTH()` function of MySQL returns the bitwise length of the value that is passed to it. Where multi-byte characters are used in the argument, multiple byte values are tabulated. Therefore, in `sakila`, we can retrieve the title and length of the title for each film. Here we use a `WHERE` clause to limit the results for the sake of space.

```
SELECT title as title, LENGTH(title) as title_length FROM film WHERE
title LIKE 'TA%E';
```

```
+-------------------+--------------+
| title             | title_length |
+-------------------+--------------+
| TALENTED HOMICIDE |           17 |
| TARZAN VIDEOTAPE  |           16 |
+-------------------+--------------+
```

The `LENGTH()` function can similarly be used in the argument of other functions. For example, if we wanted to extract the approximate middle of a value, we could divide the length by four and cull out everything from the one fourth point, the length divided by four, to the three fourth point, the length divided by four multiplied by 2 added to the value of the one fourth point. Remember that the second index value is not to a point in the value, but is added to the initial index value in order to calculate the slice. Therefore, rather than multiply by 3, we multiply it by 2 and use that value as the second index value.

```
SELECT SUBSTRING("I'm afraid not", LENGTH("I'm afraid not")/4,
LENGTH("I'm afraid not")/4*2) AS length;
```

The length of the value is 14 characters. If we divide that by 4, we get 3.5 (4 when rounded). This is our first index value. If we double that value, we get 7. Seven characters from the 4 is the end of the word "afraid". Therefore, the results are as follows:

```
+----------+
| length   |
+----------+
| afraid   |
+----------+
```

An easier way to affect this selection is to define a user-defined variable name. It is quite complicated to read.

> By using the variable name @string, we can assign the string value and not have to retype it.
>
> ```
> SET @string = "I'm afraid not"; SELECT SUBSTRING(@
> string, LENGTH(@string)/4, LENGTH(@string)/4*2) AS
> length;
> ```
>
> If we need to do this repeatedly, we could simply insert the value of @ string into a variable assignment for statement as follows:
>
> ```
> statement1 = "SET @string = "%s"" %("I'm afraid
> not")
> ```
>
> We then define the SELECT statement in Python accordingly:
>
> ```
> statement2 = "SELECT SUBSTRING(@string, LENGTH(@
> string)/4, LENGTH(@string)/4*2) AS length"
> ```
>
> We do not need to define @string if we execute both statements through the same connection. So after creating a connection and our cursor within a try...except structure, we can then execute the two statements in succession:
>
> ```
> cursor.execute(statement1)
> ```
> ```
> cursor.execute(statement2)
> ```
>
> We can then follow the execution of statement2 with a fetchall() call and subsequent processing:
>
> ```
> results = cursor.fetchall()
> ```
> ```
> for item in results:
>   print item[0]
> ```
>
> The results:
>
> ```
> afraid
> ```

We can retrieve the index location of given strings using the INSTR() or LOCATE() functions.

INSTR() or LOCATE()

Both INSTR() and LOCATE() serve to return the beginning index location of a given string. The main difference between them is the order in which the arguments are given. However, LOCATE() also supports more options.

INSTR()

INSTR() accepts the base string first followed by the pattern to be found:

```
SELECT INSTR(base string, pattern);
```

It then returns the numerical index where the first instance of the pattern begins. To illustrate, consider the following two examples:

```
mysql> SELECT INSTR('Can you find a bar in Barstow?', 'Bar') as results;
+-------+
| results |
+-------+
|   16 |
+-------+
1 row in set (0.00 sec)

mysql> SELECT INSTR('Can you find a bar in Barstow?', 'Bars') as results;
+-------+
| results |
+-------+
|   23 |
+-------+
1 row in set (0.00 sec)
```

In the first instance, we search for Bar and find it first at point 16 in the string. However, in the second instance, we look for Bars, thus avoid the word bar, and find the beginning of Barstow, instead.

You will notice that the match is not case-sensitive. Therefore, if you want case-sensitive matching, you will need to pull the results into Python. MySQL only performs case-sensitive matching when one of the strings is binary.

LOCATE()

As previously mentioned, LOCATE() supports a simpler syntax, similar to INSTR(), and a more complex syntax. To function similarly to INSTR(), we simply reverse the arguments and pass it to LOCATE():

```
mysql> SELECT LOCATE('bar', 'Can you find a bar in Barstow?') as results;
+---------+
| results |
+---------+
|    16 |
+---------+
1 row in set (0.00 sec)
```

This simpler syntax is also echoed in a synonymous operation called `POSITION()`. That function requires syntax exemplified as follows:

```
mysql> SELECT POSITION('bar' in 'Can you find a bar in
Barstow?') as results;
+---------+
| results |
+---------+
|      16 |
+---------+
1 row in set (0.00 sec)
```

As before, MySQL gives us the initial index of the first occurrence of the string. However, what if you want the second occurrence of the string? `LOCATE()` allows you to specify the beginning point of the search by stating the index point after the base string.

```
mysql> SELECT LOCATE('bar', 'Can you find a bar in Barstow?', 16) as
results;
+---------+
| results |
+---------+
|      16 |
+---------+
1 row in set (0.00 sec)
```

As with `INSTR()`, `LOCATE()` is safe for use with multi-byte characters and is only case-sensitive when one of the arguments is a binary string.

Nuancing data

In addition to performing indexing and substituting on data, MySQL also allows for several ways of massaging the data to suit your needs. Some of the more common ones are discussed in this chapter.

ROUND()

As the name suggests, the mathematical function `ROUND()` serves to round decimal values to a specified number of places. The base value comes first in the syntax:

```
SELECT ROUND(base value, number of positions);
```

So rounding an already rough approximation of Pi would look like this:

```
mysql> SELECT ROUND(22/7, 2) as PI;
+------+
| PI |
+------+
| 3.14 |
+------+
1 row in set (0.00 sec)
```

The ROUND() function will accept whatever value you give it for the number of positions. However, if the number of places exceeds MySQL's built-in abilities to calculate a value, the extra places will be filled with zeroes:

```
mysql> SELECT ROUND(22/7, 20) as PI;
+------------------------+
| PI                     |
+------------------------+
| 3.14285714200000000000 |
+------------------------+
1 row in set (0.00 sec)
```

ROUND() operates on numerical values only. In an effort to fail gracefully, it will return all zero values and a warning if you pass it a string:

```
mysql> SELECT ROUND('cat', 2) as PI;
+------+
| PI |
+------+
| 0.00 |
+------+
1 row in set, 1 warning (0.00 sec)
```

This obviously cuts against the grain of the Zen of Python's "Errors should never pass silently", so one must be wary of it.

FORMAT()

The "format" feature functions similarly to ROUND() in that it allows you to specify the number of decimal places for the results. It differs in that it will make the output of the statement more human-friendly by adding punctuation for the value. For example, division of large numbers frequently results in four or more digits to the left of the decimal point. ROUND() treats them as follows:

```
mysql> SELECT ROUND(10000/3, 5) AS result;

+------------+
| result     |
+------------+
| 3333.33333 |
+------------+
1 row in set (0.00 sec)
```

But FORMAT() makes the results much easier to read:

```
mysql> SELECT FORMAT(10000/3, 2) AS result;

+----------+
| result   |
+----------+
| 3,333.33 |
+----------+
1 row in set (0.00 sec)
```

Additionally, FORMAT() supports multiple locales. If your MySQL installation allows for more than your default locale, you can specify the format you require by including the locale as a third argument to the function.

```
SELECT FORMAT(base value, number of decimal places, locale);
```

You can find more on FORMAT() in the MySQL documentation:

http://dev.mysql.com/doc/refman/5.5/en/string-functions.
html#function_format

More on specifying locales can be found at:

http://dev.mysql.com/doc/refman/5.5/en/locale-support.html

UPPER()

In addition to the mathematical functions, MySQL also provides functions to massage the format of string data. String values frequently come as normal text—essentially a camel-backed mixture of capitals and lowercase letters. The UPPER() function makes them all uppercase and takes only the string as an argument:

```
mysql> SELECT UPPER('Can you find a bar in Barstow?') as results;

+-------------------------------+
| results                       |
+-------------------------------+
| CAN YOU FIND A BAR IN BARSTOW? |
+-------------------------------+
1 row in set (0.00 sec)
```

LOWER()

The LOWER() function is similar to UPPER() in that it performs a single function and takes only the string to be modified as an argument. As the name implies, it renders all characters lowercase:

```
mysql> SELECT LOWER('Meeting at the UN HQ in NYC') as results;

+----------------------------+
| results                    |
+----------------------------+
| meeting at the un hq in nyc |
+----------------------------+
1 row in set (0.00 sec)
```

Project: Creating your own functions

Comparing MySQL's string functions to Python's, you will notice that Python supports the capitalize() and capwords() functions. These capitalize the initial letter of the string and the first letter of each word, respectively. MySQL has no built-in capability to do this. It either returns all uppercase, all lowercase, or the original format of the string value. To put the onus of capitalization on the MySQL server, we need to define our own functions.

Hello()

To create a function, we necessarily have to go back to the CREATE statement. As in a Python function definition, MySQL expects us to declare the name of the function as well as any arguments it requires. Unlike Python, MySQL also wants the type of data that will be received by the function. The beginning of a basic MySQL function definition looks like this:

```
CREATE FUNCTION hello(s CHAR(20))
```

MySQL then expects to know what kind of data to return. Again, we use the MySQL data type definitions for this.

```
RETURNS CHAR(50)
```

This just tells MySQL that the function will return a character string of 50 characters or less.

If the function will always perform the same task, it is best for the sake of performance to include the keyword DETERMINISTIC next. If the behavior of the function varies, use the keyword NON-DETERMINISTIC. If no keyword is set for the characteristic of the function, MySQL defaults to NON-DETERMINISTIC.

> You can learn more about the characteristic keywords used in function definitions at:
> http://dev.mysql.com/doc/refman/5.5/en/create-procedure.html

Finally comes the meat of the function definition. Here we can set variables and perform any calculations that we want. For our basic definition, we will simply return a concatenated string:

```
RETURN CONCAT('Hello, ', s, '!');
```

The function obviously concatenates the word 'Hello' with whatever argument is passed to it and appends an exclamation point at the end. To call it we use SELECT as with the other functions:

```
mysql> SELECT hello('world') as Greeting;
+---------------+
| Greeting      |
+---------------+
| Hello, world! |
+---------------+
1 row in set (0.00 sec)
```

Capitalise()

A function to capitalize every initial letter in a string follows the same pattern. The main point of the function is to walk through the string, character by character, and use UPPER() on every character that does not follow a letter.

DELIMITER

Obviously, we need a way to pass the entire function to MySQL without having any of the lines evaluated until we call it. To do this, we use the keyword DELIMITER. DELIMITER allows users to tell MySQL to evaluate lines that end in the character(s) we set. So the process for complex function definitions becomes:

1. Change the delimiter.
2. Pass the function with the usual semicolons to indicate the end of the line.
3. Change the delimiter back to a semicolon.
4. Call the function.

The DELIMITER keyword allows us to specify more than one character as the line delimiter. So in order to ensure we don't need to worry about our code inadvertently conflicting with a line delimiter, let's make the delimiter @@:

```
DELIMITER @@
```

The function definition

From here, we are free to define a function to our specification. The definition line will read as follows:

```
CREATE FUNCTION `Capitalise`(instring VARCHAR(1000))
```

The function will return a character string of similar length and variability:

```
RETURNS VARCHAR(1000)
```

When MySQL functions extend beyond the simplest calculations, such as hello(), MySQL requires us to specify the beginning and ending of the function. We do that with the keywords BEGIN and END. So let's begin the function:

```
BEGIN
```

Next, we need to declare our variables and their types using the keyword DECLARE:

```
DECLARE i INT DEFAULT 1;
DECLARE achar, imark CHAR(1);
DECLARE outstring VARCHAR(1000) DEFAULT LOWER(instring);
```

The DEFAULT keyword allows us to specify what should happen if outstring should fail for some reason.

Next, we define a WHILE loop:

```
WHILE i <= CHAR_LENGTH(instring) DO
```

The WHILE loop obviously begins with a conditional statement based on the character length of instring. The resulting action begins with the keyword DO. From here, we set a series of variables and express what should happen where a character follows one of the following:

blank space & '' _ ? ; : ! , - / (.

The operational part of the function looks like this:

```
    SET achar = SUBSTRING(instring, i, 1);
    SET imark = CASE WHEN i = 1 THEN ' '
        ELSE SUBSTRING(instring, i - 1, 1) END CASE;
    IF imark IN (' ', '&', '''', '_', '?', ';', ':', '!', ',', '-
', '/', '(', '.') THEN SET outstring = INSERT(outstring, i, 1,
UPPER(achar));
    END IF;
    SET i = i + 1;
```

Much of this code is self-explanatory. It is worth noting, however, that the apodosis of any conditional in MySQL must end with the keyword END. In the case of IF, we use END IF.

In the second SET statement, the keyword CASE is an evaluative keyword that functions similar to the try...except structure in Python. If the WHEN condition is met, the empty THEN apodosis is executed. Otherwise, the ELSE exception applies and the SUBSTRING function is run. The CASE structure ends with END CASE. MySQL will equally recognize the use of END instead.

The subsequent IF clause evaluates whether imark, defined as the character before achar, is one of the declared characters. If it is, then that character in instring is replaced with its uppercase equivalent in outstring.

After the IF clause is finished, the loop is incremented by one. After the entire string is processed, we then end the WHILE loop with:

```
END WHILE;
```

After the function's operations are completed, we return the value of outstring and indicate the end of the function:

```
RETURN outstring;
END@@
```

Finally, we must not forget to return the delimiter to a semicolon:

```
DELIMITER ;
```

 It is worth noting that, instead of defining a function in a MySQL session we can define it in a separate file and load it on the fly with the SOURCE command. If we save the function to a file called capfirst.sql in a directory temp, we can source it relatively:

```
SOURCE capfirst.sql;
```

We can also use:

```
SOURCE /home/skipper/temp/capfirst.sql;
```

Calling the function

With the function loaded into memory, we can then call it:

```
mysql> SELECT Capitalise('we have a meeting a.s.a.p.');
+-------------------------------------------+
| Capitalise('we have a meeting a.s.a.p.')  |
+-------------------------------------------+
| We Have A Meeting A.S.A.P.                |
+-------------------------------------------+
1 row in set (0.00 sec)
```

Of course, we would not normally write like this. However, we can call the function as part of a SELECT statement, just like any other MySQL function.

```
mysql> SELECT CONCAT(Capitalise('we '), 'have a meeting ', Capitalise('a.
s.a.p.')) as Message;
+---------------------------+
| Message                   |
+---------------------------+
| We have a meeting A.S.A.P. |
+---------------------------+
1 row in set (0.00 sec)
```

Defining the function in Python

As you can guess by now, calling the function in Python is as simple as passing it through `cursor.execute()`. If we have a cursor defined as `cursor`, we can pass the last example of the previous section as follows:

```
statement = "SELECT CONCAT(Capitalise('we '), 'have a meeting ',
Capitalise('a.s.a.p.')) as Message"
cursor.execute(statement)
```

We then proceed to `fetchall()` the results.

Defining the function as a Python value

Defining the function is a bit different from calling it. If you try to pass the function we previously defined through Python as a value of statement, you get a programming error that reads something like this:

_mysql_exceptions.ProgrammingError: (1064, "You have an error in your SQL syntax; check the manual that corresponds to your MySQL server version for the right syntax to use near 'DELIMITER @@\n\nCREATE FUNCTION `Capitalise`(instring varchar(1000))\n\tRETURNS VARC' at line 1")

The problem is the `DELIMITER` statement. If we pull those and define statement as follows, we will have no problems (thanks to William Chiquito for the following code):

```
statement = """
CREATE FUNCTION `Capitalise`(instring varchar(1000))
RETURNS VARCHAR(1000)
BEGIN

DECLARE i INT DEFAULT 1;
DECLARE achar, imark CHAR(1);
DECLARE outstring VARCHAR(1000) DEFAULT LOWER(instring);

WHILE i <= CHAR_LENGTH(instring) DO
SET achar = SUBSTRING(instring, i, 1);
SET imark = CASE WHEN i = 1 THEN ' '
ELSE SUBSTRING(instring, i - 1, 1) END;
IF imark IN (' ', '&', '''', '_', '?', ';', ':', '!', ',', '-', '/',
'(', '.') THEN SET outstring = INSERT(outstring, i, 1, UPPER(achar));
END IF;
```

```
SET i = i + 1;
END WHILE;

RETURN outstring;

END;
"""
```

Putting function definitions into your code increases the amount of runtime resources needed and can make maintenance quite onerous. Instead, we can save it in a separate file. Note that MySQL for Python does not allow the use of MySQL's SOURCE command. So one must use alternative means to the same effect.

Sourcing the MySQL function as a Python module

We can take the preceding code and source it as a Python module. Begin it with the following:

```
#!/usr/bin/env python
## This shebang is for a Linux machine. Adjust your shebang line
accordingly

def MakeStatement():

    statement = """
CREATE FUNCTION `CapMe`(instring varchar(1000))
...
and end it:
...

END;

"""
    return statement

If we save it as capfirst.py, we can reference it as follows:
import capfirst
...
statement = capfirst.MakeStatement()
```

Sourcing the function as MySQL code

It may seem a bit excessive to put Python's function trappings around a variable assignment. A simpler way of affecting the same results is to read the MySQL file into memory as the value of statement and then pass that value through execute():

```
statement = open("/home/skipper/temp/capfirst.sql").read()
runit = cursor.execute(statement)
```

The effect is the same and the function is created in the end. Similar tactics can be used whenever you need to source a MySQL file (for example, the dump of a database).

Room to grow

This function does essentially what we want it to do: capitalizes the first letter of every word in the string. However, it still has a few drawbacks that should be addressed:

- What happens when you evaluate the string "we have a meeting a.s.a.p. in Brussels"? How would you rectify it?
- How would you handle a string such as "we were 'discussing' just that"?
- How do you write a function to load the function when you need it and get rid of it when you don't?
- The current function emulates the `capwords()` function of Python. How would you simulate Python's `capitalize()` function?

Summary

In this chapter, we have covered several of MySQL's string functions and ways to use them in Python. We have seen:

- How to concatenate two or more strings
- Ways to return only part of a string, leaving the larger string behind
- How to trim whitespaces from around a value
- Mysql's functions for replacing and inserting values into others
- How to form regular expressions for MySQL
- Ways to locate strings within other strings
- How to calculate the length of a value
- Ways to work with both numbers and character values to nuance raw data
- How to write functions for MySQL and use them in Python

In the next chapter, we will look at how to access the MySQL's metadata from within Python.

13
Showing MySQL Metadata

In previous chapters, we have moved from the basics of selecting, inserting, creating, and dropping in MySQL through Python. In this chapter, we will look at accessing MySQL's metadata through Python. We have seen a lot of this incidentally in preceding chapters. However, in this chapter, we will look at them in greater depth. By the end of this chapter, we will see the following:

- What MySQL metadata is available to us and how to access it
- How to get a list of databases and tables
- Ways to switch databases on-the-fly
- How to get columnar information

This information is very useful for creating intermediate levels of database management. At the end of the chapter, we will look at how to create a class representation of a database.

Within a MySQL session, the easiest way to access metadata is by using the INFORMATION_SCHEMA pseudo-table. By switching to it with:

```
USE INFORMATION_SCHEMA;
```

you can access a plethora of information. Doing this from within a Python program increases your program's overhead. So in this chapter, we will look at how to access metadata without switching databases.

The primary way to get MySQL to tell you anything is the SHOW command. What you get in return naturally depends on what you ask for. There are many different arguments that you can pass to SHOW, some of which appear as follows:

Arguments		
	EVENTS	
BINARY LOGS	FUNCTION CODE	PROFILES
BINLOG EVENTS	FUNCTION STATUS	RELAYLOG EVENTS
CHARACTER SET	GRANTS	SLAVE HOSTS
COLLATION	INDEX	SLAVE STATUS
COLUMNS	MASTER STATUS	STATUS
CONTRIBUTORS	OPEN TABLES	TABLE STATUS
CREATE	PLUGINS	TABLES
DATABASES	PRIVILEGES	TRIGGERS
ENGINE	PROCEDURE CODE	VARIABLES
ENGINES	PROCEDURE STATUS	WARNINGS
ERRORS	PROCESSLIST	

These are basic options, most of which can be further nuanced with the use of LIKE or other keywords to nuance or restrict the results. Some of these require different privileges than the average user. While many of these will be invaluable in accessing information about MySQL and the databases you access, many others are used infrequently, if at all. In the following discussion, we will look at key information about databases, tables, and MySQL system information that is most relevant to Python programming.

MySQL's system environment

MySQL offers access to a wide array of information about the environment in which your database is stored and the variables that impact your access to it. Of particular import for programming is understanding MySQL's engines, profiles, and system variables.

ENGINE

To understand the use of MySQL's ENGINE command, it is important to first understand what MySQL means by a database storage engine. When you create a database, MySQL defaults to storing data with the MyISAM database engine. It is a transactionless database storage engine that uses the following three files:

1 A format file (.frm).
2 An index file (.MYI for MYIndex).
3 Data file (.MYD for MYData).

MyISAM is sufficiently robust for most purposes, but there are following eight others that are worth noting:

1 InnoDB: A high-performance database engine for processing large volumes of data with efficient CPU usage and the use of transactions.
2 IBMDBI: A transaction-capable database engine designed for IBM's DB2 table format on IBM i servers.
3 MERGE: A merger of two or more MyISAM tables to function as one.
4 MEMORY (HEAP): An engine that stores all tables in memory; this is very fast but resource-intensive.
5 FEDERATED: Allows access to a remote database through a local MySQL instance.
6 ARCHIVE: An index-less storage engine that allows for efficient data storage.
7 CSV: Stores data in comma-delimited files.
8 BLACKHOLE: Receives data, but does not store it.

Oracle, the parent company of MySQL, has discussed changing the default to InnoDB in MySQL 5.5, so the default engine may change before MySQL 5.5 makes it out of beta. For other versions, the default engine remains MyISAM.

The most popular engines

While MySQL supports each of these engines, practice sees the following storage engines are used most often: `MyISAM`, `InnoDB`, and `MEMORY`. MySQL's comparison of these looks like the following:

	MyISM	InnoB	MEMORY
Multi-statement transactions, ROLLBACK	-	X	-
Foreign key constraints	-	X	-
Locking level	table	row	table
BTREE indexes	X	X	-
FULLTEXT indexes	X	-	-
HASH lookups	-	X	X
Other in-memory tree-based index	-	-	X
GIS, RTREE indexes	X	-	-
Unicode	X	X	-
Merge (union views)	X	-	-
Compress read-only storage	X	-	-
Relative disk use	low	high	-
Relative memory use	low	high	low

Additionally, many MySQL installations use networked databases referred to as **Network Database** (**NDB**), which combines several standard MySQL databases with the cluster-oriented storage engine for which it is named. You can find more about clustering MySQL databases at `http://dev.mysql.com/doc/refman/5.0/en/mysql-cluster-overview.html`

Transactions

While many of these points of comparison are self-explanatory, the use of transactions is worth further explanation because we have not used it much in this book. For the purposes of database management, a transaction is treated as a unit of work that can be compared against other units of work performed within a database management system. Put plainly, a **transaction** is effectively a collection of queries passed to MySQL in a particular order for a particular purpose.

Obviously, if you are retrieving data or inserting completely new information, the order in which the statements are executed frequently does not matter. However, if you use UPDATE or other statements that change the substance or structure of a dataset, the order matters a great deal.

Using transactions allows one to change the state of the database back to what it was before the commands were issued, and usually requires the use of the COMMIT keyword to commit the changes once they are affected. In MySQL for Python, we use the commit() method of the connection object after we have entered the data. Of the engines shown in the previous table, only InnoDB supports multiple-statement transactions and the ability to roll the state of the database back using ROLLBACK.

 For more on using transactions in InnoDB, see the MySQL manual at
http://dev.mysql.com/doc/refman/5.5/en/commit.html

Specifying the engine

To specify which engine to use, simply append the option to the CREATE statement for the table as follows:

```
CREATE TABLE mydb(myfield INT) ENGINE = <engine name>;
```

MySQL does allow each table of a database to use a different engine. For example:

```
mysql> CREATE TABLE t1(i1 INT) ENGINE=MyISAM;
Query OK, 0 rows affected (0.00 sec)
mysql> CREATE TABLE t2(i2 INT) ENGINE=INNODB;
Query OK, 0 rows affected (0.10 sec)
mysql> CREATE TABLE t3(i3 INT) ENGINE=MEMORY;

Query OK, 0 rows affected (0.00 sec)
```

This results in three tables each using a different engine.

 For information on using table spaces with InnoDB tables, see:
http://dev.mysql.com/doc/refman/5.5/en/multiple-
tablespaces.html

Whichever engine is used for a given table will naturally have an impact over how that data is stored and indexed. This can further have an impact on the choice of what backup method you use with which table (for more on MySQL disaster recovery, see the discussion in the next chapter).

ENGINE status

Each engine in MySQL is treated separately of the others. If you use InnoDB, MySQL allows you to access the log and the status information from within MySQL. To do so, we use the ENGINES keyword with SHOW.

```
mysql> SHOW ENGINE InnoDB STATUS;
```

The output will likely run off your screen. If you are on Windows or a similar graphic client to MySQL, this is usually not a problem. However, if you are using a traditional terminal on a Unix or Linux server, you would normally need a mouse to scroll through the data. A better way is to affix a \G at the end of the query. Or you can set the MySQL pager to whatever text viewing application is installed on the server that will receive piped input. On Unix machines, the text viewer more is generally available; on Linux, less is available. To pass output to the latter, use the PAGER command as follows:

```
mysql> PAGER less;
```

Now, less will be used to display output from MySQL, and the results of SHOW ENGINE can be browsed easily. Note that, because we set the PAGER value within the MySQL session, the assignment is only temporary and will refresh to the default when you next log in. Making the change persistent can be affected with the— PAGER flag, if you log in from a shell prompt (for more on this see: http://dev.mysql.com/doc/refman/5.5/en/mysql-commands.html).

SHOW ENGINES

Sometimes when working on a system that you did not set up, it is necessary to confirm, which database engines are supported by the local installation. To do that, use SHOW ENGINES. The output will be a table of all storage engines known to the current installation and their support status. For example:

```
mysql> SHOW ENGINES;
+------------+----------+------------------------------------------------
----------------+
| Engine     | Support  | Comment
|+-----------+----------+------------------------------------------------
----------------+
| MyISAM     | DEFAULT  | Default engine as of MySQL 3.23 with great
performance      |
| MEMORY     | YES      | Hash based, stored in memory, useful for
temporary tables      |
| InnoDB     | YES      | Supports transactions, row-level locking, and
foreign keys     |
| BerkeleyDB | NO       | Supports transactions and page-level locking
|
| BLACKHOLE  | YES      | /dev/null storage engine (anything you write to
it disappears)  |
| EXAMPLE    | NO       | Example storage engine
|
| ARCHIVE    | YES      | Archive storage engine
|
```

```
| CSV         | YES      | CSV storage engine
|
| ndbcluster  | DISABLED | Clustered, fault-tolerant, memory-based tables
|
| FEDERATED   | YES      | Federated MySQL storage engine
|
| MRG_MYISAM  | YES      | Collection of identical MyISAM tables
|
| ISAM        | NO       | Obsolete storage engine
|
+------------+----------+--------------------------------------------------
----------------+
```

Note that this example was run against an earlier 5.x version of MySQL. MySQL 5.5, for example, does not support the `BerkeleyDB`.

Profiling

Profiling is MySQL's form of user monitoring. When used, it tracks several aspects of system performance and the resources used in a given session. By default, it is switched off. To turn it on, key:

```
mysql> SET PROFILING = 1;
```

When profiling is switched on, you can view your session data using one of two keywords.

SHOW PROFILE

To show your profile, simply enter:

```
mysql> SHOW PROFILE;
```

MySQL will then return several statistics that will look similar to the following:

```
+--------------------+----------+
| Status             | Duration |
+--------------------+----------+
| (initialization)   | 0.000064 |
| Opening tables     | 0.000025 |
| query end          | 0.000008 |
| freeing items      | 0.00001  |
| logging slow query | 0.000005 |
+--------------------+----------+
```

SHOW PROFILES

However, if you want to view performance by query, you need to use the PROFILES keyword. This will trace your history as you switched on profiling and recount the execution times for each query you passed:

```
mysql> SHOW PROFILES;

+----------+------------+----------------------------+
| Query_ID | Duration   | Query                      |
+----------+------------+----------------------------+
|        1 | 0.00017000 | SHOW ENGINES               |
|        2 | 0.00100500 | SHOW ENGINE innodb STATUS  |
|        3 | 0.00011200 | SET PROFILING = 1          |
+----------+------------+----------------------------+
```

SHOW system variables

MySQL also provides access to a plethora of database system variables when you issue the query such as:

```
mysql> SHOW VARIABLES;
```

If you are using MySQL's default pager, the results table will usually scroll off the screen. One does not normally browse the system variables. On the contrary, one uses matching to cull out a particular value. For example, if we wanted to know which version of MySQL is in use, we would match against the value version:

```
mysql> SHOW VARIABLES LIKE 'version';

+---------------+--------------------+
| Variable_name | Value              |
+---------------+--------------------+
| version       | 5.0.51a-3ubuntu5.4 |
+---------------+--------------------+
```

If, however, we did not know the variable that we needed, we can use the following wildcard matching just as easily:

```
mysql> SHOW VARIABLES LIKE '%version%';

+------------------------+--------------------+
| Variable_name          | Value              |
+------------------------+--------------------+
| protocol_version       | 10                 |
| version                | 5.0.51a-3ubuntu5.4 |
| version_comment        | (Ubuntu)           |
| version_compile_machine | i486              |
| version_compile_os     | debian-linux-gnu   |
+------------------------+--------------------+
```

Exactly which variables are available will differ by installation and server version. For a comprehensive list of variables with links to the import of each, see:

```
http://dev.mysql.com/doc/refman/5.5/en/server-system-variables.html
```

Be sure to adjust the 5.5 (version) to read according to your server version.

Accessing database metadata

MySQL provides access to several aspects of databases, tables, or extensions thereof. Combining the various options creates the potential for interactive programs, as we will see later in this chapter. As with the MySQL environmental commands, all statements discussed here presume the use of SHOW.

DATABASES

If you are creating a wholly interactive system for database administration, you will need to access the list of databases. To do this in MySQL, we use the following command:

```
mysql> SHOW DATABASES;
```

The result is a single column table showing all known databases on the system to which the user has access. Note that the appearance of a database on the list does not indicate permission to access it. Rather, you would also need to query the privileges of the user, as we will see when accessing user information in the next main section.

Using the USE command

When you have a list of the available databases, you can access a database within the current session using USE:

```
mysql> USE sakila;
Reading table information for completion of table and column names
You can turn off this feature to get a quicker startup with -A

Database changed
```

When creating a database connection object in MySQL for Python, it is not necessary to indicate the database to be used in order to log in. Rather, one can leave that blank as follows:

```
mydb = MySQLdb.connect('localhost', 'skipper', 'secret')
```

If we want to be more overt and show that we purposely are not declaring the database, we can simply use a blank string:

```
mydb = MySQLdb.connect('localhost', 'skipper', 'secret', '')
```

or, even better:

```
mydb = MySQLdb.connect(host='localhost',
                       user='skipper',
                       password='secret',
                       db='')
```

However, in order to do anything that uses a database table, one must issue a USE statement through the execute() method of a cursor object:

```
statement = "USE sakila"
runit = cursor.execute(statement)
```

If in doubt over privileges, be sure to couch this part of your code in a try...except structure.

Accessing metadata about tables

Once you indicate to MySQL about the database you are going to use, there are several table-oriented operations that you can perform. You can also ascertain several dynamics about any given table.

SHOW TABLES

Like DATABASES, the TABLES keyword will cause MySQL to return a list of all tables in a database to which you have access. The syntax is simply:

```
mysql> SHOW TABLES;
```

SHOW TABLE STATUS

In addition to seeing the table names, we can also access several pieces of metainformation for each table using TABLE STATUS.

```
mysql> SHOW TABLE STATUS;
```

Depending on how many of the tables in the database we are allowed to access, the results can be quite long. Therefore, it is usually advisable to restrict the matches with a WHERE clause (or LIKE clause) and a parameter of equality as appropriate.

Showing columns from a table

For any given table, we can access the name, type, and default value for every field in a table. We can also see whether a NULL value is allowed, whether the field holds the primary key for the table, and any extra options that apply to the table. For example, using sakila, we can get the format of the city table as follows:

```
mysql> SHOW COLUMNS FROM city;
+-------------+-----------------------+------+-----+-------------------+----------------+
| Field       | Type                  | Null | Key | Default           | Extra          |
+-------------+-----------------------+------+-----+-------------------+----------------+
| city_id     | smallint(5) unsigned  | NO   | PRI | NULL              | auto_increment |
| city        | varchar(50)           | NO   |     | NULL              |                |
| country_id  | smallint(5) unsigned  | NO   | MUL | NULL              |                |
| last_update | timestamp             | NO   |     | CURRENT_TIMESTAMP |                |
+-------------+-----------------------+------+-----+-------------------+----------------+
```

A synonym for COLUMNS FROM is DESCRIBE. Therefore, we could get the same data with the following:

```
mysql> DESCRIBE city;
```

FUNCTION STATUS

Using FUNCTION STATUS by itself will return a list of all available stored functions known to the system. For each function, MySQL will return the following:

- The name of the database to which the function pertains
- The name of the database, its type
- The user who defined the function
- Its last modification date
- When it was created
- The role of the users who are associated with the function
- Any comments that are used to describe it

Depending on how your system is set up, this list could get quite long. So as with other operations, we can nuance what is returned by using a parameter of equality and, if necessary, a wildcard.

To return information about the function Capitalise(), defined in the previous chapter, we would use the following query:

```
mysql> SHOW FUNCTION STATUS LIKE 'Capitalise';
+-------+------------+----------+----------------+----------------------+---------------------+---------------+---------+
| Db    | Name       | Type     | Definer        | Modified             | Created             | Security_type | Comment |
+-------+------------+----------+----------------+----------------------+---------------------+---------------+---------+
| javab | Capitalise | FUNCTION | skipper@localhost | 2010-03-24 11:29:13 | 2010-03-24 11:29:13 | DEFINER       |         |
+-------+------------+----------+----------------+----------------------+---------------------+---------------+---------+
```

CREATE (DATABASE/FUNCTION/PROCEDURE/TABLE/VIEW)

Sometimes, it can be difficult to know the reason an aspect of a MySQL database functions as it does. While SHOW COLUMNS and SHOW TABLE STATUS offer a very good picture, it is not unheard of for a developer to think the database was formed with one definition when it was created with another. Therefore, MySQL allows us to see how it understands things to be and does so by giving us the defining statements of the object involved.

To view the code for the `sakila` database, for example, we would issue the following query (using a postpended \G if needed):

```
mysql> SHOW CREATE DATABASE sakila;
```

and get these results:

```
+----------+------------------------------------------------------------+
| Database | Create Database                                            
|
+----------+------------------------------------------------------------+
| sakila   | CREATE DATABASE `sakila` /*!40100 DEFAULT CHARACTER SET
latin1 */ |
+----------+------------------------------------------------------------+
```

The same goes for a table. If we are using `sakila`, we can see the following creation statement for the `film` table. Using \G will spare you a lot of the formatting, which can become noise on a smaller screen.

```
mysql> SHOW CREATE TABLE film;
+-------+----------------------------------------------------------------
-----------------------------------...(ellipses for MySQL's formatting
dashes)...
       -----------------------------------------------------------------
-----------------------+
| Table | Create Table

       |
+-------+----------------------------------------------------------------
-----------------------------------...(ellipses for MySQL's formatting
dashes)...
       -----------------------------------------------------------------
-----------------------+
| film  | CREATE TABLE `film` (
  `film_id` smallint(5) unsigned NOT NULL auto_increment,
  `title` varchar(255) NOT NULL,
  `description` text,
  `release_year` year(4) default NULL,
  `language_id` tinyint(3) unsigned NOT NULL,
  `original_language_id` tinyint(3) unsigned default NULL,
  `rental_duration` tinyint(3) unsigned NOT NULL default '3',
  `rental_rate` decimal(4,2) NOT NULL default '4.99',
```

```
  `length` smallint(5) unsigned default NULL,

  `replacement_cost` decimal(5,2) NOT NULL default '19.99',

  `rating` enum('G','PG','PG-13','R','NC-17') default 'G',

  `special_features` set('Trailers','Commentaries','Deleted
Scenes','Behind the Scenes') default NULL,

  `last_update` timestamp NOT NULL default CURRENT_TIMESTAMP on update
CURRENT_TIMESTAMP,

  PRIMARY KEY  (`film_id`),

  KEY `idx_title` (`title`),

  KEY `idx_fk_language_id` (`language_id`),

  KEY `idx_fk_original_language_id` (`original_language_id`),

  CONSTRAINT `fk_film_language` FOREIGN KEY (`language_id`) REFERENCES
`language` (`language_id`) ON UPDATE CASCADE,

  CONSTRAINT `fk_film_language_original` FOREIGN KEY (`original_language_
id`) REFERENCES `language` (`language_id`) ON UPDATE CASCADE
) ENGINE=InnoDB AUTO_INCREMENT=1001 DEFAULT CHARSET=utf8 |
+-------+-----------------------------------------------------------
-----------------------------------...(ellipses for MySQL's formatting
dashes)...
-----------------------------------------------------------------------
--------------------+
1 row in set (0.09 sec)
```

If we wanted to see the code for the `Capitalise()` function, we would issue:

```
mysql> SHOW CREATE FUNCTION Capitalise;
```

However, we must be in the appropriate database for that function. In `sakila`, we get this message back:

```
ERROR 1305 (42000): FUNCTION Capitalise does not exist
```

If we switch to the database for which we defined `Capitalise()`, however, we will get the function definition returned.

Similar operations can be performed for procedures and views.

Accessing user metadata

If you write a program that interacts with MySQL dynamically, it will need to adopt its behavior based on the server setup and the characteristic of a user's account. You will then need to be able to access what privileges have been granted to a user from within a MySQL session; you obviously cannot count on having administrator access. For this reason, MySQL provides access to user information from within a session.

SHOW GRANTS

In using SHOW GRANTS, we ask MySQL to return the GRANT statements used to grant privileges to the user. The results will show the precise tables for which permission has been granted. However, any passwords that were part of the original GRANT statement are returned as a hash.

As a user mammamia, we can see the GRANT statements that pertain to that account as shown below:

```
mysql> SHOW GRANTS;
+---------------------------------------------------------------------------------------------------------------+
| Grants for mammamia@localhost|
+---------------------------------------------------------------------------------------------------------------+
| GRANT USAGE ON *.* TO 'mammamia'@'localhost' IDENTIFIED BY PASSWORD
'*41BAD3DEEB08D03DA99724882859C3188BAEC952' |
| GRANT SELECT ON `fish`.`menu` TO 'mammamia'@'localhost'|
+---------------------------------------------------------------------------------------------------------------+
```

These results can be parsed in Python and acted upon or just cataloged.

Depending on the user's level of access, you can show grants for other users by using FOR clause added to SHOW GRANTS syntax as follows:

```
SHOW GRANTS FOR mammamia;
```

PRIVILEGES

Of course, if the user is granted all privileges as indicated by the universal wildcard (*), simply parsing the results will still keep you guessing as to what those privileges actually are. The privileges available to any user are naturally a subset of the privileges supported by the server, which are themselves configurable and vary from installation to installation. For this reason, MySQL also provides a way to learn all of the privileges supported by the server and what they do. Simply use SHOW PRIVILEGES.

What output you get for this statement depends on your server version and how the server was configured.

Project: Building a database class

When you are new to a project or just unfamiliar with a database, getting up to speed on the oral tradition of your team and (all too frequently) sparse documentation can be quite frustrating. In such instances, being able to access the technical information for a database can be quite helpful. The project for this chapter is therefore to build a database class that gives you easy access to metainformation for a database of your choosing.

As we have seen, MySQL results are not always easy to read in the aggregate. Therefore, we will also need code that will digest the results and output them in human-friendly format. The specification points for this project are thus:

- Develop a class to access MySQL metadata
- Return metainformation on a specified database using the class instance
- Reformat tabular information to be more friendly to human readers
- Print out a report of the information

We will save the boiler-plate code of creating the connection and checking the value of __name__ until the very end. First, let's look at creating the class.

Writing the class

In principle, all that is necessary is to fulfill the first item and code the several queries as methods of a class. Each method defines a statement that is then executed, returning the results. The class definition begins as follows:

```
class Database:
    def __init__(self):
        "A class representation for MySQL database metadata"
        self.database = []
```

Defining fetchquery() and some core methods

We could then write every method to execute each query within its own method like the following:

```
def tables(self, cursor):
    "Returns a list of the database tables"
    statement = "SHOW TABLES"
    header = ("Tables")
    try:
        runit = cursor.execute(statement)
        results = cursor.fetchall()
    except MySQLdb.Error, e:
        results = "The query you attempted failed.  Please verify
the information you have submitted and try again.  The error message
that was received reads: %s" % (e)
    return header, results
```

However, unnecessary repetition is the midwife of many code errors. Further, the excess code created by such repetition serves to enlarge the resources needed for the program. This may seem small, but the more the code is used the greater the drain on resources it becomes. The best way to ensure the same operation is performed the same way every time is to write it once and pass arguments to it.

It is therefore better to write an internal function and pass all statements to it. We can write a method fetchquery() to serve this purpose. The revised code would look like this:

```
# Execute straightforward queries
def fetchquery(self, cursor, statement):
    "Internal method that takes a statement and executes the
query, returning the results"
    try:
        runit = cursor.execute(statement)
        results = cursor.fetchall()
    except MySQLdb.Error, e:
        results = "The query you attempted failed.  Please verify
the information you have submitted and try again.  The error message
that was received reads: %s" % (e)
    return results

def tables(self, cursor):
    "Returns a list of the database tables"
    statement = "SHOW TABLES"
    header = ("Tables")
    results = self.fetchquery(cursor, statement)
    return header, results
```

When retrieving data based on user information, there is always a chance of an error. Therefore, we couch the execution lines of `fetchquery()` in a `try...except` structure, returning the error message if it arises.

Retrieving table status and structure

We can similarly write functions to retrieve the table statuses and structure. These we call `tbstats()` and `describe()`.

```
def tbstats(self):
    "Returns the results of TABLE STATUS for the current db"
    header = ("Name", "Engine", "Version", "Row_format", "Rows",
"Avg_row_length", "Data_length", "Max_data_length", "Index_length",
"Data_free", "Auto_increment", "Create_time", "Update_time", "Check_
time", "Collation", "Checksum", "Create_options", "Comment")
    statement = "SHOW TABLE STATUS"
    results = self.fetchquery(statement)
    return header, results


def describe(self, tablename):
    "Returns the column structure of a specified table"
    header = ("Field", "Type", "Null", " Key", "Default", "Extra")
    statement = "SHOW COLUMNS FROM %s" %(tablename)
    results = self.fetchquery(statement)
    return header, results
```

While we name the method `describe()`, we use the MySQL call SHOW COLUMNS. This is purely stylistic, and you could just as easily use the call DESCRIBE.

Retrieving the CREATE statements

Next, we can retrieve the CREATE statements for each of the database and tables. Just like executing the query, we here need to use the same code repeatedly. Therefore, we write a function to assemble the statement based on the information it receives from the calling function. Let's call it `getcreate()`:

```
# Retrieve CREATE statements
def getcreate(self, type, name):
    "Internal method that returns the CREATE statement of an
object when given the object type and name"
    statement = "SHOW CREATE %s %s" %(type, name)
    results = self.fetchquery(statement)
    return results
```

This method takes the type and name of the object and forms the SHOW CREATE statement for it. That statement is then passed to `fetchquery()`, and the results of that method are passed back as the results of this one.

For the creation statement of the database and the table, the method is:

```
def dbcreate(self):
    "Returns the CREATE statement for the current db"
    type = "DATABASE"
    name = db
    header = ("Database", "Create Database")
    results - self.gctcreate(type, name)
    return header, results


def tbcreate(self, tbname):
    "Returns the CREATE statement for a specified table"
    type = "TABLE"
    header = ("Table, Create Table")
    results = self.getcreate(type, tbname)
    return header, results
```

There are other metadata that we could retrieve, but these serve as illustrations. Next, we'll look at calling these methods and handling the results.

Define main()—part 1

We need to define the `main()` function that will serve as the brains of the program. For the moment, we will use `main()` simply to instantiate the class and run through the methods, printing out their results. The beginning of the function thus reads:

```
def main():
    mydb = Database()
```

To get an idea of what the output from these methods looks like, we can then write a series of print commands as follows:

```
print mydb.tables()
print mydb.tbstats()
print mydb.dbcreate()
for i in mydb.tables()[1]:
    print mydb.describe(i)
```

As you may note in looking at the methods, each returns a tuple in the same format as: header and results. However, the `describe()` method requires a table as its argument. So we pass the `for` loop the second part of the results from `tables()`.

A single run of this program will illustrate how unreadable the results are. MySQL for Python serves us well by turning MySQL's tables into sequences, but these are then unreadable by human users. We need to massage the data format a bit. For this we have two options—either write a custom routine or abstract the handling of results to a function. The first is illustrated, as follows, with regard to the results of `tables()`:

```
tables = mydb.tables()
print "Tables of %s" % (db)
for c in xrange(0, len(tables[1])):
    print tables[1][c][0]
print '\n\n'
```

We simply use the length of the results to form a `for` loop that prints the results in sequence. When it comes to other methods, however, it is not a bad idea to write a separate function.

Writing resproc()

What we want in `resproc()` is a method that parses the output from the `Database` methods and returns a formatted output. The first thing we need to do upon defining the function is to assign the two parts of the tuple input to different variables for ease of processing.

```
def resproc(finput):
    "Compiles the headers and results into a report"
    header = finput[0]
    results = finput[1]
```

Now we are in a position to split both parts of the input and compile them into something more meaningful to the human eye. First, we split the results and create a new dictionary out of the two called output.

```
output = {}
c = 0
for r in xrange(0, len(results)):
    record = results[r]
    outrecord = {}

    for column in xrange(0, len(header)):
        outrecord[header[column]] = record[column]
    output[str(c)] = outrecord
    c += 1
```

Next, we create a string for the results of the function. We then walk through our new dictionary and add the results to the string for a nicely formatted report.

```
orecord = ""
for record in xrange(0, len(results)):
    record = str(record)
    item = output[record]
    for k in header:
        outline = "%s : %s\n" %(k, item[k])
        orecord = orecord + outline
    orecord = orecord + '\n\n'
return orecord
```

It should be noted that the formatting used here is just for a text file. We could just as easily make it suitable for HTML or any other document format by including the necessary formatting code.

Define main()—part 2

With `resproc()` defined, we can continue with the handling of other results. For example, we can now handle the results of `tbstats()` as follows:

```
tablestats = mydb.tbstats()
print "Table Statuses"
print resproc(tablestats)
print '\n\n'
```

just as easily as we handle the results of `dbcreate()`:

```
dbcreation = mydb.dbcreate()
print "Database CREATE Statement"
print resproc(dbcreation)
print '\n\n'
```

There are, of course, other methods in the class we defined earlier. But these are done as an introduction.

The preamble

Now that we have the class and functions written, we need to include some introductory code to the head of the program. Beside the modules we use, we also need to assign a few variables and incorporate some administrative code.

Modules and variables

We obviously will need MySQLdb. However, the specification that we set ourselves previously says the user should be able to designate the database. We therefore need the sys module as well. The beginning of the program thus reads:

```
#!/usr/bin/env python

import sys
import MySQLdb

host = 'localhost'
user = 'skipper'
passwd = 'secret'
```

The database can then be set with sys.argv[] as:

```
db = sys.argv[1]
```

Login and USE

Next, we include the login and USE statements as part of a try...except structure. If we cannot login or use the specified database, we want to fail softly.

```
try:
    mydb = MySQLdb.connect(host, user, passwd)
    cursor = mydb.cursor()
    statement = "USE %s" % (db)
    cursor.execute(statement)
except MySQLdb.Error, e:
    print "There was a problem in accessing the database %s with the
credentials you provided.  Please check the privileges of the user
account and retry.  The error and other debugging information follow
below.\n\n%s" % (db, e)
```

Closing out the program

Finally, we need to check whether the program has been called directly. As usual, we do this with the following if clause:

```
if __name__ == '__main__':
    main()
```

Running the program will then produce a long report which can be ported to a file using a pipe or similar shell convention.

Room to grow

In this project, we have seen how to create a class that returns metainformation about a database. While it does what we set out to do, it does not fulfill the intent of that specification. As an exercise, the following have been left to be done:

- Create the option of an output file
- Implement the availability of options using the `optparse` module, allowing the user to specify which part of the metainformation should be returned
- Code support for handling the results from the methods that are not called in `main()`
- Build facility for retrieving the same metainformation from a remote server as from a local one
- Implement the ability to get server variables and user information

Summary

In this chapter, we have covered how to build a Python class for retrieving MySQL metainformation. We have seen:

- How to retrieve information on the engines used by MySQL
- Which system variables we can retrieve
- The several pieces of metadata about a given table that we can access
- How to retrieve user privileges and the grants used to give them

In the next chapter, we will look at one of the most important aspects of database administration—disaster recovery.

14
Disaster Recovery

In late September 2009, users of T-Mobile's Sidekick smartphone began noticing outages in the service. The Sidekick was designed to push the envelope of technology by storing most of its data remotely and requiring network connectivity for almost every function it had. Come October, the company that ran the data servers for the service, Danger, had still not restored the information. Danger had been taken over by Microsoft in February 2007, and most of the employees that started the service had left the company, leaving Microsoft's own employees to field any problems. T-Mobile consequently informed their customers on 10th October that data recovery was not forthcoming, and that they believed the data on all 800,000 customers was irrecoverably lost.

The saga was further hampered by what Reuters, citing an email from Microsoft, called "a confluence of errors from a server failure that hurt its main and backup databases supporting Sidekick users." The commercial damage was significant: T-Mobile pulled the Sidekick device off the shelves and could not sell them. By 15th October, Microsoft had found and was replacing "most, if not all, customer data", but the damage was done. Microsoft's reputation for data management was seriously damaged, and T-Mobile had sustained substantial losses in the world's largest national economy.

One thing that is certain in computing is that hardware will fail even if the software is written soundly. For this reason, a disaster recovery plan should be implemented for every database server. Even if you are not the administrator of the server, this chapter will show you how to back up the data you use. By the end of this chapter, we will have covered:

- When to implement one of several kinds of database backup plans
- What methods of backup and disaster recovery MySQL supports
- How to use Python to back up databases

The purpose of the archiving methods covered in this chapter is to allow you, as the developer, to back up databases that you use for your work without having to rely on the database administrator. As noted later in the chapter, there are more sophisticated methods for backups than we cover here, but they involve system-administrative tasks that are beyond the remit of any development post and are thus beyond the scope of this book.

Every database needs a backup plan

When archiving a database, one of the critical questions that must be answered is how to take a snapshot backup of the database without having users change the data in the process. If data changes in the midst of the backup, it results in an inconsistent backup and compromises the integrity of the archive. There are two strategic determinants for backing up a database system:

- Offline backups
- Live backups

Which you use depends on the dynamics of the system in question and the import of the data being stored. In this chapter, we will look at each in turn and the way to implement them.

Offline backups

Offline backups are done by shutting down the server so the records can be archived without the fear of them being changed by the user. It also helps to ensure the server shut down gracefully and that errors were avoided. The problem with using this method on most production systems is that it necessitates a temporary loss of access to the service. For most service providers, such a consequence is anathema to the business model.

The value of this method is that one can be certain that the database has not changed at all while the backup is run. Further, in many cases, the backup is performed faster because the processor is not simultaneously serving data. For this reason, offline backups are usually performed in controlled environments or in situations where disruption is not critical to the user. These include internal databases, where administrators can inform all users about the disruption ahead of time, and small business websites that do not receive a lot of traffic.

Offline backups also have the benefit that the backup is usually held in a single file. This can then be used to copy a database across hosts with relative ease.

Shutting down a server obviously requires system administrator-like authority. So creating an offline backup relies on the system administrator shutting down the server. If your responsibilities include database administration, you will also have sufficient permission to shut down the server.

Live backups

Live backups occur while the server continues to accept queries from users, while it's still online. It functions by locking down the tables so no new data may be written to them. Users usually do not lose access to the data and the integrity of the archive, for a particular point in time is assured.

Live backups are used by large, data-intensive sites such as Nokia's Ovi services and Google's web services. However, because they do not always require administrator access of the server itself, these tend to suit the backup needs of a development project.

Choosing a backup method

After having determined whether a database can be stopped for the backup, a developer can choose from three methods of archiving:

- Copying the data files (including administrative files such as logs and tablespaces)
- Exporting delimited text files
- Backing up with command-line programs

Which you choose depends on what permissions you have on the server and how you are accessing the data.

MySQL also allows for two other forms of backup: using the **binary log** and by setting up **replication** (using the **master** and **slave** servers). To be sure, these are the best ways to back up a MySQL database. But, both of these are administrative tasks and require system-administrator authority; they are not typically available to a developer. However, you can read more about them in the MySQL documentation. Use of the binary log for incremental backups is documented at:

`http://dev.mysql.com/doc/refman/5.5/en/point-in-time-recovery.html`

Setting up replication is further dealt with at:

`http://dev.mysql.com/doc/refman/5.5/en/replication-solutions-backups.html`

Copying the table files

The most direct way to back up database files is to copy from where MySQL stores the database itself. This will naturally vary based on platform. If you are unsure about which directory holds the MySQL database files, you can query MySQL itself to check:

```
mysql> SHOW VARIABLES LIKE 'datadir';
+---------------+-----------------+
| Variable_name | Value           |
+---------------+-----------------+
| datadir       | /var/lib/mysql/ |
+---------------+-----------------+
```

Alternatively, the following shell command sequence will give you the same information:

```
$ mysqladmin variables | grep datadir
| datadir                         | /var/lib/mysql/                |
```

 Note that the location of administrative files, such as binary logs and InnoDB tablespaces are customizable and may not be in the data directory.

If you do not have direct access to the MySQL server, you can also write a simple Python program to get the information:

```python
#!/usr/bin/env python
import MySQLdb
mydb = MySQLdb.connect('<hostname>',
                       '<user>',
                       '<password>')
cursor = mydb.cursor()
runit = cursor.execute("SHOW VARIABLES LIKE 'datadir'")
results = cursor.fetchall()
print "%s: %s" % (cursor.fetchone())
```

Slight alteration of this program will also allow you to query several servers automatically. Simply change the login details and adapt the output to clarify which data is associated with which results.

Locking and flushing

If you are backing up an offline MyISAM system, you can copy any of the files once the server has been stopped. Before backing up a live system, however, you must lock the tables and flush the log files in order to get a consistent backup at a specific point. These tasks are handled by the LOCK TABLES and FLUSH commands respectively. When you use MySQL and its ancillary programs (such as `mysqldump`) to perform a backup, these tasks are performed automatically. When copying files directly, you must ensure both are done. How you apply them depends on whether you are backing up an entire database or a single table.

LOCK TABLES

The LOCK TABLES command secures a specified table in a designated way. Tables can be referenced with aliases using AS and can be locked for reading or writing. For our purposes, we need only a read lock to create a backup. The syntax looks like this:

```
LOCK TABLES <tablename> READ;
```

This command requires two privileges: LOCK TABLES and SELECT.

It must be noted that LOCK TABLES does not lock all tables in a database but only one. This is useful for performing smaller backups that will not interrupt services or put too severe a strain on the server. However, unless you automate the process, manually locking and unlocking tables as you back up data can be ridiculously inefficient.

FLUSH

The FLUSH command is used to reset MySQL's caches. By re-initiating the cache at the point of backup, we get a clear point of demarcation for the database backup both in the database itself and in the logs. The basic syntax is straightforward, as follows:

```
FLUSH <the object to be reset>;
```

Use of FLUSH presupposes the RELOAD privilege for all relevant databases. What we reload depends on the process we are performing. For the purpose of backing up, we will always be flushing tables:

```
FLUSH TABLES;
```

How we "flush" the tables will depend on whether we have already used the LOCK TABLES command to lock the table. If we have already locked a given table, we can call FLUSH for that specific table:

```
FLUSH TABLES <tablename>;
```

However, if we want to copy an entire database, we can bypass the LOCK TABLES command by incorporating the same call into FLUSH:

```
FLUSH TABLES WITH READ LOCK;
```

This use of FLUSH applies across the database, and all tables will be subject to the read lock. If the account accessing the database does not have sufficient privileges for all databases, an error will be thrown.

Unlocking the tables

Once you have copied the files for a backup, you need to remove the read lock you imposed earlier. This is done by releasing all locks for the current session:

```
UNLOCK TABLES;
```

Restoring the data

Restoring copies of the actual storage files is as simple as copying them back into place. This is best done when MySQL has stopped, lest you risk corruption. Similarly, if you have a separate MySQL server and want to transfer a database, you simply need to copy the directory structure from the one server to another. On restarting, MySQL will see the new database and treat it as if it had been created natively. When restoring the original data files, it is critical to ensure the permissions on the files and directories are appropriate and match those of the other MySQL databases.

Delimited backups within MySQL

MySQL allows for exporting of data from the MySQL command line. To do so, we simply direct the output from a SELECT statement to an output file.

Using SELECT INTO OUTFILE to export data

Using sakila, we can save the data from film to a file called film.data as follows:

```
SELECT * INTO OUTFILE 'film.data' FROM film;
```

This results in the data being written in a tab-delimited format. The file will be written to the directory in which MySQL stores the sakila data. Therefore, the account under which the SELECT statement is executed must have the FILE privilege for writing the file as well as login access on the server to view it or retrieve it. The OUTFILE option on SELECT can be used to write to any place on the server that MySQL has write permission to use. One simply needs to prepend that directory location to the file name. For example, to write the same file to the /tmp directory on a Unix system, use:

```
SELECT * INTO OUTFILE '/tmp/film.data' FROM film;
```

Windows simply requires adjustment of the directory structure accordingly.

Using LOAD DATA INFILE to import data

If you have an output file or similar tab-delimited file and want to load it into MySQL, use the LOAD DATA INFILE command. The basic syntax is:

```
LOAD DATA INFILE '<filename>' INTO TABLE <tablename>;
```

For example, to import the film.data file from the /tmp directory into another table called film2, we would issue this command:

```
LOAD DATA INFILE '/tmp/film.data' INTO TABLE film2;
```

Note that LOAD DATA INFILE presupposes the creation of the table into which the data is being loaded. In the preceding example, if film2 had not been created, we would receive an error. If you are trying to mirror a table, remember to use the SHOW CREATE TABLE query to save yourself time in formulating the CREATE statement.

This discussion only touches on how to use LOAD DATA INFILE for inputting data created with the OUTFILE option of SELECT. But, the command handles text files with just about any set of delimiters. To read more on how to use it for other file formats, see the MySQL documentation at:

http://dev.mysql.com/doc/refman/5.5/en/load-data.html

Archiving from the command line

If you use a MySQL client with a graphical user interface, how you back up will depend on that client. Depending on your platform, MySQL ships with one or both of the following command-line programs used for archiving:

mysqldump

On every MySQL server, you will find the program mysqldump. On Windows, it is usually located in the same directory as the MySQL server executable. On Unix variants, it will be in /usr/bin/.

This program functions like an automated MySQL client. It accepts login credentials from the command line and, based on the options you give it, it will output the script necessary to recreate the database you specify. The basic syntax is:

```
mysqldump -u <username> -p --database <dbname>
```

After providing the username and database name, you are prompted for the password. This is because you have not specified it even though you have indicated with the -p flag that you will use a password to log in. This is the more secure way of running mysqldump. Optionally, you can state the password explicitly after the -p flag, but this is not advisable as it then enters into your shell command history as plain text.

Viewing the backup file

Running this command and providing the appropriate password will cause a dump of the specified database. This will almost certainly run off your screen. To save it to a file, use either a greater than sign (>) or the option --result-file= followed by the filename. A dump of the sakila database would read as follows:

```
mysqldump -u skipper -p --result-file=sql.dump --database sakila
```

After that process is finished, you could open sql.dump in your favorite text editor to see the following:

```
-- MySQL dump 10.11
--
-- Host: localhost    Database: sakila
-- ------------------------------------------------------
-- Server version       5.0.51a-3ubuntu5.4

/*!40101 SET @OLD_CHARACTER_SET_CLIENT=@@CHARACTER_SET_CLIENT */;
...
/*!40111 SET @OLD_SQL_NOTES=@@SQL_NOTES, SQL_NOTES=0 */;
```

```
--
-- Current Database: `sakila`
--

CREATE DATABASE /*!32312 IF NOT EXISTS*/ `sakila` /*!40100 DEFAULT
CHARACTER SET latin1 */;

USE `sakila`;

--
-- Table structure for table `actor`
--

DROP TABLE IF EXISTS `actor`;
SET @saved_cs_client     = @@character_set_client;
SET character_set_client = utf8;
CREATE TABLE `actor` (
  `actor_id` smallint(5) unsigned NOT NULL auto_increment,
...
  KEY `idx_actor_last_name` (`last_name`)
) ENGINE=InnoDB AUTO_INCREMENT=201 DEFAULT CHARSET=utf8;
```

So, the dump file contains all of the MySQL commands necessary to create the infrastructure of the database. If you read on, you will soon encounter the following:

```
--
-- Dumping data for table `actor`
--

LOCK TABLES `actor` WRITE;
/*!40000 ALTER TABLE `actor` DISABLE KEYS */;
INSERT INTO `actor` VALUES (1,'PENELOPE','GUINESS','2006-02-15 04:34:3
3'),(2,'NICK','WAHLBERG','2006-02-15 04:34:33'),(3,'ED','CHASE','2006-
02-15 04:34:33'),(4,'JENNIFER','DAVIS','2006-02-15 04:34:33'),(5,'JOHN
NY','LOLLOBRIGIDA','2006-02-15 04:34:33')...
```

The necessary INSERT commands are also included. The dump file is a single file backup of the database.

Other options

In addition to the options discussed previously, `mysqldump` supports several other flags. The most commonly used include:

- `--all-databases`: Dump all tables in all databases
- `--compact`: Produce more compact output
- `--databases`: Dump several databases
- `--dump-date`: Include dump date with the "Dump completed on" comment if `--comments` is given
- `--flush-logs`: Flush the MySQL server log files before starting the dump
- `--flush-privileges`: Emit a FLUSH PRIVILEGES statement after dumping the MySQL database
- `--help`: Display help message and exit
- `--host`: Host to connect to (IP address or hostname)
- `--ignore-table=db_name.tbl_name`: Do not dump the given table
- `--lock-all-tables`: Lock all tables across all databases
- `--lock-tables`: Lock all tables before dumping them
- `--log-error=file_name`: Append warnings and errors to the named file
- `--opt`: Shorthand for `--add-drop-table --add-locks --create-options --disable-keys --extended-insert --lock-tables --quick --set-charset`.
- `--quick`: Retrieve rows for a table from the server a row at a time
- `--result-file=file`: Direct output to a given file
- `--single-transaction`: Includes a BEGIN SQL statement before the data from the server
- `--skip-triggers`: Do not dump triggers
- `--tab=path`: Produce tab-separated data files
- `--tables`: Override the `--databases` or `-B` option
- `--triggers`: Dump triggers for each dumped table
- `--verbose`: Verbose mode
- `--version`: Display version information and exit
- `--where='where_condition'`: Dump only rows selected by the given WHERE condition
- `--xml`: Produce XML output

Complete documentation on mysqldump can be found at `http://dev.mysql.com/doc/refman/5.5/en/mysqldump.html`

Restoring the data

If you use `mysqldump` to create a standard MySQL backup as discussed above, you can restore the data using the SOURCE command we used in Chapter 12. For example, backing up `sakila` would use the following command:

```
mysqldump -u skipper -p --opt sakila > sakila.sql
```

After the password is entered and the database backed up to `sakila.sql`, we can login and restore the data:

```
SOURCE sakila.sql;
```

It is worth noting that the file created by `mysqldump` does not always create the database. If you want to specify the database in question, use either of the flags `--database` or `--databases`. If you are transferring the backup to another server, you will need to create a database for it first. Note, however, that the database used for the backup need not have the same name as the original. It is possible to import a backup of `sakila` into a database named `alikas`. Within the database system, the only time database names become critical is in the use of cross-database references such as triggers. Naturally, if you change the name of the database, you will need to change the references used in all of your calling applications, as well.

> Triggers are MySQL procedures that initiate an action based on an event in a table. They allow information in one table to be updated, inserted, or deleted based upon data being inserted, updated, or deleted in another table. For the MySQL documentation on triggers, see: `http://dev.mysql.com/doc/refman/5.5/en/triggers.html`

Then you will need to ensure the greater server environment is mirrored for a functioning (as opposed to simply stored) backup.

mysqlhotcopy

In addition to `mysqldump`, Unix, Linux, and NetWare servers also support `mysqlhotcopy`. This program is a Perl script that backs up live databases. Where `mysqldump` functions like a MySQL client, `mysqlhotcopy` is a server administration program. It must be run on the same host as the one that runs the database; it cannot be run remotely.

[It is worth noting that `mysqlhotcopy` only works on MyISAM and Archive tables. Therefore, you cannot use it to back up other types such as InnoDB.]

`mysqlhotcopy` works by copying the salient files for a database to the directory of your choice. Consequently, it will only work if the user who invokes it has read access to those files. This will always be the root administrator of the system but, depending on your setup, it may include others. In the following examples, it is assumed that the one has appropriate permissions to access the files.

The most basic syntax of `mysqlhotcopy` is:

```
mysqlhotcopy <database name> <path for backup>
```

While that is the most basic call of the program, it will almost never work. You must know the username and password of a user that has access to the database you are archiving. Therefore, it is more commonly called like this:

```
mysqlhotcopy -u skipper -p secret sakila /path/to/a/directory/
```

Assuming the credentials and access permissions are valid, `mysqlhotcopy` will then create a directory in which it stores copies of the files used for the database you specified.

In addition to the syntax shown above, the following options are available with `mysqlhotcopy`:

- `-addtodest`: Do not rename target directory (if it exists); merely add files to it
- `-allowold`: Do not abort if a target exists; rename it by adding an _old suffix
- `-checkpoint=db_name.tbl_name`: Insert checkpoint entries
- `-chroot=path`: Base directory of the chroot jail in which mysqld operates
- `-debug`: Write a debugging log
- `-dryrun`: Report actions without performing them
- `-flushlogs`: Flush logs after all tables are locked
- `-help`: Display help message and exit
- `-host=host_name`: Connect to the MySQL server on the given host
- `-keepold`: Do not delete previous (renamed) target when done
- `-noindices`: Do not include full index files in the backup
- `-password[=password]`: The password to use when connecting to the server
- `-port=port_num`: The TCP/IP port number to use for the connection

- -quiet: Be silent except for errors
- -regexp: Copy all databases with names that match the given regular expression
- -resetmaster: Reset the binary log after locking all the tables
- -resetslave: Reset the master.info file after locking all the tables
- -socket=path: For connections to localhost
- -tmpdir=path: The temporary directory
- -user=user_name: The MySQL username to use when connecting to the server
- -version: Display version information and exit

It should be noted that mysqlhotcopy is still in beta. Therefore, new functionality will be added, and this list is therefore not exhaustive. A convenient way of accessing the options available through your copy of mysqlhotcopy is to use either man or perldoc from a command-line:

```
man mysqlhotcopy
```

Otherwise, you can use:

```
perldoc mysqlhotcopy
```

Either of these commands will give you the manual page for your local version.

Restoring from mysqlhotcopy is a matter of copying the directory that holds the file archive to its appropriate location on your server. This is usually /var/lib/mysql followed by the database name. If in doubt, see how to access this information for your installation of MySQL in the section *Copying the Table Files* above.

Backing up a database with Python

As we have seen, there are three methods of archiving a MySQL database that a developer can use:

- Copying the MySQL table files directly
- Exporting data to a delimited text file
- Creating a dumpfile

The first and last of these require special permissions on the server. To use Python to manage the backup merely automates the process but still requires you to have access beyond SELECT.

Using MySQLdb, however, we can export the data with only basic privileges. Simply store the results of the SELECT statement into a variable, format it appropriately, and write it to a file.

Summary

It has been a long road from the beginning of this book. We have gone from merely installing MySQL for Python to doing some pretty sophisticated things with it. We have moved beyond merely using the database to using Python to do programmatic administration.

In this chapter, we have seen several ways to back up and restore a MySQL database. We have looked at:

- When it is advisable to backup a running system instead of shutting it down
- The procedure for taking a snapshot of a running MySQL server
- What backup methods are available to a python database developer
- Which privileges are required when using certain archiving methods

From here, the sky is the limit for you. You have the Python and MySQL foundation necessary to design and develop even large, database-driven applications.

Naturally, there is more to learn about MySQL. That is for the coming chapters of the book.

Index

process 170, 172
underlying code 171
EXTRACT function 258, 269

F

FEDERATED 371
feedback loop
creating 116
fetchall() 78
fetchall() method 38
fetchmany() method 136, 137
fetchone() method 135
Filemaker Pro 132
files, copying from MySQL
about 396
data, restoring 398
FLUSH command 397
locking 397
LOCK TABLES command 397
tables, unlocking 398
first-in first-out (FIFO) queue system 133
for loop 139
form() method 117
FORMAT() function 359
FROM, MySQL statements 28
FROM_DAYS() function 258
FROM_UNIXTIME() function 258
function codes, web-based administration
        project
connecting with a database 208
connecting without a database 207
database action 208
execute() 211
query action 210
table action 209

G

generators
about 142
creating, fetchone() used 142
fetchmany(), using 143, 144
GET_FORMAT() function 258
getopt module 53
GROUP_CONCAT() function
about 289
delimiter, specifying 290

maximum length, customizing 290
using, with DISTINCT 291, 292
working 289
GROUP BY, MySQL statements 30, 31
GROUP BY clause 293, 294

H

HAVING, MySQL statements 32, 33
HAVING clause
about 312
joins 321
subqueries 317
unions 319, 320
HAVING implementation
about 330, 331
HTML interface, revising 337
main() function, revising 333-335
options, revising 336
Python backend, revising 331
qaction() function, revising 331-333
Hello() function
creating 361
help() function 18, 54
HOUR() function 258
HTML output, web-based administration
        project
about 212
body() method, defining 214
definition 212
footer() method, defining 213
header() method, defining 213
message attribute 213
page() method, defining 214
HTTP persistent connections 133

I

IBMDBI 371
incorporating aggregate functions project
about 300
HTML form, changing 309
main() function, revising 305-307
options, setting up 308
qaction() function, adding 300
INNER joins 324
InnoDB 371
INSERT() function 348, 349

P

package manager 8
Pareto's Principle 134
parse_args() method 54
PERIOD_ADD() function 258
PERIOD_DIFF() function 258
POSIX 352
POSIX character classes 353
privileges, removing in MySQL
  about 233
  basic syntax, REVOKE command 233
profiling, MySQL
  about 375
  SHOW PROFILE 375
  SHOW PROFILES 376
ProgrammingError 112
Python
  access, granting 231, 232
  aggregate functions, programming with
    298, 299
  clauses, programming with 298, 299
  databases, creating with MySQLdb 194
  generators 142
  installing, on Windows 11, 12
  iterators 140
  joins 329, 330
  loops, generating 138
  REVOKE command, using 235
  subqueries 328, 329
  unions 329
Python exception-handling 105
Pythons
  errors 101-103
  warnings 101-103

Q

qaction() function 207
  about 300, 301
  new statement formation 302-305
  new variables, adding 301
QUARTER() function 258
query
  forming, in MySQL 26
  passing, to MySQL 37, 38
query() function 94

query, passing to MySQL
  about 37, 38
  results, modifying 39, 40
  simple SELECT statement 38

R

record-by-record retrieval
  issue 129, 130
  reasons 131
record-by-record retrieval, reasons
  computing resources 131
  network latency 134
  Pareto's Principle 134
REGEXP function 350
regular expression meta-characters 351, 352
REPLACE() function 347, 348
results trimming, in MySQL
  DISTINCT function, used 287
  GROUP_CONCAT() function, used 289
REVOKE command
  using, in Python 235
RIGHT joins 321
ROUND() function 357, 358

S

Sakila
  downloading 145
Sakila database
  creating 145
  structure 146, 147
SCUD 26
SEC_TO_TIME() function 258
SECOND() function 258
SELECT, MySQL statements 27
server-side sorting, MySQL
  about 292
  GROUP BY clause, using 293
  ORDER BY clause, using 294
setuptools
  installing 11
SHOW command
  arguements 370
Slashdot effect 133
sorting 304
str() function 79

Thank you for buying
MySQL for Python

About Packt Publishing

Packt, pronounced 'packed', published its first book "*Mastering phpMyAdmin for Effective MySQL Management*" in April 2004 and subsequently continued to specialize in publishing highly focused books on specific technologies and solutions.

Our books and publications share the experiences of your fellow IT professionals in adapting and customizing today's systems, applications, and frameworks. Our solution based books give you the knowledge and power to customize the software and technologies you're using to get the job done. Packt books are more specific and less general than the IT books you have seen in the past. Our unique business model allows us to bring you more focused information, giving you more of what you need to know, and less of what you don't.

Packt is a modern, yet unique publishing company, which focuses on producing quality, cutting-edge books for communities of developers, administrators, and newbies alike. For more information, please visit our website: www.packtpub.com.

About Packt Open Source

In 2010, Packt launched two new brands, Packt Open Source and Packt Enterprise, in order to continue its focus on specialization. This book is part of the Packt Open Source brand, home to books published on software built around Open Source licences, and offering information to anybody from advanced developers to budding web designers. The Open Source brand also runs Packt's Open Source Royalty Scheme, by which Packt gives a royalty to each Open Source project about whose software a book is sold.

Writing for Packt

We welcome all inquiries from people who are interested in authoring. Book proposals should be sent to author@packtpub.com. If your book idea is still at an early stage and you would like to discuss it first before writing a formal book proposal, contact us; one of our commissioning editors will get in touch with you.

We're not just looking for published authors; if you have strong technical skills but no writing experience, our experienced editors can help you develop a writing career, or simply get some additional reward for your expertise.

Python Testing: Beginner's Guide

ISBN: 978-1-847198-84-6   Paperback: 256 pages

An easy and convenient approach to testing your powerful Python projects

1. Covers everything you need to test your code in Python

2. Easiest and enjoyable approach to learn Python testing

3. Write, execute, and understand the result of tests in the unit test framework

Expert Python Programming

ISBN: 978-1-847194-94-7   Paperback: 372 pages

Best practices for designing, coding, and distributing your Python software

1. Learn Python development best practices from an expert, with detailed coverage of naming and coding conventions

2. Apply object-oriented principles, design patterns, and advanced syntax tricks

3. Manage your code with distributed version control

4. Profile and optimize your code

Please check **www.PacktPub.com** for information on our titles

MySQL Admin Cookbook

ISBN: 978-1-847197-96-2   Paperback: 376 pages

99 great recipes for mastering MySQL configuration and administration

1. Set up MySQL to perform administrative tasks such as efficiently managing data and database schema, improving the performance of MySQL servers, and managing user credentials

2. Deal with typical performance bottlenecks and lock-contention problems

3. Restrict access sensibly and regain access to your database in case of loss of administrative user credentials

Mastering phpMyAdmin 3.1 for Effective MySQL Management

ISBN: 978-1-847197-86-3   Paperback: 352 pages

Increase your MySQL productivity and control by discovering the real power of phpMyAdmin 3.1

1. Covers version 3.1, the latest version of phpMyAdmin

2. Administer your MySQL databases with phpMyAdmin

3. Manage users and privileges with MySQL Server Administration tools

4. Get to grips with the hidden features and capabilities of phpMyAdmin

Please check **www.PacktPub.com** for information on our titles

Printed in Great Britain
by Amazon.co.uk, Ltd.,
Marston Gate.